SENSE ABILITY

SENSE
ABILITY

Expanding Your Sense of
Awareness for a Twenty-first-Century Life

DORIS WILD HELMERING

Quill
An Imprint of HarperCollinsPublishers

The names of the people who were kind enough to share their stories have been changed except for Tom O'Neal and his son, Brandon. In a few stories, minor changes have been made to protect someone's identity.

Permissions, constituting an extension of this copyright page, can be found on page 251.

A hardcover edition of this book was published by Eagle Brook, an imprint of William Morrow and Company, Inc., in 1999.

HarperCollins books may be purchased for educational, business, or sales promotional use. For information please write: Special Markets Department, HarperCollins Publishers Inc., 10 East 53rd Street, New York, NY 10022.

First Quill edition published 2000.

Designed by Susan Hood

The Library of Congress has catalogued the hardcover edition as follows:
Helmering, Doris Wild
Sense ability: expanding your sense of awareness for a twenty-first-century life / Doris Wild Helmering.—1st ed.
p. cm.
Includes bibliographical references and index.
ISBN 0-688-16093-X
1. Self-perception. I. Title.
BF697.5.S43H55   1999
158.1—dc21   98-46110
CIP

ISBN 0-688-17801-4 (pbk.)

00 01 02 03 04 ❖/RRD 10 9 8 7 6 5 4 3 2 1

ACKNOWLEDGMENTS

George Bernard Shaw once wrote, "Independence? That's middle-class blasphemy. We are all dependent on one another, every soul of us on earth." Most assuredly, writing this book has again given new meaning to these words.

Skeeter, my husband, I cannot begin to enumerate all the support you have given me over the past five years as I have worked and reworked the material. You are my soul mate, my pal, my rock, my mentor, my cheerleader. Thank you.

Joann Davis, my wise, learned, brilliant editor—without your guidance and questioning, *Sense Ability* would not have been realized. I am so grateful that you took on this project. In our family, when someone does something extraordinary (and your guidance was extraordinary), we bow three times and say, "Thank you, thank you, thank you." I now bow three times and say to you, "Thank you, thank you, thank you."

Pat Gregory, bravo for always finding the exact research article or book I needed. Your sleuthing abilities are truly remarkable.

Michaeleen Cradock, both friend and colleague, a basket of

gold stars for taking such excellent care of our practice when I stole away to write. And another basket of stars for the title and the many well-grounded suggestions you made when reading the manuscript.

Linda Hinrichs, I always thought when I met you that God had sent me an angel to help with all the work I had to do. Thanks for your ear, your enthusiasm, your strength, your friendship. Thanks for being my angel.

April Winkelmann, my sweet sister, you were always there listening as I read you revision after revision. Everyone should be so fortunate as to have a supportive, loving sister like you.

More gold stars to all of you who graciously let me use your stories in this book. Without you this book would have been sorely lacking.

Bill Hendricks, I appreciate your first recognizing the value of this material. Gary Truitt and Gary Weinberg from National Press Publications, thanks for publishing *Being Ok Just Isn't Enough*, a business user's manual that contains some of the material in this present book.

Roger McWilliams and Judy Cassidy—your feedback is always excellent and on target. Much appreciation.

Sharon Endejan, Mary Schwarzbauer, and Kathy Schaefer, you all know your Bible! Thanks for identifying Bible verses.

Thank you, Michelle Shinseki, for getting the job done on time and for your joy of life.

I wish to acknowledge Jo Oberreither, my faster-than-a-speeding-bullet secretary; Anna-Mary, John, and Sheri Helmering; and Machelle Robinson for all the telephone calls and support while I was writing in the mountains; Pat Cannon for running the Tuesday evening Therapy Group; Pat Gross for all the homecooked meals; Dan Freeman, Martha Scharff, Mary Jane Lamping, Paul and Anita Helmering, and Mom and Dad for your ongoing interest and support.

And, Saint Jude, thank you for your ever-present strength in my life.

CONTENTS

1. Discovering Your Sense Ability   1
   What Is Sense Ability?   1
   Expanding Awareness   3
   Learning to Use Your Sense of Awareness   6
   Do People Really Change?   11
   A Demanding Journey   12

2. Are You Outer-Directed or Inner-Directed?   15
   Your Focus Determines Your Behavior   16
   Differences Between Outer-Directed and
     Inner-Directed   19
   Blame It on Your Genes   21
   Moving Toward a Balanced Self   23

3. Do You Know How to Love?   27
   What Is This Word Called *Love?*   29
   Love Is Listening   30
   Love Is Remembering   32
   Love Is Giving   36
   Love Is Receiving   41

Love Is Respecting   44
Love Is Confronting and Disciplining   45
Love Is Playing   50
Love Is Forgiving   52
Making a Decision to Forgive   53
Learning to Forgive Yourself   55
Do You Know How to Love Yourself?   56
A Lifetime to Love   57

4. Do You Get Too Angry?   **59**
Do I Act Like This Person?   60
The Three Main Reasons You Get Too Angry   62
How You Intensify Your Anger   66
One Event, Two Interpretations   67
An Exercise: Thinking It Through   68
Is Your Anger Genetic?   69
When Blowing Your Top Becomes the Norm   70
What Does Research Say?   71
Is There Ever a Time to Be Angry?   73
Anger-In and Anger-Out   74
Getting in Control   75
If You Must Deal with Someone Else's Anger   80
Always Remember Anger's Consequences   81

**5. How Do You Handle Suffering and
Disappointment?**   **83**
She's Had a Headache for Eleven Years   84
What Do People Do with Their Pain?   88
When You Allow Disappointment to Take Over
   Your Life   89
"Drop That Rock!"   90
When Someone You Value Is Not Available   91
When You Lose a Child   93
When You Face Chronic Illness   95
More Pain and Suffering   97
Resiliency—the Ability to Bounce Back   98

**6. Do You Monitor and Direct Your
Thoughts?**   **103**
You Are the Director   104
What Do You See?   105

Another Side to Every Story 107
Are You a Positive or a Negative Thinker? 109
An Exercise: Think Negative, Think Positive 110
Jumping to Negative Conclusions 111
Overgeneralizing 113
Obsessing 115
Is Your Thinking Past, Present, or Future Focused? 118
The Present Is Really All You Have 122
Do Your Thoughts Determine Who You Are? 123

7. Are You a Critical Person? 125
Criticism Hurts! 128
Are You a Faultfinder? 130
How Did You Become So Critical? 131
Critical Tactics 132
Is It Ever Appropriate to Be Critical? 135
Putting Away Your Criticism 136
What Is Your Higher Value? 138
Dealing with a Critical Person 140
Criticizing Yourself 141
Not Making Critical Comments Has Many Rewards 143

8. Are You Aware of Your Psychological
Boundary Lines? 144
You're Invading My Space 144
A Quiz: Discovering Your Boundary Lines 147
Hidden Boundaries 151
A Thinking Exercise 155
A Sense of Me, a Sense of You 156

9. Are You a Controlling Person? 157
Telling People What to Do 158
The "Right" to Control 161
A Quiz: How Controlling Are You? 162
When Your Own Life Is Out of Control 164
Getting Yourself in Control 165

10. Can You Override Genes and Other
Influences? 173
It's Your Nature 174
It's Your Nurture 174

An Exercise: Influences from Childhood   176
Hidden Rules of Influence   180
Dancing with Nature, Nurture, and Present Influences   188

11. **How Envious and Jealous Are You?**   **189**
The Envious Woman   190
True Confessions: Envious Feelings   190
Behaviors That Reveal Envy   191
Where Does Your Envy Come From?   193
How to Quell Your Envy   194
Jealousy—the Green-Eyed Monster   195
Better Self-esteem   196
Competing for Attention   197
Using Your Sense Ability   198
Listen to Life   199

12. **Do You Suffer from Anxiety or
Depression?**   **200**
Anxiety Can Be Healthy or Debilitating   202
Depressed—With and Without Reason   206
Dragging Yourself to Wellness   209

13. **Do You Talk to God?**   **210**
The Benefits of Prayer   212

14. **Do You Feel Oneness?**   **216**
Oneness—What Is It?   217
Thwarting Oneness   222
Setting the Stage   223

15. **Reaching for Enlightened Maturity**   **224**
Enlightened Maturity   225
A Checklist   226
Just a Few Other Requirements   229
You Can Make a Difference   233

Postscript: It Takes Four Seasons   **235**
Starting a Sense Ability Study Group   **237**
Notes   **238**
Bibliography   **243**
Index   **254**

DISCOVERING YOUR
SENSE ABILITY

*So habitual is the trance of ordinary life that one could say
that human beings are a race that sleeps and awakens, but
does not awaken fully. Because half-awake is sufficient for the
task we customarily do, few of us are aware of the dysfunction
of our condition.*[1]

Arthur Deikman, author

Several of us were waiting in line for coffee when a man
edged his way up to the counter and gave the young server
his order. The server smiled and said she would be with
him shortly. Only a few minutes had passed when suddenly the
man slammed his fist on the counter and declared, "This is ridiculous!"

The man's wife moved closer and gently patted her husband's
arm, inviting him to be patient. The man glared at her and
announced loudly that he had more important things to do.
With that, he turned abruptly and walked away.

The server, clearly upset, apologized to all of us who were
waiting. When she gave me my coffee, she apologized again.

Anyone watching the scene might think that the man was not
using the good sense God gave him. In essence, he was not using
his sense of awareness.

WHAT IS SENSE ABILITY?

Sense ability is the skill to fully use your sense of awareness. It
is the ability to observe your thoughts, your feelings, and your

behavior. It lets you see how your thinking creates many of your feelings and how your thoughts and feelings influence your behavior. Sense ability also makes you aware of others and provides real-time feedback as to how your feelings and behavior affect others—inhibiting or inviting closeness, empathy, tolerance, emotional intimacy, interconnectedness, and oneness.

If the impatient man at the coffee counter had used his sense of awareness, his sense ability, he would have noticed that the attendant was busy and that his fellow humans were also waiting. Observing that he was choosing to think negative thoughts such as, "This is taking too long" and "I have more important things to do," he would have understood that his own thoughts were creating his anger. His sense ability might have alerted him that his automatic response pattern of anger was kicking in because things were not going his way. He would have realized that he could change his thoughts to more neutral or positive ones such as, "I'm running late so I'll get coffee later," "This is a busy place," or "That coffee does smell good." By changing his thoughts, he would have changed his feelings and behavior.

If the man had used his sense ability, he might have observed that his wife was trying to comfort him as well as save herself from embarrassment. He would have seen himself rejecting his wife's reaching out. He might have determined that he had ample time to wait. And he might have had the added bonus of enjoying coffee with his wife.

In this situation the server also failed to use her sense ability. If she had, she might have realized that she was doing the best she could serving people on a first-come basis. She would have been aware that this man was using anger to try to control the situation. And she would not have felt guilty and anxious and that it was her responsibility to make everything better.

———

Your sense ability has been with you since birth. It is involved on some level in all thought processes. Although its potential is undeveloped in most people, you subconsciously make use of it many times each day. You use it to determine if you're getting your point across when talking to a mate or colleague. You use it when you listen to your child and judge what kind of a day he's having. You use it when you get up in the morning and check your mood. You use it to decide how much information to share with a new friend. You continually use the information provided by your sense of awareness to monitor, modify, and change your thoughts, feelings, and behavior.

All your senses provide your brain with hundreds of thousands of pieces of information per second. Your sense of smell allows you to identify ten thousand different odors. The human ear is capable of differentiating some three hundred thousand tones. One billion messages per second flash into your brain from the retina, allowing you to distinguish color, size, shape, texture, distance, and space. Your hand alone has seventeen thousand tactile receptors. Ten thousand taste buds inform you whether something is sweet, salty, sour, or bitter.[2] And intuition allows you to "know" without benefit of rational thought, information, or data.

As your other senses feed your brain with hundreds of thousands of pieces of information, your sense of awareness takes in that information, as well as your own thoughts, feelings, and actions, and your observations of others, and provides even more data. The more information you have about yourself—the thoughts you choose to think, the feelings you choose to feel, as well as the appropriateness and inappropriateness of your actions—and the more perceptive you are of others, the more developed is your sense ability.

EXPANDING AWARENESS

Before the advent of cataract surgery, individuals who were born with cataracts could not see. When cataract surgery was perfected, sight was miraculously given to many. However, what was startling and what no one predicted was that those who were given sight still could not see in the way one normally thinks about seeing.

For example, one man whose sight was restored could not distinguish his wife's face from that of others. He only recognized his wife if he heard her voice or felt a part of her face. When another newly sighted man was presented with a bunch of daffodils, he was mystified as to their color and what they actually were. However, when he caught a scent of the flowers, he announced happily that they were yellow daffodils. For another newly sighted person, smoke rising from a chimney into the sky seemed to split the sky in two. He mistook spots on a dog for holes through the dog. And when one man tried to set a glass of water on a table, he released the glass several feet above the table only to have the glass break and spew its contents about. Although he could see the table, he had not learned to judge distance. It took months and sometimes years before these formerly blind individuals developed the ability to fully use their sense of sight.[3]

Like the newly sighted person who has not learned to use his sense of sight, who has vision but cannot see, most people have neither recognized nor learned to fully use their sense of awareness. They have not developed the ability to see and process the information available to them. They have not mastered the use of their extraordinary, remarkable, wondrous sense ability—the sense that helps you have greater control over your thoughts and feelings and behavior. The sense that helps you have strong, healthy, lasting relationships. The sense that helps you attain contentment, peace, and a feeling of well-being. The sense that allows you to feel your interconnectedness and oneness.

————

When I started writing this book, my intention was to help people better understand themselves, to become more aware so they would have fewer problems and healthier relationships. I wanted people to have a book that they could pick up any time and find information on how they might deal with a particular problem. Having seen more than fourteen hundred people in psychotherapy, having logged over forty thousand hours as a psychotherapist in the last twenty-eight years, and having written over nine hundred newspaper columns and seven books that focus on relationship problems both at home and at work, I knew firsthand that the real key to life, happiness, and strong healthy relationships starts with the individual's sense of awareness.

What people needed was more awareness. They needed specific, concrete techniques to help them become more aware. This book was written to fill that need.

———

Let's start by looking at two pictures drawn by artist and writer Larry Kettelkamp.

It is evident that the first drawing is a portrait of Abraham Lincoln.[4] If you look closely, however, you will see more than Lincoln. You'll find a picture of a mouse, a camel, a goose, a clown, a profile of a face, a dog's head, and a snail, all contained within Lincoln's portrait.

How many of these figures are you able to find?

Looking at the second picture,[5] what do you see? Why, a clown, of course.

Now turn the book clockwise 90 degrees. The clown has turned into an entire circus: a circus tent, a juggler on a unicycle, an animal balancing a ball, and along the perimeter of the circus ring, elephants and horses. One horse even has a rider standing on its back.

This exercise demonstrates that your awareness was somewhat limited when you first saw the pictures. But as you looked more closely, your awareness expanded.

In Chapter 6, "Do You Monitor and Direct Your Thoughts?", you'll be asked to look at several more pictures. Since you've had the experience of looking at Lincoln and the clown, when you look at the next set of pictures, you'll be searching immediately for more than originally meets the eye. You'll be operating from an expanded sense of awareness.

In addition, once you read the material in this book, I believe you will find that your sense of awareness will have expanded. You won't be able to see yourself or live your life the same. You will be different.

LEARNING TO USE YOUR SENSE OF AWARENESS

One way to develop and use your sense of awareness is to learn to step out of yourself, so to speak, and to consciously watch yourself in your mind's eye. As you watch yourself, you do not interpret or evaluate or judge. You simply observe. As you do this you become the *Impartial Observer*.

When you are the Impartial Observer, you are in the present watching yourself in real time. You move outside yourself and see yourself clearly. You observe yourself interacting with your husband. You see how you automatically raise your voice when he disagrees with you. You watch yourself berate your child when he refuses to go to bed. You see how you point your finger to emphasize what you're saying. You see yourself slumping in a chair and feeling as if no one cares because you don't have anything to do on Sunday. You watch yourself eat too much and get stuck obsessing on an event that happened years ago. You watch as you harshly criticize others at a meeting. You see yourself take on more and more tasks, then watch as you moan and groan to everyone that you have too much to do. You observe your impatience at the checkout line. You watch as you exaggerate and make yourself more important in the retelling of a story.

As the Impartial Observer, you detach yourself from the event and you watch. You discover if your thoughts are positive or negative and if they are about the past, the future, or the present. You see which feelings you are most likely to feel and how you often regulate their intensity with your thoughts. You see yourself acting rudely, jealously, lovingly. It's as though you are watching yourself in a movie.

As your awareness grows, you begin to recognize that instead of being autonomous and free, you have a particular response pattern that you use over and over. With watching comes a new understanding of yourself. It's as though you awake from a dream. You no longer see with the eyes of a sleepy child, but with the eyes of an awakened, mature adult. When you are the Impartial Observer, you are using your sense ability.

––––

"Yesterday was horrendous," said Joan. "So when I got up this morning I decided to take a long soak in the bathtub. And guess what? There was no hot water. I was instantly mad at my husband. He must have realized when he took his shower the pilot light had gone out on the water heater. But he didn't care enough to go down to the basement and fix it and he knows I can't do it. I've never figured it out. After all I do for the family, I can't even get a hot bath."

If Joan had switched to the Impartial Observer that morning, if she had used her sense ability, she might have seen how she made an assumption that her husband knew the pilot light was off. She might have watched herself move toward feelings of helplessness and anger when she learned there was no hot water. She might have observed how she interpreted this event in such a way that it took on more and more negative meaning. If Joan would routinely place herself in the Impartial Observer mode, over time she might discover that her automatic response patterns are less than satisfactory.

After self-discovery, if Joan went to take a bath and there was no hot water, she would see it simply as an event. There is no hot water. The pilot light must have gone out. Joan would then choose to take a cold bath or skip her bath. She might even learn to light the pilot. No feelings of being a victim. No anger at her husband.

Once you learn to become an Impartial Observer and use your sense ability, you will experience more and more insight because you no longer let your thoughts or feelings run away with you. You don't jump to conclusions and make assumptions. You are able to see the whole picture. As a consequence, you respond to the event in its entirety without prejudice.

If you've ever studied another language, you know that in the beginning you have to think painstakingly about each and every word. However, as you became more proficient in the new language, you no longer have to translate word for word. You simply find yourself thinking in another language.

The same phenomenon occurs when you take up a sport or musical instrument. In the beginning you have to concentrate and think about the way to hold the racket or position your fingers. But soon you find you are doing it automatically. The same holds true of becoming an Impartial Observer. At some point moving to this position will become automatic.

By being an Impartial Observer and using your sense ability, you will disentangle yourself from life's fears, hurts, depressions, and yearnings. Anger, jealousy, greed, obsessional thoughts, and unfulfilled desires and fantasies will no longer dominate your waking hours. Events will become only events. Your perspective of life will expand exponentially. You will become the master of your thoughts, feelings, and behavior.

———

Another way to start consciously using your sense ability is to preface your thoughts, feelings, and actions with the words, *"I am aware. . . ."*

For example, *I am aware* that I am listening to the rain falling on the roof. *I am aware* that as I hear the rain, I'm beginning to feel a sense of well-being. I am aware that I'm resisting getting out of bed. I am aware that I'm making up excuses to tell people why I've come late to the meeting. I am aware that I'm thinking about my telephone conversation last night. I am aware of feeling anxious because of everything I have to do today. I am aware that I am reprimanding myself because I forgot to send a birthday card to Aunt Susan.

Within a day of using this technique, you'll find yourself more calm, and your usual mental banter will have subsided. You'll also find that you are more accepting of events and that your negative feelings are less intense. When you find that your husband didn't put out the trash and you say, "I am aware that George didn't put out the trash," it becomes only an event, with few interpretations or feelings attached. You won't race to think that you can't count on George, that he never does what he promises, or that he doesn't love you.

———

A third way to tap into your sense ability is to say an affirmation over and over. The one my clients have found most helpful is *I choose to live each moment in an accepting, relaxed, and conscious way.*[6]

You might want to say this phrase a few times right now, allowing yourself to feel its strength.

"I choose to live each moment in an accepting, relaxed, and conscious way."

"I choose to live each moment in an accepting, relaxed, and conscious way."

By repeating this affirmation a few hundred times throughout the day, you will keep yourself focused on the present moment and you will experience more and more awareness. Your mind will become quiet. The constant chatter will cease. And the stillness you feel will give you even greater awareness.

If you're thinking, "No way. This is just one more chore I have to deal with," I urge you to try saying this affirmation anyway. Do it just for a day or two. By seeing yourself more clearly, you'll be better able to disengage from the aggravations, irritations, and psychic pains that invade your life. Also, you won't feel as harried and you'll have more energy.

The number-one reason people seek therapy is because they are in pain. And they want out of their pain. A good therapist helps provide insights and new strategies for dealing with these problems. By regularly and consciously using your sense ability, you can begin to become your own therapist. In your mind's eye you are seeing yourself. Once you see yourself and how some of your thoughts and feelings and actions are not helpful or productive, you can make the appropriate changes.

Remember: Intelligent behavior is not responding instantly but sorting out the best response in each situation. And you can't do this until you are able to see yourself and are free from your automatic response patterns.

A man and wife would sit and meditate each morning before allowing the day's events to take over their lives. Every day as they were meditating, they would hear the impatient honking of a horn next door, signaling the arrival of the neighbor's car pool.

One morning after meditating, the man said to his wife, "If I had the power, I would will that all four tires of that honking car would go flat every day as that guy got in his car."

The wife replied, "My, my. That's rather drastic."

After thinking it over, the man said, "If I had the power, I would will that the horn on that car would never work and could never be fixed."

The wife's response, "That's still a bit drastic."

Some hours later the man came back with a slight smile and said, "If I had the power, I would will that the horn wouldn't work, but only in front of our neighbor's house."

The wife said, "That's better."

That night as the couple got into bed the man said, "If I had the power, I would be so intently involved in my meditation that I wouldn't even hear the horn."[7]

What I admire about this man is his willingness to continue to search for the best response. He went from thinking vindictive thoughts and "Why can't the other guy change?" to focusing on himself and what *he* could do differently. The man used his sense ability, he looked at a variety of responses, and he changed.

———

Here's another way to tap into your sense ability: Any time you use the word *why* to explain your actions, switch the word to *how*. For example, suppose you are the impatient type. If you ask yourself *why* you are impatient, you might say because you are tired, you have too much to do, and you come from a family where everyone was impatient. When you ask yourself *how* you are impatient, you might say you cut people off in midsentence, you drive fast, or your tone of voice is often curt. Already, with one small technique, by changing the word *why* to *how*, you have started becoming more aware. You are developing your sense ability.

DO PEOPLE REALLY CHANGE?

Often, when I see someone in therapy or give a talk, a person will say, "People don't change. You can't change a person."

My response is, *"Oh, yes. People change."*

I've had people leave therapy and tell me they are different people, inside and out. They think differently, feel differently, and behave differently. People gain control of their anger. They learn to manage their feelings and stop making critical and sarcastic comments. They learn to give compliments. They learn responsibility, doing what they say they'll do, staying within their budgets, or stopping the affairs. They control their drinking or give it up entirely. They stop procrastinating. They go back to school, change jobs, or start dating. They learn to be generous. They learn the true meaning of love.

No one stays the same throughout life.

Are you the same arrogant or scared kid you were in high school? No way.

Have you learned a new sport or taken up a new hobby in the past ten years? Of course you have.

Have you learned to use a computer, set a VCR, get information from the Internet, program your answering machine, send a fax, use an ATM machine? Probably so.

Remember Alice in Wonderland? She's talking to the Caterpillar:

"Who are you?" said the Caterpillar. . . .

Alice replied, rather shyly, "I—I hardly know, sir, just at present—at least I know who I was when I got up this morning, but I think I must have been changed several times since then."[8]

By reading this chapter, you have already begun the process of change. You have already started to become more aware, to use and expand your sense ability.

A DEMANDING JOURNEY

You will be asked a number of questions in each of the chapters that follow. For example, "Do you get too angry?" "Do you know how to love?" "How do you handle suffering and disappointment?" "Are you an inner-directed person or an outer-directed person?" "What do you obsess about?" "Are you aware of your psychological boundaries?" "Are you a critical person?" "Are you jealous?" "Are you controlling?" "Do you perform acts of selfless service?" "Do you talk to God?"

These are the issues in life that demand awareness. These are the issues that limit or expand your sense ability. These are the issues that make or break relationships, that govern job success, that determine whether you live life in sadness and misery or whether you live your life in contentment, peace, and enlightened maturity. These are the core issues that define your life.

Because of the importance of these issues, I ask that you answer all the questions that are asked of you throughout this book. Take the time to answer them in your head or write the answers in the margins, because in the very process of answering these questions, you will be developing, using, and expanding your sense of awareness.

Humans have a wonderful urge, a special drive, to make things better in their lives and in the lives of others. This book was designed to help you do that.

The methods and techniques for awareness and change suggested in each chapter have been used with successful results by many therapists, and most are backed by research. Some techniques will not appeal to you, or you'll doubt their efficacy. But, as Mom used to say, "Just try it once. You might like it." Research also shows that even the smallest of changes, using one simple technique, can have an enormous effect on a person's life.

You will find instructive stories from Christianity, Judaism, Buddhism, and Hinduism. Each story was chosen to help clarify and teach the principles in this book.

The stories of others that are used throughout *Sense Ability* will help you see that you are not alone in your struggles or in your desire to give meaning to your life. By reading these stories, I believe you will get answers for your own life, and you will gain hope and comfort and a feeling of oneness.

You may find this book hard work. It's a demanding journey and not for sissies. It requires you to focus carefully on your life, to take responsibility, to stretch out, to try new ways of thinking, feeling, and behaving, to become aware, to use and expand your sense of awareness.

Most of us spend much of our life sleeping, as in a dream. This book is a wake-up call to learn to love yourself, to love others, to control your anger, to put away your criticisms, to better cope with disappointment and suffering, to quell the constant stream of desires, to conquer your depressions and anxieties, to do away with petty jealousies and envy and impatience. This book invites you to gain mastery over the issues that define and shape each day of your life. It invites you to have healthy and loving relationships, to see your interconnectedness, to become totally aware, to see, to awake. Or, as Saint Paul said, "Wake up, sleeper, rise from the dead. . . . " (Eph. 5:14) It's time to discover and use your sense ability.

2

ARE YOU OUTER-DIRECTED OR INNER-DIRECTED?

What lies before us and what lies behind us are small matters compared to what lies within us.

Henry David Thoreau, author

I was at a board meeting, waiting patiently for the proceedings to start, when another member walked in. He greeted everyone good-naturedly, took his place at the table, and then said, "Can't a guy get a cup of coffee around here?"

Without missing a beat, a woman got up, asked the fellow what he took in his coffee, and fixed it for him.

The man, who was covertly asking to be waited on, was at that moment inner-directed. His focus of attention was himself.

The woman who got the coffee was outer-directed. Her focus of attention was on someone other than herself.

People constantly shift their focus of attention from the outside world of others to the inside world of themselves. At the same time people are genetically programmed one way: to focus most of their attention either outward or inward. This trait is readily observed early in life and is remarkably persistent throughout life.

Because people tend to be somewhat polarized, there is a noticeable difference in the way an outer-directed and an inner-directed person thinks, feels, and behaves. Although no one is entirely outer-directed or inner-directed, each type exhibits a distinct, observable pattern of behaving.

In your quest to expand your sense of awareness, you will come to understand if you are outer-directed or inner-directed. As you understand the differences, you will see not only why and how problems arise in your relationships, but also how you can avoid these issues by thinking and behaving differently.

YOUR FOCUS DETERMINES YOUR BEHAVIOR

The following three scenarios describe three people who have very different ways of focusing their attention and consequently behaving. You probably have a number of characteristics similar to one of these people.

Maggie's focus of attention and consequent behavior is mainly directed toward others; she is outer-directed. Bill's behavior reveals that he is mainly focused on himself; he's inner-directed. Al has very different behaviors from Bill, but he is also inner-directed.

As you read, ask yourself: *Am I like this person? And if so, how? Do my behaviors reflect an outer-directed or inner-directed orientation?*

Meet Maggie

Maggie is thirty-six years old, has two children, and is a computer scientist. When Maggie wakes up in the morning, the first thing she thinks about is the children's schedule. When she remembers that Pete's soccer game is at 5:30, she immediately plans how she's going to juggle her time so she can leave work early.

When she hears on the radio that the temperature is dropping, she calls to her daughter to take a jacket. She goes outside to cut some roses before the cold weather finishes them off. Maggie knows that Shirley, the office receptionist, loves roses.

As Maggie fixes coffee, she telephones her mother to remind her of Pete's game. She gives the cat fresh water and adds food to his bowl. She pours herself coffee, calls to Pete to hurry, and reminds him not to forget his soccer shoes.

When Maggie gets to the office, she gives Shirley the roses and tells her she likes her blouse. She hands a fellow engineer an article she cut out for him the night before. She works at her terminal with few breaks.

If someone has a technical problem, Maggie is the one who can be depended on to figure out a solution. If people seem unhappy in her department, she brings them little presents and offers advice. Sometimes her advice is unsolicited, but it is always well meaning.

Because Maggie is so aware of others, she could easily name a number of things people could change about themselves. Because she understands that she has a tendency to be critical, she works to control her negative comments, although she's not always successful.

Maggie sees it as her job to help people. Maggie has a hard time saying no, and sometimes she gets so tired and stressed with everything she takes on that she can be found in the washroom crying.

Are you like Maggie? Do you know anyone else who thinks and acts like her?

Meet Bill

Bill is forty-seven years old, married, has two teenagers, and is an attorney. As soon as the alarm sounds, Bill's out of bed. He throws on his running clothes, does a few warm-up exercises, and flies out the door. By the time he gets back from running, the family is up. When Bill notices that his wife is about to take her shower, he gives her a sheepish grin and says, "You don't mind if I go first, do you, honey?"

After his shower, he fixes himself cereal and asks his son what's happening. As his son talks, Bill reads the newspaper and only half listens. When he's finished eating, he jumps up, grabs his briefcase, and says flirtatiously, "Doesn't anyone here have a kiss for me?" His family gives him kisses and he's off.

When Bill gets to work, he meets with one client after another. Because he overschedules himself, he often runs late. When he makes a promise to do something, he frequently forgets because he gets busy with other things. He sometimes starts conversations in the middle of what he's thinking, and people are often forced to figure out what he's talking about. Those in his firm see him as bright, funny, high energy, and a go-getter. On any day of the week, however, someone is annoyed with him, and Bill just can't understand why.

Recently Bill telephoned me (we talk every couple of weeks), and when I answered the phone, he said, "I've been trying to reach you for an hour. Where have you been?" I shook my head and smiled. I do love Bill—we've been friends for years—but he sure operates as though he's the center of the universe.

Are you like Bill? Who else do you know who acts like him?

Meet Al

Al's married, has three children, and is an insurance adjuster. Getting ready for work, Al only half listens as the television reports the events of last night. When his wife asks if he's going to be able to make it to their youngest son's soccer game, he says he's not sure. He gives no further thought to her question.

When his daughter rushes in to ask if he can pick her up from swim practice, he says, "Probably."

When she insists, "Daddy, I've got to know. I have to make plans," he responds, "I guess I can."

As he pours himself coffee, he asks, "Has anyone seen the milk?" His wife says, "It's here on the table."

He eats his breakfast quietly and half listens as his wife checks schedules. When she leans down to kiss him goodbye, he turns his cheek so she can kiss him. When she says, "Say, what do you think of my new dress?" he notices it for the first time, smiles, and says, "It's nice."

Al is a hard worker. His co-workers think he's a nice guy, but no one knows him very well because he doesn't talk or share much about himself. Even in a brainstorming session that involves his department, he rarely makes a comment. He doesn't get angry. He's not critical or sarcastic. He's not rude. He simply goes with the flow.

People in Al's social circle also like him. But here too, no one knows him very well. He just doesn't share himself. Nor does he remember to ask about someone else.

Are you similar to Al? Do you work with anyone like him or have friends who act like him?

As you can see from these three scenarios, if you are outer-directed, you're simply more aware of others and what's going on around them, whereas if you're inner-directed, you are more aware of and tuned into yourself. Each focus has its pros and cons.

DIFFERENCES BETWEEN OUTER-DIRECTED AND INNER-DIRECTED

Here are some interesting differences that social scientists have observed about inner-directed and outer-directed people. Read the list with yourself in mind.

- An outer-directed person feels love when giving; an inner-directed person feels love when receiving.
- An outer-directed person feels powerful when she does things for others; an inner-directed feels powerful when he gets others to do things for him.

- An outer-directed person is very concerned with the opinions of others; an inner-directed person doesn't concern himself too much with what others think.
- An outer-directed person lectures, gives advice, corrects, analyzes, and forever wants to change people; an inner-directed person doesn't want to change and has no need to change others.
- An outer-directed person often loses sight of self; an inner-directed person is aware of self.
- An outer-directed person gives energy; an inner-directed person takes energy.
- An outer-directed person is good at reading body language; an inner-directed person tends to be less in tune with nonverbal communication.
- An outer-directed person often wants togetherness and strives for interdependence; an inner-directed person primarily wants independence.
- An outer-directed person pursues people; an inner-directed person allows himself to be pursued.

Note that I used the pronoun *she* when describing an outer-directed person and *he* for an inner-directed person. This is because more women focus their attention outward on others and more men focus their attention inward on themselves. There are, however, outer-directed men and inner-directed women.

Keep in mind also that you focus your attention both outward and inward. It's just that your tendency, your genetic inclination, is to focus mainly in one direction.

You might compare this difference in focus to being right- or left-handed. A right-handed person will use his left hand, but less frequently. And a left-handed person will use his right hand, but not as often as his left.

Sometimes people think that an outer-directed person is outgoing and talkative and an inner-directed person is shy and quiet. This may or may not be so. An outer-directed individual may be very shy and an inner-directed individual very talkative. An outer-directed person may be low energy and an inner-directed person high energy. An outer-directed person may be selfish and not very loving. An inner-directed person may be altruistic and loving.

Having an outer or inner focus should not be confused with being extroverted or introverted, although some sharing of characteristics between extroversion and outer-directedness and introversion and inner-directedness does occur.

———

The differences between outer-directed and inner-directed people do account for an interesting polarity in behaviors of men and women. For instance, women are generally better gift givers, while men frequently miss the mark. Why? Because the outer-directed woman is generally more in tune with the person she's buying for, whereas the inner-directed man is not focused on others and what they might enjoy.

When making social arrangements, an outer-directed wife checks with her husband before finalizing plans because she views this as caring, responsible behavior. An inner-directed husband may make plans without checking first because he wants some independence and checking is an interdependent behavior.

Outer-directed women tend to take on the role of emotional cheerleader in the relationship. They want to talk and spend time together. Inner-directed men sometimes view this as an infringement on their life. It's as if women are always chasing men, and men are always running away.

BLAME IT ON YOUR GENES

Your focus of attention has a biological basis. At birth, you have a predisposition to be either outer-directed or inner-directed. Then a variety of other factors come into play that determine how strongly outer- or inner-directed you are. These factors include your parents' expectations, how you are nurtured, and our culture.

If you're female, your parents may have expected you to take care of your siblings, both physically and emotionally. As a result, you honed your ability to look outward. If you are male, your parents may have had few expectations. As a consequence you probably did not develop your ability to look outward but developed more fully your ability to know what you want in life.

Our culture also influences how strongly outer- or inner-directed you are. Because boys receive more attention than girls in our society (some studies report two to three times as much), men come to expect to be the center of attention. It's what they have always known. Because little girls see little boys getting more attention, they fall into step, focusing outward and *giving* attention.

Sometimes an unexpected event will modify a person's focus. For example, an inner-directed man who loses his job may come to look more outside himself and be more sympathetic to others who have had job difficulties and financial reversals. An inner-directed man who experiences a major illness may become more conscious of his family. On the other hand, an outer-directed woman may become more inner-directed if she has a problem at work or if she becomes ill.

Perhaps we adjust our focus during a time of crisis, with inner-directed people turning outward and outer-directed people turning inward, because our usual way of thinking and behaving seems to have failed us.

Many women have told me that when they were in their twenties and thirties, they were too outer-directed, often worrying about others to the exclusion of themselves. By their early to midforties they started to focus more on themselves and what they wanted in life.

Conversely, many men often start out being extremely inner-directed, and by their early to midforties, they were focusing more on others. Through time and experience, most people adjust and modify their focus, but their basic center of attention does not change. This was made clear in a most poignant way some years ago.

———

My friend Betty was dying of cancer. It was a Wednesday evening, and I had the strongest urge to see her. When I walked into her bedroom, she said, "Doris, I'm dying."

I said, "I know, Betty. What can I do?"

She looked at me and said, "Will you please clean my bedroom and bathroom? I know that must sound silly, but please will you?"

I said, "I understand." I got busy and dusted her dresser, folded her robe, and straightened some magazines and papers. I went in her bathroom, cleaned the sink and mirror, and emptied the wastebasket.

When I walked back into Betty's bedroom, I asked if there was anything else I could do. By this time her daughter had come into the room. She asked if her daughter would put *Madame Butterfly* on the stereo. The three of us sat silently, listening to an aria. Betty looked at us, smiled, and said, "Now I'm fine."

Several hours later she died.

What Betty needed first was to have her outside world in order. Once this happened, she was able to relax and turn inward.

MOVING TOWARD A BALANCED SELF

Inner-directed	*The Balanced Self*	*Outer-directed*

● ● ● ● ● ● ● ● ● ● ● ● ● ●

Looking at the line above, take a pencil and mark the area where you perceive yourself to be—far right, far left, only a little to the right or left, or somewhere in the middle.

The farther you are from the middle—the Balanced Self—the less awareness and harmony you have in your life. As you develop and use your sense of awareness, you will move toward the center, toward balance, harmony, and wholeness.

Too Outer-Directed

Many people, particularly women, think that being outer-focused is better, more admirable and virtuous. Certainly it is a better world when people look out for each other and are generous, giving, and responsive to others' needs. But sometimes outer-directed people go overboard and do *too* much for others to the exclusion of themselves. Then they feel taken advantage of, overwhelmed, and not appreciated. Also, when you do too much for another, your giving sometimes becomes smothering and detrimental.

I'm seeing a woman in therapy who is too centered on her young son. If he's happy and things are going well for him in school and with his friends, she's happy. If her son does poorly on a test, has a run-in with a teacher, or is snubbed by another child, she takes his side and goes into action. She does too much to ease his pain. She might call the teacher and plead her son's case. She will take him to a movie, plan an overnight with some of his friends, run him to the music store to pick out a few CDs, or go to the library and help him with a paper. This child is not learning how to handle problems and disappointments and take responsibility for himself. He's not building his own resources, which he will need. This woman's happiness is too dependent on her son's happiness.

————

The following story shows the pitfalls when one is too outer-directed:

"A monkey was sitting in a tree looking at the water below. All of a sudden, the monkey hopped down, grabbed a beautiful salmon from the water, and placed it on a high tree branch.

"The monkey's friend looked at her and said, 'What on earth are you doing with that salmon?'

" 'I am saving it from drowning,' the monkey happily replied."[1]

Are you like this monkey, jumping in to the detriment of others?

If you're smiling in recognition, start by taking better care of yourself. This is essential if you are to develop your sense ability. I ask all outer-directed people to set aside a half hour each day for themselves because they rarely take time for themselves. Your eventual goal is to reach an hour each day and five or six hours each weekend, even if you have young children.

Also think about what you've always dreamed of doing. Going away for a month to write? Taking a drawing class? Starting to play the piano again? If one of your children or your mate had such a goal, you would most likely be supportive and help figure out how he could reach it. How about directing that energy toward yourself?

Becoming aware, developing your sense ability, requires time and attention directed toward yourself.

Too Inner-Directed

If you are too inner-directed, you must learn to look outward more often, taking others into account, if you are to develop awareness.

Several days after I had given a talk on this subject, the president of a corporation telephoned and introduced himself. He said, "I recognize myself. I'm one of those types who's been accused of always doing what I damn well please. What's the cure?"

I half laughed and said, "You have two assignments. These assignments are easy for some people and difficult for others. For you, they will be difficult."

He said, "I can handle it."

"Okay," I said. "The first thing you do—every time you make a decision to do something, be aware of how your decision is going to impact or affect other people. If others are going to be adversely affected, consider an alternative plan. In this way you'll be taking others into account.

"The second thing—keep all promises. If you promise to telephone someone on Monday, do it. If you promise to be home by six, be home by six. No excuses."

I've never heard from him again and often wondered if he was able to keep his assignment.

If this were your assignment, would you have difficulty doing it?

If you're inner-directed and passive, and your style of behaving is quietly doing your own thing, not sharing yourself or your ideas, you also must become more outer-directed if you are to expand your sense of awareness. Otherwise, others become responsible for the directing, planning, and decision making that affect your life. Also, you miss out on being an integral part of someone else's life and having others be a part of yours.

Ed, who was inner-directed and passive, came to see me because his wife was threatening to leave him. He seldom talked or shared and rarely gave of himself emotionally. I put him in a therapy group where he learned to interact with others. He had three goals: (1) to reveal something about himself each week, (2) to initiate a conversation and learn something about another's life, and (3) to give his wife three compliments a day. For one year Ed kept a written record.

The night he graduated from his group, Ed said, "I thank you. My wife thanks you. My children thank you." I will never forget how pleased he was. I gave him a pat on the back and knew that his thank-yous were about becoming a more introspective, sharing, giving, balanced human. Ed had learned to use his sense of awareness.

Ask yourself: *Do my thinking and actions imply an "I-count-you-count" philosophy? Is my focus in life a balanced one?*

Once you are able to focus outward on others and inward on yourself, you are developing and using your sense ability.

DO YOU 3 KNOW
HOW TO LOVE?

If I speak in the tongues of men and of angels, but have not love, I am only a resounding gong or a clanging cymbal. If I have the gift of prophecy and can fathom all mysteries and all knowledge, and if I have a faith that can move mountains, but have not love, I am nothing. If I give all that I possess to the poor and surrender my body to the flames, but have not love, I gain nothing.

1 Corinthians 13:1–3

Dick came to see me because his wife was going to leave him. It was our first therapy session, and he was in great emotional pain.

One of the first things I asked Dick was if he knew why his wife wanted to leave him. He said he wasn't sure. I asked what his wife had complained about through the years. He said his wife thought he always had to have everything his way.

"Is this true?" I asked.

He said, "Not always."

He related that when he was a child, his father was in charge of the decision making. He guessed he had some of those same tendencies.

I asked if he could think of any specific incidents when he insisted on his way. He said his wife wanted to put an addition

on their house with money she had inherited from her grandmother, but he had nixed the idea. He said that at one time she
wanted to go back to school and finish her education. He was
against it, so she never went back. In retrospect he's sorry that
he didn't encourage her.

"Have you ever told your wife that you've regretted taking
that stance?" I asked.

"No," he said, "I've never brought it up. My philosophy is to
let sleeping dogs lie."

I said, "Sometimes they're not sleeping." He smiled in recognition.

I asked Dick what other complaints his wife had. He said she
thought he had a bad temper.

"What do you say?" I asked.

"Sometimes I do," he admitted.

I questioned whether he had ever hit his wife when he was
angry. "Never," he said indignantly. "I would never touch her."

"How about name calling or intimidating looks?"

"Sometimes," he admitted.

I asked if he was a pouter. He looked at me and said, "How
did you know?" I said that often when a person thinks he should
be in charge, he uses a variety of behaviors to get his way.
Pouting is one of them.

Dick said, "My wife's sarcastic and she's very critical."

My response, "That doesn't make you want to be with her,
does it, Dick?" I could see the wheels turning.

"So how long can you pout, Dick—a couple of days?" I asked.

"I've been known not to talk for a while," he said.

I pushed. "What's a while, Dick?" He grinned at having been
caught. "A couple of days, maybe a week," he said.

I asked what other reasons his wife might have for leaving him.

"Golf," he said. "She thinks I like golf better than I like her."

"Do you?" I asked.

He laughed and said, "No."

"How much do you play?" I inquired.

He grinned and said, "Every chance I get. I love the game."

He proposed that maybe his wife was mad because he forgot her birthday. She had given him a surprise party for his birthday, and then he forgot hers. "But, honest," he said, "it wasn't intentional."

When I asked what he'd done to make up for forgetting her birthday, he said he thought he had apologized. And he sent her flowers, which she promptly threw in the trash.

I kept pushing. "Anything else your wife complains about?"

"She's always saying I don't love her."

"If you did love her, what would you be doing differently?" I questioned.

"I guess I'd listen more. Maybe spend more time doing what she wanted. Tell her I love her. That's a big one. I'm not a bad guy, you know. I just don't think about those things."

"So why not, Dick? I bet your wife has told you plenty of times," I countered.

"You're right," he said, "she's told me plenty."

Unhappily for Dick and his wife, Dick does not know how to love. Perhaps if he had known what love involves, perhaps if he had listened to his wife, been more introspective and aware of his behavior, this lonely man would not be sitting in front of me.

WHAT IS THIS WORD CALLED *LOVE*?

Many people think they know the meaning of love because they have allowed themselves to fall in love, perhaps many times. They have experienced the merging of their ego state with that of another, like two rushing streams converging. Each person felt tremendous physical attraction and passion for the other. They were carried away with hormones and chemistry. They idealized each other, listened to each other's stories, supported one another, did things for each other, provided for one another, and excluded the world. Romantic love.

When each person stepped back and regained a sense of self,

when each took a more in-depth look at the other, each sometimes decided that yes, something greater than romantic love was developing. Each felt the love growing and made the decision to remain together.

Other times, after taking a more in-depth look at each other, one or both of them turned away and declared, "I am no longer in love."

Some say they know the meaning of love because they feel it in their bones, in their very soul. When they think of their mate or children, parents or special friend, they feel an overwhelming sense of closeness. For a moment in time they are one with the other. This is how love "feels."

Love also means *doing*, performing acts of kindness, selfless service, munificence. The performance of these loving acts—this is what expands your sense ability. This is what determines if you truly know how to love.

Think of love as an active verb: dynamic, attentive, aware, vigilant, thoughtful. Think of love as something one person does for another because he believes that the other person has value and worth. Love is listening. Love is remembering. Love is giving, receiving, respecting, confronting, and disciplining. Love is playing. Love is forgiving.

In the process of using your sense ability, you will undoubtedly find some areas where your love is great, perhaps in the giving area. You will also uncover areas where your love is somewhat lacking, maybe in the area of listening. Interestingly, using your sense of awareness helps you become a more loving person, because when you love, you become less judgmental, less critical, less controlling, obsessive, and jealous. And as you love, you expand your sense ability.

LOVE IS LISTENING

If you know how to love, you listen.

When someone talks, you don't merely hear their words, you

listen to that person. Your purpose is to discover something new. You step back from what you think and feel and try to understand what the other person thinks and feels. You do not rush to judge, problem-solve, analyze, or lecture. You listen with your face, your eyes, your mouth, your whole body. You don't fill in words when the other person hesitates or wait for a chance to break in and tell your story. You focus on what the other person is saying. You ask thoughtful questions that are in keeping with the topic. You say, "Uh huh," nod, smile, laugh, and try to put yourself in the other person's shoes. You don't glaze over, make a to-do list in your head, or mentally take a trip to Bermuda. You travel along with the person talking. You listen.

———

My husband runs a company. Sometimes he shares a problem, and I immediately want to tell him what I think he should do. Instead I ask, "Do you want my feedback or do you want me to simply listen?" Usually he says, "Listen."

I think, "Oh heck." But if I'm being respectful of him, I do what he wants. I listen.

———

As I was writing this book, my friend Linda called every so often to find out how it was going. She would say, "Want to read me a few pages?" And sometimes I did.

As she listened, she'd interject, "Yes . . . yes . . . good . . . go on." Linda knows that when I write my first and second draft of a book, all I want is hurrahs and encouragement. By the time I get to the third or fourth draft, I look to Linda for suggestions and feedback. Because she listens, she understands what I need and when.

Whenever I telephone Linda, she's enthusiastic. She knows how to make me feel special. She's a true friend. She gives time, attention, and compliments. If you're in trouble and call Linda,

she doesn't put you on hold. She listens. She seeks to understand. Linda knows how to love.

———

A woman was telling her husband about having dinner with their
oldest son and how grown-up he seemed. As she was talking,
her husband interrupted and said, "Did you tell him to wear
sunscreen?" She said, "Sunscreen? What are you talking about?"

The husband said he had just seen a show on television about
skin cancer and how everyone who's out in the sun should wear
sunscreen. Needless to say, this man had not been listening to
his wife.

Perhaps it's because we have so many places to go, things
to do, and people to see that we've lost the art of listening.
It's always a treat for me to watch someone listen and not interrupt. If you're having problems with a relationship, listen to
the person, seek to understand, and you'll see the relationship
improving. When you listen you give the other person the gift
of self-esteem. You convey to him that he is important and
loved.

Do you know how to love—how to listen?

LOVE IS REMEMBERING

If you know how to love, you remember.

If your friend has a job interview or a major presentation, you
find out how it went. You remember. Your remembering says,
"What is going on in your life is important to me."

You make a point to remember the courses your child is taking, her teachers, and the names of her friends. If your memory
isn't good, you write the information down and review it periodically.

You remember a friend's favorite color, favorite flower, what
she likes to eat, the type of books she enjoys reading. If she

E-mails you a note, you E-mail back. If a favorite book of hers is made into a movie, you bring it up as a subject of conversation. If she completes a project, is awarded a contract, makes a big sale, you offer congratulations.

———

A man forgets his wife's birthday. The wife is crushed. She interprets her husband's forgetfulness as not caring. She says, "He doesn't love me. If he did, he'd remember." A forgotten birthday or anniversary is certainly not the end-all, but it's an indication that the husband doesn't love enough. He needs to remember, to love.

Some men tell me they're forgetful, and birthdays and special events just don't mean that much to them. I say, "That's because no one has ever missed your birthday, so you don't really understand." I ask how many times they've forgotten to attend a football game. They say that's different. Is the difference because one is important and one is not? And which is really important?

Some people say they don't remember "this stuff" because they have a bad memory or they aren't the sentimental type. If you have a bad memory, put a note on your calendar. If you're not sentimental, okay. But remember anyway. Your goal is to discover ways in which you might become more loving. Remembering someone on *her* special day is a way to love, a way to expand your sense of awareness.

———

Saying thank you is another way to remember, to love. For example:

"I love the pin you gave me, Martha. I wear it all the time."

"Thanks for the wonderful dinner, Mary Jane and Jack."

"Thanks, Mom and Dad, for taking such great care of our children."

Some people say thank you automatically. It's part of their

automatic response pattern. Others are less free with their re-
membrances. But each time you say thank you, each time you
remember, you are being loving.

———

Every time I do something special for my niece, Machelle, she
sends me the same thank-you card because I enjoy it so much.
The card by Gibson features characters from the comic strip
Mother Goose and Grimm:
    On the front it says, *"To: Your Royal Thoughtfulness"*
    On the inside it reads, *"From: Your Humble Thankfulness!"*
    I've never gotten tired of receiving this card.

    Right now, look around you. Who do you want to remember to thank?

    I was talking to my friend Michaeleen while sucking on a
piece of hard candy. All of a sudden Michaeleen looked at me
and said, "Doris, can you speak?" I shook my head no. She turned
me around and did the Heimlich maneuver several times. Out
flew the piece of candy that had lodged in my throat.
    That weekend I went and found a necklace for Michaeleen
that had about twenty gold stars on it. It also had some silver
ones and some with rhinestones. It's pretty glitzy, I must admit,
but Michaeleen frequently wears it. Each time I see her wearing
it, I'm reminded of how she saved my life. Each time she wears
it, she's reminded of what she did. We remember.

———

I wrote a newspaper column about my mother this past year that
was reprinted in many newspapers around the country, and many
readers wrote me saying how it brought back memories of their
own mothers. The column follows:

    Hi Mom. Happy birthday!
    When I looked on the calendar and found that your birthday
fell on the day my column runs, I decided to write my column

about you today. So sit back, and I hope you enjoy because I'm going to talk about how great you are.

I think my earliest memory of you, Mom, was when you slipped on the ice on the front steps and couldn't get up. I was three, and you had me go to a neighbor's house to get help. It was you and me in that little house; Dad was away in the war. I remember loving you so hard.

I remember the day you enrolled me in kindergarten, and I got sick, and you carried me four blocks because I couldn't walk. You were so worried.

Remember when I would come home for lunch when I was in grade school, and we'd sit at the table and eat soup? We'd listen to *Rex Davis and the News* and then that radio soap opera that started with "Can a girl from a small mining town in West Virginia . . . ?" I loved coming home for lunch and being with you.

I remember, too, that every day about four o'clock you'd go wash up and put on make-up because Dad was coming home. I used to secretly admire you as I watched you put on your lipstick. You were so pretty. You still are beautiful, Mom.

I remember one night I was not a very good girl, and you told me that when the ice cream man came, I was not going to get an ice cream. I was sure you were going to change your mind. You went out to that little truck and got everyone but me an ice cream. I was so sad when you didn't get me one. I knew then I better behave. Thanks, Mom, for having the courage to discipline me.

I remember all the times you took me to swim practice and all the malts we drank afterwards. Mom, do you know how many fat grams are in those malts? They were sure good, weren't they?

Remember all the meals you prepared? Pork chops with mashed potatoes and applesauce and peas. Fried chicken, mashed potatoes, white gravy, spinach, beets, and salad. And pie for dessert. And when you made liver for Dad, you made us girls bacon because we couldn't get the liver down.

Remember how I used to read that Betty Crocker cookbook and cook all summer long? You ate everything I made, even my first cherry pie when you had to tear the crust because it was so tough. You were my friend.

Remember when I had our son John? I couldn't get him to sleep for anything, and you'd come over and rock him, and he'd go to sleep. That's when I realized experience was everything.

I remember when I started writing my newspaper column years ago. Anna-Mary was a baby. If I got writer's block, you'd come over and play with her or take her for a walk so I could get it together.

I remember, too, all the times you babysat John and Paul and all the swimming outings and fishing trips you took them on. And how you'd save your money for Christmas to be able to give everyone a special gift.

Mom, you have given me so much. You taught me to say "please" and "thank you" and "I'm sorry." You taught me to give hugs and freely say "I love you." You gave me the gift of liking to work. You gave me a belief in God and a religion and you taught me to pray. You gave me the courage to try new things and be adventurous. You gave me the love of cooking and eating and having family gatherings. You taught me how to take care of others and to be responsible. You taught me to smile and laugh and enjoy life and make each day count. You are a wonderful wife, a sweet grandma, a special human being and my mom. I love you!

Do you remember when? Do you let others know that you remember? Is there someone you might remember today?

LOVE IS GIVING

Mary and her husband had been living apart for almost a year. She was in the process of divorcing him. For years he had been verbally abusive and unfaithful. They were within two weeks of their divorce when her husband called her. He said he had been diagnosed with leukemia and would probably live less than a year.

Mary helped her husband move back into her home and took care of him for the next five months until he died. He continued to be abusive and ungrateful.

When her friends asked why she put up with the jerk, she replied, "You don't have to be in love to be loving. I'm doing it for our children, for myself, and for him because he needs help."

Mary knows how to give, how to love.

———

Peter was twenty-seven and dying of prostate cancer. He had been working for his company for two years as the assistant buyer for merchandizing. He had been off work for three weeks because of surgery and treatment. When he went back to work, the head of the company sat down with Peter and said, "Whatever you need, let us know. You'll get your full pay, no matter what. Just get yourself well."

Peter struggled to go to work, sometimes only a few hours a day. Everyone in his department pitched in and took up the slack. Until the day Peter died, he received a paycheck. The boss and the people in Peter's department knew how to give, how to love.

———

Author and therapist David Reynolds suggests a number of maxims for people to live by. I think my favorite is "Give and give until you wave goodbye."[1]

In some relationships a psychological withdrawal occurs long before the end of the relationship. If each member would give right up to the end, perhaps there would be no end. And if the end did come, each would have fewer regrets.

———

One year at Christmas I asked my mother what she would like Santa Claus to bring her. She said without hesitation, "A bicycle." I asked with enthusiasm, "And what kind of a bicycle would you like Santa to bring?" She said she'd like an exercise bicycle.

I thought, "Oh darn." I wanted to buy her a real bicycle, one she could pedal around. I knew she didn't have a bike as a child. Maybe she would like to go with me to the store and ride a real bicycle? She said no. What she wanted was one that didn't go anywhere.

In the end I got her what she wanted. One of my all-time favorite pictures of Mom shows her smiling happily in a red dress and high heels, perched on her brand new bicycle that didn't go anywhere on Christmas Day.

Do you give others what they want instead of what you want?

———

When I do marriage counseling, one of the things I'm most struck with is the lack of generosity between partners. They don't give to each other. The husband doesn't tell his wife she looks nice, or she has beautiful eyes, or he loves her sense of humor. The wife, on the other hand, doesn't remind her husband that she loves his hair, or ruddy complexion, or the fact that he's so darned smart.

When I talk about the importance of giving compliments, I'll often ask the husband to give his wife five compliments right there in the session. He can't do it. He stumbles and stammers, and I have to help him think of nice things to say to the woman he's been living with for years.

When I ask the wife to give her husband five compliments, she's able to do it immediately, but her compliments often have a critical undertone. For example, she'll say, "It's nice that you finally got the gutter fixed," or "I like your hair now that you've got it cut." Her compliments are prickly. Prickly compliments limit your sense of awareness. Prickly comments are not loving.

———

I'm seeing a couple in therapy who recently married. He's fifteen years older than his wife. They have just bought a house. Although he's a multimillionaire, he refuses to put his new wife's name on the house. When I ask him why, he says, "It's my money. I earned it; she didn't. If her name's on the house and we divorce, she'll get half the house."

I realize that some marriages end in divorce and an antenuptial agreement safeguards a person's assets, as well as his children's inheritance. At the same time, why is this man not willing to put his wife's name on the house, making it *their* home? He wants her to share his bed, to share herself, to help maintain and decorate his house, entertain their friends and his children, but he is unwilling to share his house. She is not asking for his business or other assets, only that her name be added to the deed for the house.

Another problem is she has no children and would like to have a child. He says he's done having children. He has four. She says, "You promised me we would have a baby."

He says, "I changed my mind."

This man is not giving or loving.

———

A friend complains to me that her mother, now in her mid-eighties, talks almost exclusively about the past.

When my friend tells her mother, "Mom, you've told me that story," her mother says, "I know, but I want to tell you again. It makes me feel better."

I've known the mother for years. She's been a giver all her life. She raised two children and ran a restaurant with her husband. Every day they were up cooking by 6 A.M. When this woman came to her daughter's house for a visit, she'd pitch in and cook, clean, and iron. Now age has beaten her down. She's all bent over and can barely walk. She's become forgetful. Perhaps the only thing she can give is her story.

If you are a grown child who feels frustrated by an aging

parent's repetitive story, show your love by listening. If you can't
bear to hear the same story again, allow yourself to drift and
daydream without becoming impatient or annoyed. Remember:
The only gift your parent may have to give is her story.

———

Dr. Joan Borysenko writes of Mother Teresa:

> I have never seen the power of unconditional love more pow-
> erfully demonstrated than in a documentary film about Mother
> Teresa in which she is shown ministering to sick and dying
> children. When asked why she bothers to care for children who
> will soon die anyway, she replies simply that love is the birth-
> right of every person. It's what we're all here on earth for.
> There's a particularly moving part in the film where Mother
> Teresa is caring for a severely spastic child who is dying of
> malnutrition. His wasted face and limbs are contorted in a
> twisted mask of pain and fear. Mother Teresa begins to "lay on
> hands" with great tenderness, smiling her love into the fright-
> ened eyes. Within minutes, the child's limbs have miraculously
> relaxed, and his face is full of peace and love. The Natural Child
> in him, temporarily asleep, is reawakened by her love.[2]

———

Love is giving your child's hair a rumple when you pass. Love
is bringing your husband a cup of coffee. It's jumping up and
taking care of your little ones while your mate sleeps in. It's
inviting your folks for dinner. Bringing the office gang dough-
nuts on a cold November morning. Visiting someone in a nursing home. Smiling at the grocery clerk. Baby-sitting for a friend's
child. Pitching in and helping a colleague at work. Snuggling in
bed with your grandchildren. Getting someone to laugh.

Love is sharing an idea, sharing money, giving time, giving
someone a pat, a compliment, a hug, kisses, smiles, presents, and
cards. Love is offering counsel, solace, empathy, and your time.

LOVE IS RECEIVING

Love is being able to receive.

When I was in the third year of writing my newspaper column, a new editor decided to drop my column. The day I found out I was being canceled, I couldn't stop crying. I cried all day, all night, and all the next day. The only two people I told were my husband and my partner, Serra. Neither had seen me in such a state. Both of them held me and let me cry. Through my tears I whimpered, "I'm not going to tell anyone."

Serra, the wise mother-of-reason, said, "Doris, people will see that your column isn't in the newspaper. They will ask you about it. Go to the paper and see if there isn't something you can do."

I finally shut off the tears and blew my nose for the hundredth time and decided I just couldn't let this happen. I called the managing editor of the newspaper and made an appointment.

When we talked, he said, "Columns come and go, and readers like new things."

I said, "But the column is well read. It's reprinted in school newsletters; it hangs on company bulletin boards. It helps people in their daily lives."

He said, "Have some people write and tell me how much they like the column and we'll reconsider."

I said, "Fine."

I now had the task of asking people to write letters. What I discovered was that I didn't know how to ask for help. I knew about giving. I was a wife, a mother of three children. I was a therapist. I was responsible for training graduate students to do group therapy. I gave talks in the community. I advised my friends. But I didn't know how to receive.

In the next two weeks I learned a lot about humility and pride and asking for help. It was very painful. I asked people to write letters, and a friend got up a petition to save my column. Soon after, the managing editor called me and said, "Okay. You've got your column back."

I think people are adept either at giving or receiving. Outer-directed people tend to be better at giving. Inner-directed people tend to be better receivers. Also, our culture schools women to give and men to receive. Unfortunately, this sad polarity of give and take has been the demise of many relationships. Some people need to receive more, and others need to give more, but even this disparity waxes and wanes through the years. Difficulties do arise, however, when one only receives and has little idea how to give back, or when one gives and gives, and then feels hurt and emotionally unnourished.

If you do not know how to receive very well, ask yourself, *"How* do I not receive?" If you'll recall from Chapter 1, "Discovering Your Sense Ability," asking *how* instead of *why* invites more observation and increasing self-awareness. This Gestalt technique immediately helps you tap into your sense ability.

When one woman was asked, "How don't you receive?" she answered: "Well, when something needs to be done, I don't wait for others to do it. I take care of the job myself. In fact, my husband is always saying, 'You don't give me a chance to do anything for you.' And he's right. I guess I need to be more patient. More understanding of his schedule, his rhythm.

"Another way I don't receive—I think sometimes I don't see or value what others really do for me. I'm rather particular, sort of fussy about gifts and how things should be. When I receive something that isn't me, I think I don't count it. I think on some level people know I'm hard to please so they're reluctant to give to me.

"Maybe I don't receive so well because I like to be in charge. When others do for me, I'm no longer in charge. Like not letting anyone bring dessert when I'm having a dinner party."

In one brief session this woman had gained great insight. She now understood that others wanted to give to her. Perhaps now, in addition to giving, she will be able to receive. All she needs to do is open her heart and arms and learn to accept their gifts.

If you're stuck at the opposite end of the spectrum, and you're not much of a giver, ask yourself, "How don't I give?" Such questions help you open sleepy eyes, become more loving, and expand your sense of awareness.

––––––

Do you have trouble saying the words *I love you?* Perhaps you never learned to use these words, or you have fallen out of the habit, or you're too embarrassed.

I know a man who hated to say, "I love you," to his wife. When his wife told him, "I love you," he became annoyed. When I asked him why he was annoyed, he said, "When she says she loves me it's really for her, because she expects me to say it back."

Certainly he had a point. When we tell someone, "I love you," often there's some expectation, some small demand, that the other person say it back. At the same time, saying "I love you" may be one of the most perfect forms of giving and receiving. When someone says, "I love you," the person is giving. When someone says, "I love you, too," he or she is giving back.

A woman told me that her husband is finally walking with her. She extracted a promise from him that for one month the two of them would walk around the neighborhood after dinner. Now, some months later, they are still walking. While walking, they talk of their children, share their worries, lovingly brush up against each other, and laugh at how wonderful and difficult life can be. In the very act of giving, this man has received.

––––––

An old rabbinic tale addresses the importance and fulfillment of being able to give and to receive.

The Lord said to the Rabbi, "Come, I will show you Hell." They entered a room where a group of people sat around a huge pot of stew. Everyone was famished and desperate. Each held a spoon that reached the pot but had a handle so long that it could not be used to reach the mouth. The suffering was terrible.

"Come, now I will show you Heaven," the Lord said. They entered another room, identical to the first—the pot of stew, the group of people, the same long spoons. But there everyone was happy and nourished.

"I don't understand," said the Rabbi. "Why are they happy here when they were miserable in the other room, and everything was the same?"

The Lord smiled. "Ah, but don't you see? Here they have learned to feed each other."[3]

LOVE IS RESPECTING

If you know how to love, you are respectful.

You do not tell someone you will do something and then not do it. You do not make people wait unless you have a valid reason. You return telephone calls. You do not name-call, make sarcastic comments, or use a hostile tone of voice. You do not hit, push, try to intimidate by raising your voice, or refuse to talk because you are angry. You do not lie, try to dupe another, or ignore your marriage vows.

You let go of all mean-spirited behaviors. You are never rude. You are a courteous driver. You are polite to waitresses, sales-clerks, solicitors, cabdrivers, airport attendants, and repair people. You treat others with kindness. You strive to be considerate, thoughtful, and mannerly. In your presence, others feel worthwhile and valued.

If you are an employer, you pay people a fair salary. You do not pile more and more work on them. You recognize their contributions to the company. You provide a healthy and pleasant work environment. You do not lose your temper or degrade an employee. You do not set up a situation where people feel threatened and competitive with one another. You know how to take charge if a situation calls for it. You understand your management style. You do not misuse your power. You know how to be a leader.

If you are an employee, you don't take advantage of your company. You do what is expected, and you meet deadlines. You do not slough off your job, pad your expense account, roam the halls, spread rumors, procrastinate, or take too much personal time. You work to the best of your abilities. You try hard to get along with everyone and help establish an environment of trust and cooperation.

———

In your quest to develop and use your sense ability, ask yourself again: *Do I respect others? Is there someone I need to be more respectful of?*

LOVE IS CONFRONTING AND DISCIPLINING

If you know how to love, you confront and discipline when necessary.

You do not sit by while your mate drinks himself to sleep at night, or your friend gains a lot of weight, or your sister never visits your parents, or your co-worker carries off the company's supplies, or your child always has money and you have no idea where he's getting it. You take the risk and talk with the person.

Unfortunately, if you decide to take charge and confront an individual, you risk having that person turn the confrontation around and become annoyed or angry with you. People have a habit of wanting to kill the messenger. At the same time, confronting and disciplining are important parts of love, and if you never take the risk, you should question how loving you are.

———

I have a friend who is hoping to transfer out of her department because she can't stand her boss. Why? Her boss refuses to take charge. "He never has an opinion," she says. "When we're having a meeting, he lets people talk on and on. And whoever yells the loudest gets her way. The other problem—he won't let anyone else make a decision. The upshot is, everyone feels helpless. Eventually everyone transfers out of the department or leaves the company."

Needless to say, this boss is not loving.

I had a woman tell me that bosses don't need to be loving. I say, "Oh, yes. Bosses are people, and all people need to be loving." Teachers, supervisors, salesclerks, secretaries, parking attendants—no one is exempt.

If a person calls in sick, a boss can say, "Feel better. And come back quickly. We need you." With these statements, the boss extends comfort to his sick employee while showing concern for the company. He is a loving boss. If the boss believes a particular employee calls in sick too often, he can later confront the situation.

If a boss sees someone is not doing her job, it's his job to care enough about the company and the other employees to confront the person. This is love. If the person does not alter her behavior, the boss may need to fire her, which again is loving. Love is confronting and disciplining.

———

Here's another example of people who did not know how to love, how to confront, when that was the very thing that was called for.

A woman was having her license renewed. She appeared to be close to eighty. She was using a cane and had difficulty walking. Another woman, presumably her daughter, had to help her. When the elderly woman got to the counter, she had a hard time understanding what the clerk was asking.

When it was time for the eye test, she was uncoordinated and had trouble putting her head against the machine. She took at least five minutes to complete the test; most people finished in thirty seconds. The woman kept saying she couldn't see. Finally the clerk said, "Okay. Go get your picture taken."

The woman who was renewing her license is not loving to

others. She is thinking only of herself. The clerk who allowed
her to renew her license is not loving. She probably wanted to
get the woman out of the bureau and get on with her job. She,
too, is thinking only of herself. The daughter who helped her
mother is not loving. She would rather be passive, allowing her
mother to renew her license, than confront her mother and perhaps take on the added responsibility of a mother who does not
drive.

All three of these people could see the risk of the mother's
continuing to drive, but none of them was caring or loving
enough to confront it. Only after someone kills a family or runs
her car into a school bus do we say, "She should never have
been driving."

No one wants to hang up his car keys. Sometimes people must
love others enough to confront themselves and say, "It's not safe
for me to be behind the wheel." Sometimes a grown child must
be the one to say to his parent, "No more driving, Dad. I love
you. That's why I can't let you drive." Sometimes a professional,
such as a doctor, must take the risk and tell his patient, "No
more driving. Your eyesight is too poor."

It was prom night, and some of the high school juniors and
seniors chartered a bus to take them to the dance. During the
bus ride they drank beer and whiskey. By the time they arrived
at the dance, a number of them were drunk.

The school decided to suspend these students for eleven days.
The students were allowed to go to the school district's alternative discipline center where they could work on their assignments under teacher supervision. Several of the students' parents
protested the suspensions, complaining that the school was being too harsh.

The parents who protested may be loving parents in many
ways, but their unwillingness to support the school in its disci-
plinary decision was not loving.

I suspect each of these parents would gladly lay down his or her life in exchange for the life of their child. And yet, these parents could not see that the principal's decision to suspend the children for their reckless behavior was a way to show love. There would be no record of the event put in the students' files. The seniors would be allowed to graduate with their class. But their irresponsible behavior was duly noted and had a consequence. The principal knew how to love.

———

Some years back I wrote a column about not allowing your underage child to drive.

After the column appeared, a woman called my office and said she had allowed her fifteen-year-old daughter to take the car for a drive, and the girl was killed.

The woman wanted to know if I thought she was a bad parent. I first had her tell me about her daughter and their relationship. Then we talked of discipline and love and how difficult it is to teach responsibility to strong-willed adolescents. In the end I told her that she sounded like a loving parent who had made a mistake, who should not have allowed her daughter to drive.

She cried for a long time and said she'd been waiting for someone to tell her that. She knew she had been wrong.

I said it was now time for her to work on forgiveness. She agreed to find a therapist in her area and work on forgiving herself.

———

Liz's mother was in excruciating pain, dying of bone cancer. Liz spent days taking her mother to the hospital for treatment, waiting on her, sitting by her bedside, and comforting her father. Liz's husband, Alan, never went to the hospital, never offered to help out. He offered no support to his wife or in-laws.

Some months after Liz's mom died, Alan's mother became ill

and needed to be taken to the hospital for treatments. Because Alan's father was in his eighties, the couple needed help. Liz again was loving and took it upon herself to help.

Alan remained distant from his mother during her illness, as he had from his mother-in-law. Additionally, he chose to go on a two-week ski trip with an old college roommate and the roommate's girlfriend.

When Liz complained to Alan's therapist about Alan's lack of support, the therapist responded, "Alan needs to take care of himself during this period. He's confronting his own mortality."

Liz's response: "What about confronting his responsibility?"

I wonder why the therapist did not confront Alan on his lack of caring for his wife, his in-laws, and his own parents. Was it easier for the therapist to be supportive of Alan's fears than confront Alan on his responsibilities? Good therapy requires both.

How could Alan justify offering little to no support to his wife when her mother was dying? And what about supporting his in-laws? Through the years they had been there for him. And his own parents—why was there so little love shown to them? In the process of developing his sense ability, Alan will need to confront himself, to ask of himself, "In the hour of my wife's and parents' needs, how might I have been more supportive, more loving?"

———

Emily, age sixteen, thought she was too old to have a curfew. She also thought she shouldn't have to report where she was going or who she'd be with. Emily's mother believed otherwise. She thought it was important to know her daughter's whereabouts and set curfews. Typically, when Emily's mother asked her daughter about plans, the daughter gave her halfway answers and used a get-out-of-my-life tone of voice.

Whenever the father heard the two of them bickering, he would say to the mother, "Leave her alone. She's only young once." To his daughter he'd say, "Don't mind her. You know your mother. She's always complaining about something."

Confronting children is love. Teaching them responsibility and manners is love. Having expectations, guidelines, and rules is love.

Are you loving enough to your children? Is there someone you need to be confronting?

LOVE IS PLAYING

Sometimes when I walk in the park I'll notice a family playing together. They may be engaged in a game of Frisbee or touch football. They bump into each other and laugh and push and shove good-naturedly. I've seen a mother down on all fours giving her daughter a pony ride while watching a father run around in circles with one child clinging tightly to his back and another screaming and laughing, trying to tackle dad around his legs and bring him to the ground. I've watched an old man feed the ducks and two women sit on a bench and laugh.

How wonderful that God has given us the ability to smile, to laugh, to relax in each other's company. How wonderful to see the world in all its glory, to feel an interconnectedness with others, with nature, with God.

Play expands our appreciation of life. It swells our joy. It relaxes and yet energizes and stretches us to become more than we presently are. Play helps us grow. It gets us to take a break from suffering, disappointments, and worry. It sets the stage for feelings of intimacy.

Thich Nhat Hanh says, "People of our time tend to overwork, even when they are not in great need of money. We seem to take refuge in our work in order to avoid confronting our real sorrow and inner turmoil. We express our love and care for others by working hard, but if we do not have time for the people we love, if we cannot make ourselves available to them, how can we say we love them?"[4]

Becoming a truly loving person requires, demands, that you play.

How much time do you spend playing? Having lunch with co-workers, going fishing, playing golf, playing cards, going to the movies, reading for pleasure?

How much time do you spend with your mate? Going to the symphony, playing tennis, sailing, dining out, making love?

How much time do you spend actually playing with your children? Not running them from activity to activity, but going to the zoo or having a picnic on the family room floor?

Do you notice any imbalance?

Do you spend too much time focusing on your own activities while ignoring your mate?

Is there too little time for you and too much for your children?

A man told me his wife would be a good golfer if she would only concentrate and listen to what he said. She shot back, "You get too critical. Even our friends feel sorry for me on the golf course."

He said, "Hasn't your game improved since I've been telling you what to do? And when you play lousy, you come home mad. You're not a stupid woman, but you've got to con-cen-trate. Con-cen-trate." His voice was gruff as he pointedly enunciated his words.

He looked at me and said, "Do you play golf?" I told him I drive the cart and cheer. He dismissed me with, "My poor dear, you don't get it."

Am I the one who doesn't get it?

If a sport makes you miserable, it's not play. If you get angry with others while golfing, playing cards or a board game, this is not play and it's not loving. Screaming harshly at your children from the sidelines to "Get that ball" is not play, not love.

I looked up the word *play* in a thesaurus. What I found was "frolic, rollick, frisk, romp, caper, lark about, flounce, skip, dance, cut up, horse around, fool around, carry on."

Do you skip and lark about with your wife? Romp with your children? Cut up with your co-workers?

Do you need to spend more time at play?

LOVE IS FORGIVING

Forgiveness is love. It means letting go of anger, hostility, and resentment; letting go of hurt and sadness; letting go of the right to get even.

When Suzanne told her husband she was going to put some school papers in his briefcase for him to copy for her, he told her to set them on top of his briefcase and he'd take care of it. Suzanne instantly felt something was wrong.

After her husband fell asleep, she looked in his briefcase. There she found a letter written on a legal pad. It talked of love and commitment. Suzanne felt guilty for not trusting, and tender feelings welled up for her husband. When she turned the page over and continued to read, however, she realized the letter was for another woman.

"My heart started pounding, and I gasped for air," she said. "I thought I was having a heart attack. My crying was so intense I broke a blood vessel in my eye."

After learning of her husband's affair, Suzanne demanded he move out of their house. Because her husband wanted the marriage, he readily complied. He also gave up the affair immediately. And apologized over and over. During that time Suzanne debated whether she wanted the marriage and could ever live with her husband again. Every day was a rollercoaster ride among feelings of hurt, anger, and rage. Because they had young children, she decided to give it a try.

It's been three years since Suzanne learned of her husband's affair. The two of them have been through marriage counseling, group therapy, and Retrouvaille, a program designed to help troubled marriages.

Today their marriage is stronger than most. But trust and forgiveness remain problems for Suzanne. Some days she's able to be forgiving and say to herself, "He didn't have the affair to hurt me. He had it to take care of himself."

Other days, hurt and anger overwhelm her. She thinks, "I was a good wife. Why did he betray me? I'll never be able to forgive."

Suzanne is forgiving her husband. It's just that her forgiveness is happening a little at a time.

MAKING A DECISION TO FORGIVE

Forgiveness begins when a person makes a conscious decision to forgive. Often this decision is reached because it is just too painful, too awful, to keep obsessing about the injustice. You see life going on around you, and it calls to you to join in and partake. You know that others have suffered and survived. On some level you understand that to be whole, to regain your peace and your freedom, you must work to forgive.

Sometimes you decide to forgive because the person who has wounded you is a family member and you don't want others in the family to suffer. Or you must deal with the person on a daily basis, and it's just too heavy a burden to continue to carry the anger and hurt.

When someone sees me for therapy because he feels resentful and has been unable to forgive, I have him tell me his story uninterrupted. I listen and let him know I understand. I then have him tell me his story again. And sometimes again. Not because I haven't listened, but because in the second and third telling, he softens. He doesn't have to convince me that he's been wounded. In the retelling he is less dramatic, less hostile, less full of details.

I ask how he has kept his suffering and bad feelings in the forefront of his daily life. How many other people has he told his story to? How often does he fight in his head with the person?

I get him to look at the consequences of holding on to his resentment—restless sleep, poor health, less ability to enjoy others and feel joy. If he does not let go of his anger, he hurts himself.

I ease him into telling me about the goodness of the other person, the joy he or she provided in his life. Sometimes I ask him to write down the other person's good qualities.

Depending on the offense, I may ask him to take the role of the other person and tell me the story from the other person's point of view. This is most difficult and rarely works well in his first telling. When he can gain insight into why the other person may have acted as he did, however, he sometimes starts to heal.

If he is religious or spiritual, I ask him to pray for help to forgive. If he's Roman Catholic, I sometimes give him a Saint Jude novena book. I once gave a book to a woman I thought was Catholic because I knew her sister was Catholic. Several weeks later when I saw her again she said, "Who is that Saint Jude person? I think he really helped me."

I talk about the Buddhists' belief in lovingkindness and how when you are hurting, you are asked to see in your mind's eye all the people you love. I ask if he can see the person who has offended him, and if he can kindle lovingkindness toward that person.

We talk of how forgiveness is about his pain and not about the other person who has offended him. We talk of how he wants an apology, how he sees it as his right, but that he does not need the other person to apologize for him to be able to forgive.

I remind him of the Lord's Prayer: "Forgive us our sins, as we forgive those who have sinned against us." (Matt. 6:12)

I remind him of what Lewis Smedes says in his book *The Art of Forgiving*: "Vengeance is personal satisfaction. Justice is moral accounting. Forgiving surrenders the right to vengeance, it never surrenders the claims of justice."[5]

We talk of retribution and how when you forgive, you give up your right to get even. You do not give up your right to justice. If you have been hurt in an accident because of someone else's carelessness, if you have been raped, if someone has physically or psychologically damaged one of your children or taken advantage of you financially, you may choose to extract a penalty, demand reimbursement, or ask that the person do a community service.

We talk about the fact that life is not fair. And sometimes family, and friends, and bosses, and co-workers take advantage and step hard on your heart. Sometimes justice never seems to be served. But in the end, it is how you deal with the injustice that limits or expands your sense of awareness. It is how you deal with the injustice that makes a difference in your life.

LEARNING TO FORGIVE YOURSELF

Over the years, Patty has secretly spent more than thirty-five thousand dollars of her family's savings. She is guilt-ridden and remorseful.

How did she spend the money?

If the family went to dinner and the bill was thirty dollars, Patty said it was twenty. She was fearful that if her husband found out the true cost, he would be angry. When she bought a birthday gift for someone, she lied about the cost. This way she could give what she wanted and not have to face her husband's wrath over the gift's cost. If they had to buy extra food because they were entertaining, she would supplement the food budget out of savings.

When Patty's husband learned that she had spent their savings and was secretly taking from his IRA by forging his name, he immediately filed for divorce.

Patty feels guilty because she did not have the courage to confront her husband about the way he controlled with money. She feels great sadness over the loss of her family. She hopes that her ex-husband will forgive her and tell her that in many ways she was a good woman, a good wife. Although this would be wonderful, her ex-husband may never have enough love to forgive her. What Patty must do is come to terms with what she did. She must forgive herself.

———

In order to forgive yourself, you must stop denying that you hurt another and that somehow your reasons were justified. You must cut off your stream of explanations and rationalizations. You must take responsibility and say, "I did it, it was wrong of me, I caused another pain." If possible, you must apologize and then make amends, which might translate into being more loving to the person, saying over and over you are sorry, paying back money if need be, or doing volunteer work in the community. Giving and doing for others is one of the best roads to the forgiveness of self.

Forgiving is hard work, whether it's forgiving yourself or another. And often you don't forgive all at once. It's more like chipping away at your sadness, hurt, and resentment. Sometimes it takes years, perhaps a lifetime. Yet there is nothing you can't forgive. And in the process of forgiving you regain your freedom, you reclaim your soul.

DO YOU KNOW HOW TO LOVE YOURSELF?

If you truly know how to love, you know how to love yourself. You *listen* to yourself. If something does not feel right, you trust your feelings. If you're tired, you let yourself rest. If you're hungry, you take the time to eat.

Loving yourself means you *remember* that you like popsicles, popcorn, apricots, and peach jam and you keep them around and treat yourself. You remember to wear your favorite cologne or put on your favorite tie. You remember that as much as you like watching your grandchildren, you get tired and you need backup if they're to be with you all weekend.

Loving yourself requires that you *give* to yourself. You look in the mirror and say, "Hi, what a great smile you have. What beautiful eyes you have." You pat yourself on the back for a job well done. You take a day off to play.

You love yourself by letting others care for you. You allow yourself to *receive*. When someone offers to help you with a report, clean your garage, or help rebuild your porch, you let him. You have learned to feel comfortable letting others help you out.

To love yourself means you are *respectful* of yourself. You don't give yourself to someone sexually so he will like you. You don't go to a party and drink too much. If you have a drinking problem, you go to AA, Rational Recovery, a treatment program, or a therapy group. If you're overweight, you exercise and eat differently.

Your list of things to do for the day is reasonable. You do not put it on yourself to run to the nursing home every day to take care of a parent. You give yourself certain days off each week. You pursue goals and know your limitations.

You care enough about yourself to *confront* yourself on behavior that you need to change. You stay home from work and go to the doctor when you're ill. You take time to *play* a little every day. You *forgive* yourself.

A LIFETIME TO LOVE

Learning to love takes a lifetime. Most people know how to love in some areas but not in others. A father may be wonderful at giving to his children but not good at disciplining. A woman may be giving to her children but not giving to her husband. A man may be forgiving toward his family but not respectful of his co-workers. Parents may provide the best that money can buy for their children but never listen to their hopes and fears.

In your quest to develop your sense ability, what have you learned about love and the way you love? How will you be different?

DO YOU GET
TOO ANGRY?

If you are patient in one moment of anger, you will escape a hundred days of sorrow.

Chinese proverb

Many people get too angry. If someone says or does something they don't like, they instantly try to take control by becoming angry. It's as if no one else counts but them. There is no room to see things differently. No time to explore, to talk, to understand.

A person may handle his anger by getting a mean look on his face, using a threatening tone, or raising his voice. He may make rude comments, shout obscenities, and degrade the person who he thinks has crossed him. The angry person may simply shut another out, pout, and refuse to talk or even acknowledge another's existence, sometimes for days or weeks or a lifetime.

As a society we have allowed ourselves to be rude, sarcastic, hostile, mean-spirited, litigious, and violent. Instant hostility and verbally abusive behavior are everyday occurrences. A father grabs his daughter in a fit of temper, calls her names, pinches her arm, and later apologizes and tells her he loves her. A husband or wife thinks little of spewing out cutting remarks and using four-letter words with his or her spouse. Today it is commonplace to call your mate, the person you share your life with, a jerk, a bitch, a son of a bitch, an asshole, and then expect to make love a few hours later.

Grown children write letters to their parents and in-laws berating them for some perceived injustice. They withhold grandchildren from parents because they don't like something the parents said.

People are impatient with salesclerks and waitresses if they take too long. People cut each other off on the highway and then wave a fist or make an obscene gesture. Body language speaks of intolerance and hostility. Tone of voice conveys disdain. People are out of control with their anger.

———

When I give talks on anger, I often ask the audience, "How many of you get too angry?" Consistently, over half the people raise their hands.

When I ask how many people have to deal with someone who gets too angry on a regular basis, almost everyone in the audience raises a hand.

When I see an individual growing red in the face, pointing his finger, raising his voice, enunciating each word, trying to bully another with his anger, I wonder, "Doesn't he understand how hurtful he's being? Does he think everyone was put on this earth to serve him, to think and act like him?" I also think, "How can he justify such meanness?"

DO I ACT LIKE THIS PERSON?

In the following stories you will meet many people who have problems with their anger. As you read, ask yourself: *Do I act like this person?*

If you know you do, use the techniques spelled out in this chapter to control your anger. No one has to have a bad temper.

———

"Jim wanted to get a dog," said his wife. "He pushed to get a dog. But I was hesitant. I knew from past experience that Jim probably wasn't going to be much help. But in the end I agreed, and we got a dog.

"When the dog didn't behave the way Jim thought she should, like when she had accidents on the carpet, Jim would take her outside and beat her. Naturally the dog became afraid of him, so Jim refused to take care of the dog.

"If I had to go out of town, I'd have to take the dog to a kennel. Once I had to leave on short notice and I forgot to make arrangements. Jim called me that night and was furious that the dog was there. He said, 'I sure hope you're coming home tonight because I'm not going to take care of this dog. She'll just have to go without food and water until you get home.' There I was, over 250 miles away, feeling helpless.

"Not too long after the dog incident, Jim asked me to tape a show for him on the VCR. Somehow I missed the first half hour. When he went to play the tape, he was outraged. He kept screaming at me, 'I can't count on you for anything. You're so stupid.' He then took the tape and ripped it up, yelling, 'Now no one can watch it.'"

If you met Jim, you would probably like him. Responsible, educated, articulate, funny, good looking, and sometimes very generous and kindhearted. But if something doesn't go his way, he closes off his sense of awareness and becomes mean, aggressive, and hurtful.

———

A man and wife came to me for marriage counseling. I started by asking each of them if he or she wanted to stay married. The woman nodded her head and said yes. The man asked me what the hell that meant.

I explained that sometimes people come for marriage counseling and they're not sure if they want to stay married. They have reservations. Other times one of them wants out of the marriage. The way a person answers this question gives me a good deal of information about how I'll focus the session— which spouse is unhappier, who at that moment has the leverage, and if marriage counseling is appropriate for them.

After my explanation I asked the man what *he* saw as the main problem in his marriage. He said, "Communication." He then screwed up his face, turned toward his wife, and said sarcastically, "My wife doesn't talk to me. She doesn't think I'm good enough to talk to." As he said this, his voice was loud and he enunciated each word.

I said to him, "You're getting too angry."

His response, "You're damn right I'm angry." Then he attacked me. His words were "And who do you think you are, asking me if I want to stay married? I'm getting out of here and seeing somebody who knows what they're doing." With that announcement, he jumped up, stomped out of the office, and slammed the door behind him.

Needless to say, this man has an anger problem.

THE THREE MAIN REASONS YOU GET TOO ANGRY

How about you? Do you get too angry? You know if you get too angry. You might not like to admit it. You may downplay your anger's intensity and frequency, but you know if you have an anger problem. What you may not understand is what drives your anger, the consequences of getting too angry, and what you can do to change.

You Think Negative Thoughts

The number one reason you get angry is that you think negative thoughts. When an event happens, instead of putting a neutral or positive interpretation on it, you put a negative interpretation on it. By thinking negative thoughts, you can actually create your own anger. You can give meaning to an event in less than a second. Within a few seconds you can have a number of negative thoughts.

When Lou walked into his kitchen one afternoon and saw a stack of college books on the table and a schedule with his wife's name on it, he became furious. Lou's negative thought was that his wife was going to school to finish her education so she could divorce him! The way Lou interpreted the situation created his anger.

If a friend had walked into the kitchen with Lou that day, the friend would not have responded with anger. When he saw the stack of books he might have thought, "I wonder who's taking classes?" This is a neutral thought. He might have read the titles with interest. He might have even had a positive thought such as, "Those were the days."

———

Suppose you tell your daughter you want her to clean the kitchen while you're gone. She says okay. A few hours later you come home, and the kitchen is still a mess. You immediately think a negative thought: "I can't count on her for anything." Your next negative thought: "She never does anything around here that I tell her to do." This thought is rapidly followed by a third negative thought: "What a brat." And another negative thought: "She's never going to amount to anything." In less than a few seconds you have had four negative thoughts and you're angry.

Now let's examine more closely what happened. First, you asked your daughter to clean the kitchen, and she agreed. Several hours later when you came home, the kitchen was not clean. You have no further information. All the other thinking you did was conjectural and negative.

Because in the past your daughter has agreed to do something and then not followed through, you *assume* that she blew you off and didn't clean the kitchen because she was talking on the telephone or watching television. But you really don't know.

Maybe the neighbor had an emergency, and she ran over to watch the neighbor's child. Maybe her girlfriend hit a deer with her car, came by the house to call the police, and in the commotion your daughter didn't have a chance to clean the kitchen.

I bet you're thinking, "Oh sure, her friend hit a deer."

Well, my daughter's friend hit a deer, and the friend did come to our house to call the police. So it's not impossible. Until you have all the information, you're making assumptions that create your anger.

Without these negative thoughts, you'd be the first to admit that sometimes your daughter does do chores around the house. In fact, just yesterday she mowed the lawn and helped fold laundry. And, yes, sometimes she doesn't follow through on her promises. But do you really think she's never going to amount to anything?

You Perceive a Threat

Along with thinking negative thoughts when things don't go the way you expect them to, you feel thrown off balance, threatened, fearful, challenged, or not in control of the situation.

Going back over the previous examples:

Jim, the guy who refused to take care of the dog, felt confused and off balance when he walked in from work and saw the dog. Things were not the way he imagined they would be. He had not expected the dog to be at home. He also was threatened because he had to deal with a dog that didn't like him. When he discovered that his wife hadn't recorded the television show properly, his plans were interrupted. His world wasn't the way it was supposed to be.

Lou, the man who overreacted to the college books, was thrown off guard when he saw the books. He felt a vague sense that he was losing control. When he made a negative interpretation that his wife was going to get her degree and leave him, his fear increased.

The man who walked out of marriage counseling felt threatened because he was in an unfamiliar, uncomfortable situation with someone he didn't know. And I had challenged him regarding his anger.

You Have a Physiological Response

Once you put a negative interpretation on an event, which takes less than a second, you have an immediate physiological response. Adrenalin rushes through your bloodstream, your heart beats faster, your respiration increases, your blood pressure goes up, your muscles become tense, your digestive processes stop, your skin temperature rises, and sugar is released into your bloodstream. You're ready to do battle!

———

Some people are extremely resistant to believing their anger is generated by what they think. They want to believe other people cause their anger. If you hold to the notion that others cause your anger, then you can take the position that you're not responsible for it. It's the old he-made-me-do-it excuse. However, if you come to understand that your anger is almost always generated by what you think, the way you interpret an event, you become responsible for controlling your anger.

Some researchers believe that an intense emotion such as fear or anger or enjoyment sometimes does occur prior to thought or simultaneously with thought. But even if this is the case, "the full heat of emotions is very brief, lasting just seconds rather than minutes, hours, or days . . . For emotions to last longer the trigger must be sustained, in effect continually evoking the emotion, as when the loss of a loved one keeps us mourning."[1]

If on occasion your anger is automatically present in full force without any prior thoughts, and your adrenalin is running, which can happen in thousandths of a second, you still must think negative thoughts in order to sustain your anger beyond several seconds. You must keep feeding it or it will dissipate.

HOW YOU INTENSIFY YOUR ANGER

Additional negative thoughts that you may use to help you feed and intensify your anger include name calling, exaggerating, and using a should-and-ought belief system.

You Name-Call

You would probably admit in your off-anger hours that most people are not all good or all bad but a combination. Even the most vicious person can show lovingkindness and compassion. And the kindest, most loving person can exhibit very mean behavior.

But when you're angry with someone, you put him in the bad-guy category and you label him. You call him a jerk, an idiot, stupid, dumb, a brat, a bastard, an asshole, or whatever colorful word you can think to spit out. Once you've labeled the person, he loses his humanity. He becomes the label you've put on him, and he's now your enemy.

When Jim's wife did not record the entire television show, he screamed at her that she was stupid. In his rage he blocked out that she has many skills and talents and holds a business degree.

What is the name you call others when you're angry?

You Exaggerate

Along with name calling, you exaggerate the seriousness of the event. The event becomes the only thing that matters. You block out all other information you know about the person. You erase all the good times you've had with him. The only thing that counts is the event.

Because Jim's wife didn't tape the show properly, he tells her she's stupid and can't do anything right. When thinking rationally, he knows of many things his wife does very well. He also exaggerates the seriousness of the situation. Yes, his plans have fallen through, but he has options. He could watch the tape anyway, check the television guide and find something else to watch, rent a movie, or read the newspaper.

When Lou sees his wife's college books, he leaps to the conclusion that she's planning on divorcing him. In reality, his wife was going back to school to be better able to help with approaching college tuition for their children.

You Think in Terms of *Shoulds* and *Oughts*

You have a belief system about how people *should* act, right? And when people don't do what you think they should, you become righteous and indignant. You think it's your right, your moral obligation, to tell them off. In this way you fuel your anger by running out a lot of shoulds and oughts. For example, Jim thinks, "She *should* have put that stupid dog in the kennel. She *ought* to know how to use the VCR!"

ONE EVENT, TWO INTERPRETATIONS

When presented with any event, you make an interpretation. In the following story, a husband and wife had two very different interpretations, which resulted in two very different feelings.

Bob told me that he and his wife, Carol, had gone out of town for the weekend. Somehow Carol's grown children misunderstood when they would return. When they came home and listened to their answering machine, they found that her children had left a number of messages, such as "Where are you?" "We're trying to reach you," and "Call us as soon as you get home."

Immediately Bob thought, "Why don't those kids leave their mother alone? They're so demanding." Along with these negative thoughts, he felt threatened—his life was being interrupted by these children. Within less than a second of hearing the messages and making his interpretation, Bob had a rush of adrenaline. His heart started pounding, and his blood pressure went up. He interpreted the rush he felt as anger because the children had called so often.

When Carol heard the messages on the machine, she immediately thought, "The kids must have been worried sick that something happened to us. I guess I didn't make it clear to them when we were coming home." Along with these thoughts, she also had a rush of adrenalin. Her heart started pounding, and her blood pressure went up. Carol interpreted the rush she felt as anxiety over having caused her children so much concern.

Because Bob interpreted the rush he felt as anger, he was tempted to say something negative about the children. Because Carol interpreted the rush she felt as anxiety over having put the children through unnecessary worry, she wanted to telephone them immediately and reassure them that all was well.

AN EXERCISE: THINKING IT THROUGH

To help incorporate what you have read and to reinforce that your anger is primarily the result of your own thinking, answer the following questions:

1. In the past week, what situation or event occurred where you became angry?

   _____

   _____

   _____

   _____

2. When the situation occurred, what negative thoughts did you have?

   _____

   _____

   _____

3. What neutral thoughts might you have had instead?

   _____

   _____

_____

_____

4. If you had neutral thoughts instead of negative ones, would
   you have felt angry?

   _____

   _____

   _____

   _____

If you have an anger problem, I suggest you hang these four
questions on your refrigerator. Every time you become angry,
run through the questions. Before long you will be using your
sense of awareness and you will understand that you are gen-
erating your anger.

IS YOUR ANGER GENETIC?

Is your anger biologically based in your genes? The answer is
yes, your anger has a genetic basis. That's why two people from
the same family, who each have his or her own unique genetic
makeup, can experience the same event and feel differently. One
becomes irate, and the other doesn't feel much of anything and
wonders, "What's all the fuss about?"

If you are quick to anger, you probably have inherited a predisposition, a temperament, to be angry. You have inherited
emotionality that causes you to react *intensely* to events. And you
have inherited impulsivity so that you respond *instantly* to an
event.

However, as Carol Tavris explains, "Any inherited predispo-
sitions we have are more diffuse and generalized than those of
lower animals: genes merely provide us with a reaction range,
and environmental events determine where in the range an individual will fall."[2]

In addition to inheriting emotionality and impulsivity, people who are quick to anger often have a high energy level, and that's what's so "juicy" about them, says Pema Chodron. The idea is not to get rid of your anger—it's part of you—but to learn "to see it with precision and honesty," and not act on it.[3]

You must come to the realization that simply because you are more emotional and excitable than someone else, you do not have to respond sharply, have a hostile tone in your voice, explode, name-call or pout and refuse to talk. You must come to the realization that spewing out anger as well as pouting is mean and hurtful and does not serve you or others. You must come to the realization that even though you feel anger, you don't have to express it. You must face that you are responsible for controlling your anger.

WHEN BLOWING YOUR TOP BECOMES THE NORM

Sometimes a person who has an anger problem was raised in a family where one or both parents had a similar problem. If a daughter sees her father blowing his top or refusing to talk when things don't go his way, she may come to imitate that behavior, particularly if she has the genetic makeup. But if she doesn't have a high excitability and irritability quotient, she's not likely to follow her father's modeling.

Sometimes a child is born with a high irritability and excitability quotient, and unfortunately no one teaches him to control his anger. No one makes him accountable for his temper. No one takes him on, makes him stand in the corner, gives him time-outs, or demands a cooling-off period in his room. Most important, no one teaches him to look at an anger-provoking situation from several perspectives. He then grows up and continues to tyrannize people with his angry behavior.

Another reason people who have a high irritability and excitability quotient give themselves permission to get angry is that they live or work with people who frequently get too angry. It becomes the norm, the standard operating procedure, to get angry when things don't go their way.

WHAT DOES RESEARCH SAY?

Since the mid-1950s it became fashionable to express your anger and "let it all hang out." This idea was supported by many health care professionals who preached that it was healthy to express your anger. People were told that repressed anger would give them high blood pressure, ulcers, and possibly breast cancer. People were told that depression is anger turned inward, so they needed to get in touch with their anger and start expressing it.

Research shows that getting angry actually raises your blood pressure and stresses your heart. It also shows that ulcers are not the result of repressed anger. In nine out of ten cases ulcers are caused by bacteria. As for repressed anger causing breast cancer, only one study indicated a link, and the study has been refuted because a number of variables were not taken into account, such as the hopelessness, helplessness, and depression these women felt in their lives. And depression is not anger turned inward. Depression is a result of a chemical imbalance or various stressors in one's life.

Research also shows that people express anger because it has an effect. It's a learned strategy to get your way, not a biological inevitability.

Expressing your anger by raising your voice and yelling does not reduce your anger. In fact, expressing anger frequently intensifies the feeling. In addition, regularly expressing anger makes you a hostile person. The more often you give yourself permission to get angry, the more things you'll find to be angry about. If you give yourself permission to get angry in the morning, you're more likely to get angry later in the day. Anger sets the stage for more anger.

Getting too angry undermines your self-esteem, as well as the self-esteem of the person whom you've chosen as your target. Most people do not feel good about themselves after they explode. The people who experience the explosion certainly don't feel good. And children who grow up with angry parents suffer for years with insecurity issues.

Anger is short-lived, only a few seconds, unless you keep fueling it with negative thoughts. You can be in a vicious argument with your husband or wife, but when the telephone rings, you pleasantly say, "Hello," have a nice conversation with your friend, hang up the receiver, and can again be furious and ready to fight. Why? Because you have reflooded yourself with negative thoughts.

People who are quick to express anger are generally less tolerant and flexible than those who keep their anger in check. They are so busy being angry that they are unable to hear or see other options or viewpoints. They do not seek to understand.

Sometimes a person actually feels better after she rants and raves because she has lessened her physiological arousal—her heart doesn't pound as fast, and her blood pressure drops. However, ranting and raving to lessen your physiological arousal level is a learned cathartic habit. You can achieve the identical effect by taking a brisk walk or listening to music.

Most people have been led to believe that men get angrier than women. Men are more prone to violent behavior, but women express anger every bit as much as men. Men do pout more, however, and hold grudges longer.

People are more likely to express their anger with their mates, children, and co-workers, people they see as equal or less important than themselves. People are more likely to check their anger with their bosses, bankers, lawyers, or doctors, people they view as having more power than they have.

And the most popular place for people to allow themselves angry outbursts? Unfortunately, it's in the home. The place where they are most conscious of controlling their anger is on the job.

IS THERE EVER A TIME TO BE ANGRY?

Sometimes I read, "You need to get out your anger." I believe that this is bad advice. There is no storage box marked "Anger" inside you. As I have noted, your thoughts almost always generate your anger. Turn off the negative thoughts and your anger will dissipate.

The question, Is there ever a time to be angry? has been debated for centuries. Some philosophers and moralists say yes, others say no, and many hedge.

Anger is a feeling, and I believe all feelings are meant to be expressed at times. Feelings are a part of our humanity, and sometimes getting angry is helpful to get a point across. Always, however, you should be in control of your anger. Always your anger should be coupled with reason.

So the better question might be, How much anger is okay, and under what circumstances?

If your six-year-old runs into the street, you're going to instantly feel fear, which more than likely will be followed by anger because you have repeatedly told him not to go into the street. Pointedly saying with emotion, "Never, ever, chase your ball into the street," will more than likely get his attention.

If your fifteen-year-old son comes home drunk, you're going to have some angry feelings. This is appropriate. But expressing your anger when he's drunk isn't going to do either of you much good. The next day when you revisit what happened the previous night, you will more than likely feel angry again. His knowing that you are angry over his behavior is a way to signal, "I care. I'm concerned. It's not okay what you did."

If you learn your husband has been having an affair, you're going to feel anger. You will probably give yourself permission to yell and scream. But you will not give yourself permission to call his boss or his parents or wake up the children and tell them their father is a cheat.

If your co-worker procrastinates and doesn't complete his part of the project, which keeps you from meeting your deadline, you'll want to let him know you're irritated. At the same time, as in all these instances, you will always want to run the show with your thinking.

"The Christian-based *A Course in Miracles* teaches that we should never express anger toward others because we are, in that moment, unable to see clearly our interconnectedness with others. If we saw clearly, if we knew all the dimensions of our feelings, we would see that our anger is fear-based, that the situation would be best handled by clear explanation of need rather than outrage."[4]

Whether it's ever okay to express anger will continue to be debated. But there is no question that if you express anger, it must be coupled with reason.

I think the words of Saint Augustine also invite contemplation: "It is better to deny entrance to just and reasonable anger than to admit it, no matter how small it is. Once let in, it is driven out again only with difficulty. It comes in as a little twig and in less than no time it grows big and becomes a beam."[5]

ANGER-IN AND ANGER-OUT

A person usually has several styles of anger. An anger-out style manifests itself as yelling, shouting, ranting, raving, kicking the furniture, and slamming doors. An anger-in style is displayed by pouting, sulking, holding a grudge, refusing to talk, and withdrawing.

———

Carl, the boss, asked Rosie if she knew anything about data communication. Rosie said she didn't know much but would look into it. When Carl reviewed Rosie's time sheets two weeks later and found she had put in twenty hours researching data communication, he went ballistic. He ranted and raved and wanted to know what the hell she was doing. This was not what she should have been working on!

Rosie also became furious. She, however, said nothing. She got her car keys and left work. The next three days she called in sick. Two weeks later she gave notice that she was leaving the company.

Carl's anger style that day was anger-out. When he saw Rosie's time sheets, he had negative thoughts, felt threatened, had a rush of adrenalin, and, unfortunately, gave himself permission to blow.

Rosie's anger style was anger-in. When Carl confronted her on her time sheets, she had negative thoughts, felt threatened, had a rush of adrenalin, and, unfortunately, closed up and withdrew.

What's your style? Are you an anger-out or an anger-in person when you're at work? What about when you're at home with family? How about with someone in authority? How about with your co-workers?

Unfortunately, neither of these styles, anger-out or anger-in, is productive. The best style? Using your sense ability to control, adjust, and regulate your anger.

GETTING IN CONTROL

I've been guilty of too much anger in the past. I used to get angry when I couldn't find my keys. I'd race around the house yelling, "I can't find my keys. Where are my keys? Help me find my keys." I expected everyone to drop what they were doing and look for my keys. I'd get angry at the children for leaving messes. I'd get angry at parents who didn't discipline their children at church or at a worker who failed to show up. Because I've struggled with my anger, I know what people who are quick to anger are up against. I don't believe you have to experience every pain to be able to help, but sometimes it gives you an edge.

Almost always, when I see someone who has an anger problem, I suggest several methods to control it. Choose the one that has the most appeal. But do choose one. If you use any of them on a regular basis, you will be controlling your anger instead of allowing your anger to control you.

"I Choose to Control Myself, My Negative Thoughts, and My Anger"

One of the most important and neglected aspects of learning to control your anger is the work you must do *before* you are presented with an anger-provoking situation. Those who have a high excitability and irritability quotient are angry within less than a second of perceiving that they have been crossed. That's why telling someone who has an anger problem to count to ten before he gets angry doesn't work. He's angry by the time he gets to number one. It's too late to count.

No one would think of running a marathon without preparing for it. It's the same with anger. You must work to control your anger before the anger-provoking event occurs.

One technique I always suggest is to say to yourself several thousand times throughout the day, *"I choose to control myself, my negative thoughts, and my anger."* Start when you put your feet on the floor in the morning. Repeat it in the shower, as you're brushing your teeth, as you're commuting or you're sitting in traffic, and when you're on break. Any time you're doing a mindless task, repeat this affirmation to yourself.

Within several days you'll notice a remarkable change. Now when you are presented with a situation that would ordinarily have you red-faced and boiling, you'll respond differently.

Here is what you can expect. Someone will cross you. You'll immediately think an angry thought such as, "How dare she!" This thought, which took less than a second, will be followed by a physiological rush. At the same time, if you've been saying your affirmation a few thousand times a day, doing your homework, the thought, *"I choose to control myself, my negative thoughts, and my anger,"* will immediately come into your head. This thought will help stop further negative thoughts, your physiological arousal will lessen, and you'll be in control.

"Yeah! It Works"

"I came into therapy because of my anger," said Ron. "I had a heart attack and I'm only forty-six. I had to get in control of myself. And my wife was thinking about leaving me because I was mad all the time.

"I'd lose my temper with salespeople after asking them repeatedly to do something if they still didn't get it right. One of them would come up and not have what they needed and I'd go ballistic. I verbally abused them. I was mean. I'd say, 'How long have you been working for us? Why the f—— can't you get it straight? How many times do I have to tell you how to do it this way?'

"I cringe now when I think what an ass I made of myself and how I berated people.

"My honest reaction when I was told to say that phrase a couple of thousand times a day was that there was no way this was going to work. My thought process was that if I fly off the handle so easy, how could saying something two or three thousand times a day slow me down. But I tried it. Yeah! It worked.

"After several weeks I changed the phrase to that other one you give, *'I choose to live each moment in an accepting, relaxed, and conscious way.'* After several months people at work started coming up to me and saying they hadn't seen me lose my temper. I used to lose it every day. In the last year I have not lost it once. That's not to say I haven't raised my voice, but I was appropriate. I did not fly off the handle."

"I've Thrown Clubs Forty or Fifty Feet Up the Fairway"

Here's another testimonial that says you can learn to control your anger by repeating a phrase.

"I was the type of person who, when I got mad," said Tom, "would grab the closest thing and go at it. I'd smash tools, kick the car, throw golf clubs. I've thrown clubs forty or fifty feet up the fairway into the trees and had to get someone to get them out for me. It didn't matter who I was with. Then I'd refuse to talk.

"Once I was in the backyard and I couldn't get the lawn mower to start. The thing just would not start. I finally picked it up by its handle and smashed it against the iron patio supports. I then tore off the handle and threw it out in the yard. Then I tore off each of the wheels. Later my neighbor told me she had been watching and she said, 'I never saw anybody beat up a lawn mower before.'

"More recently my wife and I were on vacation and walking along a very crowded street. This kid was carrying a plate of food and eating. When we tried to pass, he sort of blocked our way and cursed. So I took his plate of food and smashed it in his face. Then I punched him. I was also the type who would jump out of my car and say, 'You want to go at it? Okay, let's fight.'"

Tom came with his wife for marriage counseling and then agreed to come into one of our therapy groups.

"It took me about three months to realize why I was there," said Tom. "I blamed things on my wife and other people. Then one night I talked about my anger and I was told to say that phrase, *I choose to control myself, my negative thoughts, and my anger,* several thousand times a day. I said, 'If that's what it takes.'

"After a few weeks I changed the phrase to *I will not allow anger to ruin my life or anyone else's.* I say it slowly every day in the shower. I also say it when I look in the mirror and shave. When I'm at my office or in the car or doing something around the house and I feel the tension build, I will say it. I suspect I'll have to say it the rest of my life.

"Controlling my anger put the joy back in Christmas this year. It's really put the joy back into my life."

———

As you can see from these two stories, both men had severe anger problems. By using an affirmation regularly, several thousand times a day, they were able to control their negative thoughts and change their automatic response pattern of spewing out anger.

Other affirmations you might use:

"I choose to control my anger and expand my awareness."
"I choose not to be angry. I choose to stay in control."
"I am a patient person who practices lovingkindness."
"It's my interpretation of the situation that's driving my anger."

The Cultivation of *Metta*

In the Buddhist tradition it is believed that if you continually recite a thought of lovingkindness (*Metta*), in which you hope for another's well-being, eventually animosity and hatred will become less a part of your life. Two such *Metta* meditations follow:

May I be happy, may I be peaceful;
May you be happy, may you be peaceful.

Breathing in, I know that anger makes me ugly.
Breathing out, I do not want to be contorted by anger.
Breathing in, I know I must take care of myself.
Breathing out, I know lovingkindness is the only answer.[6]

Perhaps you'll choose to memorize one of these poems and say it throughout the day.

An *X* Marks the Deed

Sometimes when someone is starting the process of controlling his anger, I'll ask him to put an *X* on his calendar each time he allows himself to pout or fly into a rage. Marking down each time you allow yourself to become angry will increase your awareness and make you accountable. You can also see how many days you've made yourself and someone else miserable because of your anger.

A similar technique is to keep an anger diary. Simply write down when you became angry, what negative thoughts you had at the time, who your anger was directed toward, and how might you have handled the situation differently. Again, recognition and accountability lead to controlling your anger.

"I'm Mildly Annoyed"

On occasion I'll suggest to someone that instead of yelling, "I'm furious," or "I'm so angry," or "I'm pissed"—all phrases you use to announce your anger and help escalate yourself—try yelling instead, "I'm mildly annoyed." Try it right now in your head.

No matter how loud you try to yell, "I'm mildly annoyed," this phrase is not going to rev up your anger. But it will help you turn on your brain and probably it'll bring a smile of recognition.

I once read that we are all five minutes from death—a heart attack, an aneurysm, an inability to breathe, a car accident. Ask yourself as you're thinking negative thoughts, "Is this incident worth dying for? Is it worth getting myself all revved up over? Is this event worth becoming mean and ugly to another of God's children?"

IF YOU MUST DEAL WITH SOMEONE ELSE'S ANGER

Suppose you don't have an anger problem yourself, but you have to deal with a mate, boss, or co-worker who does get too angry.

If it's your mate who's ranting and raving at you, start by saying in your head, *"He's turning on his anger in order to scare me so he has control. He's turning on his anger in order to scare me so he has control."* Saying this phrase will help you keep your brain turned on. And it will immediately move you to become the Impartial Observer. Once in this mode, you are not likely to get defensive and snared by the remarks he's making.

If it is your boss who gets furious, listen to what she is saying. If you believe there's little relevance or validity to her comments, you might say, "Let me think about what you're saying." When she's no longer angry, bring up the incident and the two of you can discuss the issue.

If there's some truth to what she's saying, agree with the part of the confrontation that is accurate. For example, if she says, "You're always late with your reports, and they're full of errors," you might say, "I have been late and I have made mistakes. I'll work to correct the problem." Agreeing with the part of the confrontation that is accurate often has an immediate calming effect on the person who's making the confrontation.

If the person is a co-worker or friend or someone else who attacks you with anger, try to listen to what is being said as opposed to how the message is being delivered. Sometimes making the statement, "I can see what you're saying," helps the other person calm down because he feels he's being heard. This comment also buys you time and allows you to consider if there's something you should change.

If the person expresses his anger by pouting and refusing to talk, you might say amicably, "I'd really like to solve this problem. When you're ready to talk, let me know." Then stop focusing on him and start focusing on you and your life. When he comes around, be available to talk. When the relationship is on track again, ask if he'll make an agreement that the next time there is a problem, he'll think about talking sooner, because it is in talking that sticky wickets get solved.

ALWAYS REMEMBER ANGER'S CONSEQUENCES

Often when people have an anger problem, they will make vows that they are never going to allow their anger to get the best of them again. Then several days later, they break their vows. It's not that they plan to mess up, but they do. The reason is that they have not been doing their homework. They have not been saying their affirmations, or working on thoughts of lovingkindness, or putting an X on their calendars and keeping diaries, or using the phrase "I'm mildly annoyed."

Sometimes a person says her life is too busy and she doesn't want another thing on her plate. But if you desire to be good at fly-fishing or tennis, you practice, practice, practice. The same is true of controlling your anger.

Remember: Continually getting angry sets the stage for people to fear you and dislike you. Your anger is simply too hard on their self-esteem. It's also hard on your self-esteem because most people who get angry do not respect themselves afterward. Your anger also creates a situation where people don't trust you because they're never quite sure when you'll turn on them.

When angry, you close out all possibility of love. It's impossible for you to love when you're angry and impossible for another to love you. And when you're finally done with your tantrum, you have the additional job of making amends. But this gets harder and harder because those around you probably don't believe that this is your last tantrum.

Ask yourself the following:

Why would I continue a behavior that plays havoc with my self-esteem and the self-esteem of others?

Why would I want people to fear me, dislike me, not trust me, not respect me, not love me?

With conditioning and work, you can control your anger. And in controlling your anger, you will be moving one step closer to fully developing your sense ability.

5
HOW DO YOU HANDLE SUFFERING AND DISAPPOINTMENT?

To everything there is a season, a time for every purpose under heaven.

Ecclesiastes 3:1

No one escapes life without pain and disappointment. This is the first noble truth that Buddha taught. Life is pain. Life is suffering.[1]

I look around me. Every person I know has had pain—physical pain and emotional pain. The death of a child. A chronic illness. Loss of a mate. Loss of a parent. Affairs. Lost jobs. Divorce. Problems with friends. Financial problems. Betrayals. Lawsuits. A difficult child. Alcohol problems. Car accidents. Broken bones. Cancer. Infertility. In-law problems. Problems with aging parents. I could fill several books with my friends' sufferings and ten more with some of the sufferings my clients have had to endure.

And life doesn't provide us with only big hurts; it also gives us plenty of little thumps and bumps along the way. For example: A child won't cooperate and do his homework; the toilet stops up; the electrician doesn't come when you've taken off work; your fourteen-year-old "borrows" the family car;

your mother is overly critical; a mate rejects you sexually; the car breaks down; the hot water heater goes out; a friend burns a hole in your furniture and pretends she didn't do it. This is life.

Some months, some years are better. I sometimes think, "This is good. Everything is fine, only a little suffering these last few months."

When pain comes into your life, how do you deal with it? Do you get angry? Cry? Withdraw and feel depressed? Put one foot in front of the other and keep on marching? Focus on something new? Obsess and think, "Why me?" and "It's not fair"? Do you look for insight in reading and talking with others? Do you ask God for help? Do you work with a therapist? Do you push the sadness away by refusing to think about it?

How you deal with your pain is what makes the difference. How you deal with it is what limits or expands your sense ability.

SHE'S HAD A HEADACHE FOR ELEVEN YEARS

Amanda has had a constant headache for over eleven years. Every day she's in pain. She started having headaches in the early eighties. By the late eighties, they were daily occurrences. In the beginning Amanda attributed her headaches to stress. She had three teenagers, a busy preschooler, and a demanding full-time job as a graphic designer. She took a lot of over-the-counter medication and tried to ignore her aching head.

"In the morning when I opened my eyes there was pain," she said. "On the way to the shower I'd be taking my medication. I'd think, 'I'll get in the shower, and my headache will get better.' "Then I'd think, 'I'll eat something and it will get better.'

"I'd get to work and think, 'I'll get a cup of coffee and it will get better.'

"I'd then say to myself, 'It's not getting better. But maybe after I eat lunch.'

"Finally I couldn't ignore my headaches any longer."

Amanda's internist sent her to biofeedback sessions with a psychotherapist and to a psychiatrist. "The psychiatrist tried some of this medication, and more of that, and less of this," she said. "Nothing worked."

She went to a university pain management program. There Amanda worked with a physical therapist who helped her with upper-back exercises, thinking the problem was muscular. The pain specialists also had her go to an aerobics class three times a week. Nothing worked.

She had sinus surgery because her sinus cavity was misshapen and the doctors thought perhaps that was causing the problem. "My sinus surgery was the most painful experience I've ever had," she related. "Worse, it didn't help the headaches.

"I went to several eye doctors to make sure the problem wasn't visual. I saw my dentist for the possibility of temporomandibular joint dysfunction. I had two MRIs and a CAT scan.

"I went to a special headache clinic. They put me on a tyramine-free diet and presently regulate my medication. But I still have the constant pain.

"Sometimes I think if a doctor told me to get up on the table and bark like a dog, I'd do it.

"I've had acupuncture. I've seen allergists, chiropractors, a reflexologist, a hypnotherapist, and several massage therapists. I've even visited a psychic. I've used relaxation techniques. I've had medication in every category that is prescribed for headaches. I've counseled with my minister. I'm now attending a therapy group to keep me from getting discouraged."

A year and a half ago Amanda had to take a permanent leave of absence from her job.

When I asked Amanda how she deals with the pain, she started crying. Along with her tears, she half laughed and said, "Well, I cry. The only problem with crying is that it makes my head hurt more."

She also said, "I go to bed with an icepack. I read books on headaches. I do neck-stretching exercises. I pray about one hundred times a day saying, 'Please, God, take this pain, I've had

enough.' I get mad at my headache and push myself to do house-
work or take my daughter to gymnastics. I take hot showers that
beat on my head. My family gives me head and neck massages.
At this point I'm willing to do anything that seems reasonable.
I'm waiting for the miracle."

I've known Amanda for fifteen years, before she was married,
had her baby, got her first design job. I love Amanda. Sometimes
in a childish way I say, "Okay, God, I'll take Amanda's headache
today. Give her a day off."

But that's not the way it works. We can't take another person's
pain. But we can stand by her and give comfort and support.
We can pray for her. We can make dinners, sit and hold her
hand, give her a foot rub, read the Bible with her, and search
the Net to see if there is any new treatment for her illness.
Sometimes our efforts can take the edge off her pain. In the end,
however, everyone must face his or her own pain.

———

"I loved my boss," said Marie. "She was respected by everyone.
She thought highly of my work. She thought I was smart. Then
my boss left the area and I was assigned a new boss. This boss is
unbelievably difficult to work with. She acts as though I'm stupid
and I can't do anything right. She's always on my case about
something. Not a day goes by when she doesn't make some snide
remark or send me a memo that implies I'm an imbecile.

"I like what I do and I don't want to quit my job, but my job
is very stressful because of this woman. The way I cope—I try
to ignore her rude comments. Sometimes I get very determined
and I put in extra hours trying to please her, to show her what
a good worker I am. I tell myself, 'I'm a good person no matter
what she thinks.' Sometimes I call my sister in the evening and
complain to her. I count the people on the job who like me,
and once in a while I go to lunch with my old boss, who helps
me feel good about myself."

———

When Joan received an anonymous phone call informing her that her husband was having an affair, she said that she couldn't breathe. "I think the phone call confirmed what I vaguely suspected," she said.

"My husband, who had always been easygoing, had became hostile." When Joan tried to find out why he was leaving so early in the morning for his job or what time he was coming home from work, he acted as if it were none of her business. "He also bought himself some new clothes—sweaters and pants, tennis shoes, and loafers." When Joan shared information about her life or the children's, her husband would act uninterested.

"I was also spending a lot of hours at work, so I think I dismissed the changes that were occurring."

After the phone call, Joan started checking her husband's long-distance phone bills. She looked more carefully at the checkbook and the charge card bills. There were bills from florists and restaurants. "Restaurants we never went to. Flowers I never saw," she said.

At first Joan thought of killing herself. "I just couldn't make sense of it because I thought we had a good marriage. My husband even said we had a good marriage."

When Joan confronted her husband, he gave up the affair reluctantly. He said, however, that he had never thought of getting out of their marriage. He bought his wife gifts, apologized, and tried to reassure her. When Joan would get angry and berate him, he'd take it. He refused to fight back and he kept telling her he was sorry.

After two or three years, Joan said she brought up the affair less and less. "I could actually get through an argument and not mention the affair. I still have pain, but I no longer obsess on how my husband could do this to me."

———

Jake is living with a different kind of pain. Jake's wife left him and is pursuing a divorce.

"At first I thought my wife was ridiculous and was being too influenced by a friend who recently divorced. But through my therapy group I've come to see how difficult I've been to live with.

"I've done a lot of crying. A lot of soul-searching. Talking to other people. Reading books. My group has been setting me straight, telling me I get too angry and that I'm too controlling. I've lost my wife, but I believe I'm becoming a better person."

WHAT DO PEOPLE DO WITH THEIR PAIN?

Physical pain, emotional suffering—how do these people cope? What can you learn from their stories? How do they go on?

Amanda handles her pain by trying various options. She goes to one doctor, tries the treatment for five or six months, and then, if it doesn't work, she searches for another option. She talks to people, picking their brains to see if they've heard of something she hasn't. Sometimes she bulldozes her way through the day, trying to ignore her physical pain and to focus on someone else. She listens to a problem her husband is having and cooks a meal for a sick friend. She weeds the garden. She uses prayer to give her hope. And sometimes she gives in to her pain and allows herself to tune out the world and go to bed.

Marie tries to deal with the pain of having a difficult boss by working hard, by trying to ignore the rude comments her boss makes, by complaining on occasion and using her sister as a sounding board, by telling herself she's a good person, and by remembering those who do like her.

Joan continues to struggle to trust her husband because of his affair. Chances are she will never regain all the trust she once had, but as time goes on, more trust will return. She says that she and her husband have changed. He's become kinder, more giving of himself. He shares more, puts his arms around her more. Joan has become careful not to criticize. "I think I had been too free with my criticism," she said. She started doing more things for herself and putting less emphasis on working. "I had been the giver, the accommodator, the workhorse," she said. "Now it's more balanced."

Jake, who was not able to save his marriage, is dealing with his pain by trying to understand what went wrong—how he was a difficult person to live with, how he was too controlling, how he got too angry. By reading, listening to others, and going to therapy, he is working to change and lessen his pain.

WHEN YOU ALLOW DISAPPOINTMENT TO TAKE OVER YOUR LIFE

Sadly, some individuals continually think about and obsess on their pain. They never got a college degree, or they lost their business, or they were fired, and they can't seem to move beyond the event. They can't or won't let their disappointments go.

Margaret's husband walked out on her and their three children ten years ago. The week his company announced that he would be made president, he moved out of the house and filed for divorce. Three months later he moved across the country with his secretary to take his new position. Margaret was devastated. Her whole life was upside down. She was forced to dig in and finish raising the children as a single parent. Margaret had to go through the humiliation of being left, change her view of what her future life would be, and quiet her love for her husband.

Margaret has done a yeoman's job with her children. She moved to a new neighborhood, made new friends, took up walking, has a job she enjoys, and is dating several men. Outwardly she appears to have moved on with her life and dealt with her sadness.

If you talk to her, however, you will hear about her ex-husband. You will hear her ask, "How could a man just pack up and leave his family?" If you spend any time with her, you'd think her ex-husband left her a year or two ago, not ten years ago.

Louis was fired twelve years ago. He was a good employee, but a new regime came in and he was part of the old one. He found a different job, but he has never been able to find one as high paying or as prestigious as his old job. Every conversation you have with Louis contains derogatory remarks about how his old company mistreated him. When I talk with him, I think, "He's suffered enough. Why does he choose to keep fighting with 'them' in his head, making himself miserable?"

His old job made him feel worthy and good about himself. When he lost that job, he lost a lot of his self-respect. His fight with the company is about respecting himself. What Louis fails to understand is that he's causing himself more grief and pain by keeping the fight going in his head.

Margaret and Louis are each classic examples of people who are still suffering from events of long ago. They responded to the painful situations by doing some of the things they needed to do to get their life on track, but they failed themselves by continuing to fight in their heads. Inadvertently, they have not used their sense ability and they have continued their pain.

"DROP THAT ROCK!"

I sometimes tell my clients who get caught in their pain the following story.

A man is swimming across a river and in one hand he's holding a big rock. As he nears the middle of the river, the people on shore can see the man's in trouble. He's choking and sputtering. "Drop the rock!" yells a man on the shore. "You'll be able to swim better." Still the man in the water holds on to the rock. Everyone on shore who is watching can see the man is drowning. "Drop the rock!" the people shout. "Drop the rock!" Finally the man turns and with his last breath says, "I can't. It's mine."[2]

Are you holding on to a rock that you need to drop? How often do you pick it up, examine it, and make yourself feel miserable?

Sometimes people are able to lessen their pain by claiming the part they played in their present suffering. For example, if a woman is suffering from a failed marriage, she can say, "I know I ignored him for the last five years of our marriage, and I overspent, and I often turned him down for sex." This softens her, helps her see herself less as a victim, and acknowledges wrongs on both sides. By taking some responsibility herself for her failed marriage, she is starting the process of letting go and moving on.

WHEN SOMEONE YOU VALUE IS NOT AVAILABLE

Anyone who has had to deal with a close friend or a child moving away, a spouse who is emotionally unavailable, or the heartache of not being able to find a partner understands the anguish of loneliness.

When Lynn's married daughter moved out of town, Lynn was crushed. She and her daughter had always spent a lot of time together—shopping, cooking, and taking Lynn's children to the park. They had an easy back-and-forth relationship. They referred to each other as soul mates.

Lynn's first reaction after her daughter moved was to feel depressed. For weeks she moped around. Nothing made her happy. She simply went through the motions when she was with others.

"I forced myself to stay involved," she said, "but on the inside I felt hollow."

Lynn swam twice a week, became active in a study group, and renewed old friendships. She put one foot in front of the other and kept going.

"But I was miserable. I'd go somewhere and couldn't wait to get home," she said. "Then one day it dawned on me that I hadn't thought of my daughter, not once. My day had been good. I felt content."

Lynn changed gears. She felt lonely and depressed because

her daughter had moved away, but she didn't give in to her feelings. She used her sense of awareness and made herself stay involved. She forced herself to pursue various interests. It took about fifteen months for her to shake her sadness, but now she's content with life again.

Notice I wrote, "Lynn *made* herself; she *forced* herself." Switching gears, changing directions is not easy, but it's one of the most valuable assets we have as humans, and it's one of the most important techniques for getting over a hurt or disappointment.

A To-Do List

When I'm working with someone like Lynn in therapy, I will often assign a to-do list of activities. Doing something is the last thing the person wants to do at the time. As she takes a painting course or becomes interested in herb gardening, however, her attitude about life becomes more positive. In the eastern part of the world there is a saying, "First we do, then we feel."

I use this same philosophy when a woman no longer feels in love with her husband. She doesn't want to leave the marriage because she doesn't want to share custody and have someone else parenting her children. Financially and socially the marriage works. She simply is not interested physically or emotionally in her husband.

I can't make her fall back in love, but I can help her set the stage. We set the stage by coming up with some activities that she and her husband will start doing together. I extract a promise that she will find out one new thing about her husband each week, then share it with me. She might get him talking about a favorite teacher he had in grade school, or what his mom served for dinner when he was a child.

She's also given the assignment to flirt with her husband, because as she's changing her behaviors, her husband automatically and unconsciously starts changing some of his. For every action there is a reaction. And sometimes the woman will report that she's—well, maybe—starting to fall back in love.

WHEN YOU LOSE A CHILD

Losing a child is arguably the worst pain a person can face. Talk to any parent. What is his or her worst fear? The loss of a child. For any parent who has lost a child, there is no getting over it. It gets better over time—six, seven, eight years later—but the pain never fully goes away. Yet some parents recover enough to live healthy, vital lives. What do these parents do with their suffering? What might we learn from them?

I talked with a man about his twelve-year-old daughter who was killed in an auto accident two years ago. I asked him, "What do you do, Jim, to keep the pain of your daughter's death from consuming you?" He said, "I choose the time to think about her each day. It's usually in the morning when I'm at church. Then I don't let myself think about her anymore that day. If a thought comes that is about her, I push it away. I don't allow myself to go over the details of the accident, or when the police came to get me, or when I went to the hospital to identify her. I couldn't handle it. I shut it out. I concentrate on my wife and our other children.

"I loved her so much. Oh, it hurts. But I can't let myself dwell on it."

Jim has done two valuable things for himself. He goes to church each morning, where he prays and recognizes his loss. Then, through great determination, he puts thoughts of his daughter away and leaves church.

Is what he does easy? No. Never. Each time a thought of his daughter comes into his head, it takes a herculean effort to push the thought from his mind. It would be so easy for Jim to think of her beautiful smile, her swimming at the lake, her opening presents at Christmas, her giggling, mischievous face. But to allow himself to think about her during the day is torture and leaves him too depressed. And it doesn't bring his beautiful child back.

Jim honors his child by going to church and praying for her

each morning. He also honors her by going on with his life and taking care of the other members of his family.

———

"My husband used to fly the kids back to school in his plane when they were in college," a mother explained. "My daughter Stacy was in her senior year. My son was a sophomore. There was another girl on board. They ran into bad weather fifteen minutes before they were to land, and the plane went down.

"The other family, who lost their daughter, found out before I did. They called my parish priest, and he called me. When I heard, I went outside. I looked up in the sky and kept saying to God, 'You made a mistake. You made a mistake.' Stacy had just sent in her paperwork to be a missionary.

"I also said, 'This is too big for me to handle, God. Now you must take care of me.' After I said that, a prayer shot through my head: 'May the body and blood of our Lord Jesus Christ, being offered in all the tabernacles of the whole world, bring me, not condemnation, but heal my mind and body.'

"I repeated that prayer over and over. As people talked to me about the accident, I kept repeating that prayer. I also prayed for my daughter and son and husband. I said, 'Lord, Jesus, have mercy on them.'

"I knew I would be okay. I closed the family office supply business and went back to teaching. I stayed only a semester and then opened up a Catholic bookstore.

"People send people to me who are having problems. People who are desperate. I give them that prayer.

"Saying that prayer after the plane accident, I knew I could handle it, I could make it. People would come up to me and say, 'I couldn't do it,' and I would console them. It is my faith that has gotten me through this.

"Of course everyone kept telling me to get help, see a therapist. I said, 'My psychiatrist is upstairs.' "

———

This woman has made it her life's work to take care of others in their suffering. Is she happy? Sometimes. But mostly she is calm, she is at peace.

All religions talk of the importance of selfless service to others. When someone goes through a great tragedy, the most helpful thing that person can do for himself or herself is to give to others.

I believe that those who have suffered great losses on this earth, and then turned their sufferings into compassion for others, have awakened because they are one with others.

————

I worked with a woman who had lost her child three years earlier. She could not stop thinking about her daughter Julie. Morning, noon, night. I had no doubt that this woman was literally dying of a broken heart.

One day I asked her what Julie had to say to her. She looked at me startled and couldn't understand what I was saying. So I asked again. "When you talk to your daughter, what does she tell you?" She said her daughter never talked to her.

I said, "Oh, Virginia, you must let your daughter talk to you." She asked, "How?" I said, "Give your daughter words. Say something like, 'Julie, tell me you're okay.' And then let her answer you."

From that time, whenever Virginia thought of Julie, she had a back-and-forth conversation with her. When Virginia learned that her daughter was okay and that she could converse with her in her head anytime she wanted, she was able to bear the loss of her daughter and start living again.

WHEN YOU FACE CHRONIC ILLNESS

Being chronically ill or living with a mate or child with a chronic illness is another type of suffering many people must face. An estimated one hundred million chronically ill people live in the United States.[3] Are you one of them? Or do you live with a mate or take care of a child who is chronically ill? How do you cope?

When Frank and Cece danced at their wedding twenty-five years ago, neither of them could have predicted that by middle age they'd be sitting on the sidelines watching their friends out on the dance floor. After a disc ruptured in Frank's back, affecting his sciatic nerve, he suffered chronic, often debilitating lower-back pain.

"It's been a nightmare," says Cece. "We used to go camping and fishing with the children. After Frank's back problem he couldn't pitch a tent, so the boys and I had to do it. He couldn't walk the river bank. He never said much, but it saddened me to watch him. Finally we gave up camping.

"He used to play tennis with the children and basketball in the backyard. That had to end. We used to have friends over for barbecues and parties. We still have friends to our home, but almost all the work is mine. I must do the preparation, the serving, and the cleanup. It's exhausting. I know some of our friends don't call us when they get together to go on an outing. Frank would have to sit in the car or on a bench, and that would make them uncomfortable.

"Frank is unable to lift anything and has trouble walking. Standing for even a few minutes is painful. He still works as an accountant, but by evening he's exhausted.

"He comes home and falls asleep watching the news," says Cece. "I try to be supportive, but sometimes I think, 'It's not fair. Frank is a good person. I'm a good person. Why us? Why can't we be on the golf course with our children? Why can't we go apple picking with our family? Why can't we be on the dance floor? I'm young, I want an active life.' Then I think, 'Cut that out. You're not helping yourself or Frank. Stop that thinking.'

"Mostly I count the good things I have. A husband who loves me. Wonderful children. Parents who are healthy. Good friends. Financial security. Faith in God.

"I've started walking by myself in the evening. I think Frank likes that I'm doing this, but I think he's also sad that we can't walk together.

"One thing that pulls me out of feeling sorry for myself is when I think about Frank and his disappointments in life. He's in pain most of the time, yet he never complains. He can't hike or garden. Even waiting in line for the movies is tough. He's had to give up so much. Everyone should meet Frank. They would look at their lives differently."

Frank deals with his disappointment with resignation and quiet acceptance. No complaining, no feeling sorry for himself, no thinking about what life was like in the past or could have been in the future. He lives in the present, doing what he can.

Cece struggles more with her disappointment. On some days she accepts Frank's illness and tries to make the best of their life. She mentally reviews what she does have. She says, "I wouldn't trade Frank for anything." On other days she thinks about what she's missing in her life and she feels sad.

MORE PAIN AND SUFFERING

Here are some additional problems that people I've known have had to face. Ask yourself, "How would I cope? Would I exchange my pain for their pain?"

Barbara's husband had a six-year affair with her sister. The marriage has survived, but Barbara still catches herself agonizing over it. She has never told anyone else in the family. And she still sees her sister at family functions. "I'm quiet about what happened so as not to hurt my mom or to break up the family."

Jane is forty-seven years old. Four years ago her husband was in a car accident and is brain damaged. Jane's life is caring for him and their two children.

Richard and Rachael's only son married a woman out of their faith. They originally protested the marriage, and their daughter-in-law has never forgiven them. She reacts badly when her husband wants to spend time with his family or take their children to visit. Richard and Rachael have apologized many times to no avail. The son mostly stays away.

Emily is seventy-six years old. Her only son came to her apartment and told her he and his family would no longer be inviting her for the holidays because his wife doesn't like her and it causes too many problems. She asks me, "Where do I go? Most of my friends are dead or in poor health. Other families don't want me."

———

Would you trade your problems for those you have read about? Unless you have lost a child, I think not. Sometimes comparing your problems and pain with those of others helps you understand that every human has pain.

I once read, "Be kind, for everyone you meet is fighting a hard battle." Today I have this quotation printed on the top of my stationery. It helps me be patient and reminds me that we're all in this world together. Sometimes when people are rude or not so nice, I think, "I wonder what battle they're fighting, what suffering they're struggling to overcome."

RESILIENCY—THE ABILITY TO BOUNCE BACK

Why do some people seem to deal so much better with their disappointments and suffering in life?

Some people are simply more emotionally hardy. Some people are true survivors. It is believed that this quality of hardiness is based partly in biology and partly in your attitude. One might say people who are hardy have an attitude of hardiness.

You can't change your biology, but biology is only 50 percent of the equation. The other 50 percent you can change. You can develop hardiness.

The first requirement of hardiness is to become a truly authentic person. This means that you are not tied in to your worldly possessions or your career or where you live or go on vacation. You are comfortable within yourself.

When I see someone who is unhappy with herself, I will have her write down one hundred things she likes about herself. Usually I'm met with a storm of protest. A hundred things? After the initial resistance, however, she finds she rather likes making the list. Then I have her read it each night before she goes to bed. It's remarkable how this one small exercise increases one's self-esteem. Perhaps you'll try it.

———

Remember the discussion about being authentic that took place in the story *The Velveteen Rabbit?*

Velveteen Rabbit is talking to Skin Horse:

> "Does it hurt?" asked the Rabbit.
>
> "Sometimes," said the Skin Horse, for he was always truthful. "When you are Real you don't mind being hurt."
>
> "Does it happen all at once, like being wound up," he asked, "or bit by bit?"
>
> "It doesn't happen all at once," said the Skin Horse. "You become. It takes a long time. That's why it doesn't often happen to people who break easily, or have sharp edges, or who have to be carefully kept. Generally, by the time you are Real, most of your hair has been loved off, and your eyes drop out and you get loose in the joints and very shabby. But these things don't matter at all, because once you are Real you can't be ugly, except to people who don't understand."
>
> "I suppose *you* are Real?" said the Rabbit. . . .
>
> "The Boy's Uncle made me Real," he said. "That was a great many years ago; but once you are Real you can't become unreal again. It lasts for always."[4]

Another requirement of hardiness is a belief in God, a belief in some Higher Power who is there to help you get through your pain. If you talk to God regularly and ask him for help, you are strengthening your ability to deal with adversity.

Hardiness also requires a Balanced Self. You must have the ability to look inward at what you believe you need coupled with the ability to look outward to others for their love and support.

People who are hardy also have a history of being able to deal with curve balls. That's why I object when parents want to make everything easy for their children. When children go through struggles and some adversity, they become resilient.

Hardy people are also doers. They are involved with life. When hardy people are given challenges, they may moan and groan, but they rise to the occasion.

Think of all the challenges that you have been given in the last six months. Have you risen to the occasion?

Tom, a television personality, was negotiating a new contract. The station offered to renew his contract, but the pay would have to be less. Tom said he could not respect himself if he accepted. Regretfully, he resigned.

When a newspaper reporter asked him about the pain he must be feeling leaving such a visible job in the community, Tom said he'd been through pain before. And there was no pain that could compare to the pain he had felt when he held Brandon, his dying seventeen-year-old son, in his arms.

"Brandon was so tough in the way he dealt with things," said Tom. "I would start to feel down and then I'd think, 'What right do I have to mope around?'

"Brandon went through chemotherapy three times. Lost weight, lost his hair, was constantly sick to his stomach. Because his platelets were so low from the chemotherapy, he'd bleed from his mouth and nose.

"One day I came into the hospital and he was lying there. One eye was swollen shut because a blood vessel had broken, his nose was packed, and his hair had started falling out. It was all over the pillow. The poor kid. When he saw me he said, 'Now I'm starting to look like you, Dad.'

"Brandon taught me a lot about living and dying. I think I have helped others through Brandon. I work for the Leukemia Society. I started with fund-raisers when he was still alive. I also run a fund-raiser on my own. It's called the 'Brandon O'Neal Charity Party for Leukemia.' We get hockey sticks and bats and hats signed by various athletes. I have wonderful friends who help.

"All of us are only here for a short amount of time. For Brandon it was seventeen years. Everything he was going to do he was going to do in that time. He was so involved in hockey. They named an annual hockey game after him. He left his mark. I'm glad I got to be his father."

Tom is authentic. Tom is hardy.

I've known Annie for years. When I was in college, I taught her four boys to swim. I met Annie again when she called my office because she and her husband, Bert, were fighting terribly over their youngest son, Kevin.

"Bert could see Kevin had a problem," said Annie. "I had my head in the clouds. I couldn't believe Kevin was into drugs. Finally he got in trouble with the law, robbed a house, so I had to change my tune.

"Bert and I disagreed on how to handle Kevin. Bert moved out, and I took over. It was a nightmare. Through counseling I learned to discipline the children and also not to get so upset when Bert was critical. We got back together and lived on pretty good terms for another eight years before he died."

Two years after Bert's death, Annie was diagnosed with ovarian cancer.

"I went through chemotherapy and lost all my hair. It came back curly. That was good."

Several years later Annie was diagnosed with breast cancer and had a mastectomy. She was also in bad financial shape. A mutual friend called and told me Annie was in trouble, so I called her. I said, "I've got a great therapy group that meets on Tuesday nights and I have one spot left."

That was three years ago.

"My group has given me a lot of support," says Annie. "My grandson has cystic fibrosis. He just celebrated his sixteenth birthday.

"My group has seen me through the death of my thirty-one-year-old daughter-in-law, who died of a rare form of breast cancer.

"My group supported me through several more biopsies. The doctors found cancer again. More chemotherapy, a staph infection that almost did me in, blood clots in my legs, and the loss of my curly hair. But now I'm just fine.

"I'm making my granddaughter jumpers for school. I dressed four dolls for my church to give to poor families at Christmas. I have six grandchildren and lots of friends. I have my flowers to take care of.

"I tell you, every day is an experience. I think you get out of life what you put in. You can be happy, sad, angry. I elect to be happy. I program myself to be happy. I say, 'You have today, let's see what you can put into it.' "

Annie has suffered. But Annie is hardy.

———

As David Reynolds writes, "There is nothing ennobling about pain and suffering. But in *striving while suffering* we move beyond ourselves to become new creatures."[5]

If you live, you will have pain. You will have disappointments. You will suffer. No one escapes. But if you use your sense ability, you will move beyond your pain and beyond yourself and you will find new meaning for your life.

DO YOU MONITOR
AND DIRECT
YOUR THOUGHTS?

You just think lovely wonderful thoughts and they lift you up in the air.

Peter Pan

Thousands of thoughts bombard you daily. For example: "I need to have the car inspected . . . I wonder how Mom's doing? . . . How am I going to get everything done? . . . I'm so fat . . . I wonder what the stock market did? . . . Why can't somebody do something about this traffic! . . . I didn't sleep at all last night . . . Maybe I'll give Jim a party for his birthday . . . Oh, I need gas. . . . "

Thinking is somewhat like breathing. You're always doing it. But unless you get short of breath or someone suggests you focus on your breathing, you forget that you're doing it. It's the same with your thoughts. You simply don't think about the fact that you think approximately sixty thousand thoughts a day.

Some thoughts you think are positive, some negative, some neutral, some are about the past, some about the future, some you obsess on, some come and go and you take no note, some invite you to feel sad and gloomy, some infuriate you, and some bring a smile and give you a sense of well-being.

The way you think defines almost every feeling, action, interaction, and behavior in your life. It is not other people or their actions or what happens or doesn't happen to you. It is the way you think, the thoughts you choose to focus on.

As pointed out previously, on occasion a feeling comes before a thought, such as when you are startled and instantly feel fear. This is because you are hard wired for survival, and fear is intricately and elaborately built into every cell. But even the reflex of fear is very short-lived, about three seconds, unless you feed it with additional scary thoughts.

Another exception is the feeling of instant pleasure when eating or having sex. Here, too, you are exquisitely wired to feel pleasure because these two activities are essential for the survival of the human race.[1]

But in most instances, when you experience a feeling, it is your thoughts that are directing and determining what you feel. It is your thoughts that ultimately determine your behavior.

YOU ARE THE DIRECTOR

Because thoughts follow one another in such rapid succession, it's easy to forget that you are creating and then directing them. You also don't say to yourself, "I think I'll link a few thoughts together to entertain myself." You simply go about setting up a story line where you're the hero, the villain, or the victim. You automatically link thought after thought as you develop your plot.

You take a story that has already unfolded in your life, such as when your first husband left you, and you continue to change, adjust, and fine-tune the dialogue that some day you plan to have with him.

You have a thought about something in the present. For example, you think, "We have to get Mike to study more." And then you add another thought, "I don't understand him and why he won't study." And then several more thoughts, "Maybe if we get him a tutor, or maybe if we give him $25 for every B, we could get him interested in school." You may have conversations in your head with your son, his teachers, the school counselor, your husband. You then think, "How come I'm always the one trying to figure out a solution?" You start to feel anxious and annoyed. You pick up your cell phone to call your husband.

What happened? You allowed one thought—"We have to get Mike to study more"—to snag you. Then you built on it until you felt frustrated and helpless. To relieve those feelings, you acted—you picked up your cell phone to call your husband.

Maybe a conversation with your husband will help you come up with a new idea for solving the problem. Maybe it will help you dissipate your bad feelings and provide you with hope. Perhaps it will help you let go of thoughts of Mike, school, poor grades, and the educational system. But maybe you're headed for more negative thoughts and feelings about the situation as you talk with your husband.

WHAT DO YOU SEE?

Now look at these three pictures. Study them carefully. What do you see?

Is the first picture[2] a rabbit, or is it a duck? It's both. If you look at the face on the right, it's a rabbit. When you look at the face on the left, the drawing becomes a duck. Can you see both at the same time? No, but both the rabbit and the duck are there for you to see. The animal that pops out at you, the one you see, depends on your focus of attention.

The second sketch, drawn by the caricaturist Al Hirschfeld, is titled, *The Boys from Syracuse*. There are two boys, one looking to the right and one looking to the left. Initially the boys appear as if they are dancing with one boy's face hidden behind the other. But if you look very closely, you will see that the boys share a single face. If you have trouble seeing that they share the same face, take your fingers and cover both the boys' bodies including their heads, but don't cover up the face.

In the third sketch,[3] do you see a man with a rather large nose? Or do you see a woman holding a baby? Both are there. Again, it's your focus of attention that determines what you actually see.

———

Did you approach these pictures a little differently than you approached the pictures in Chapter 1? Chances are you did because you had already had the experience of looking for something more than originally meets the eye. You were already operating from an expanded sense of awareness.

These pictures demonstrate that what you choose to focus on determines your next thought. For example, in the third picture, if you saw only the man, your next thought might have been that the sketch is rather primitive. But when you spied the mother and child within the same drawing, your succeeding thought might have been that the artist was rather clever.

These pictures also illustrate that your way of seeing and thinking about something is based solely on your perceptions. Often there is more information that is just as valid as what you choose to focus on. As you develop and use your sense ability, you will find yourself looking at issues from a wider perspective.

———

I've been a fan of Sherlock Holmes since I was a little girl be-cause he always seems to note what I miss. In *The Adventure of Silver Blaze*, Holmes and Colonel Ross are talking:

Colonel Ross: Is there any other point to which you would wish to draw my attention?
Holmes: To the curious incident of the dog in the nighttime.
Colonel Ross: The dog did nothing in the nighttime.
Holmes: That was the curious incident.[4]

Again, our thinking, our focus of attention, determines how much of the whole picture we actually see. Holmes notices not only that there is a dog, but also that the dog does not bark.

ANOTHER SIDE TO EVERY STORY

A twenty-nine-year-old woman smokes. She has been smoking for years but has never let her parents know she smokes. She's gone to great lengths to hide her smoking.

She says, "I don't tell my parents because it would cause them to feel anxious about my health."

A friend of hers thinks otherwise. He says, "She doesn't tell her parents because she's afraid they'll lecture and try to extract a no-smoking promise."

Is there a right or wrong? No. It's simply that each of these people interpret, think about, the situation differently.

———

One of the partners in a company told me that when a customer calls and complains to him that a piece of their equipment is not working, he immediately thinks, "I wonder what we did wrong? I wonder if the design is faulty?" On the other hand, when the other partner in the company hears there's a problem, he says, "That customer must be doing something wrong." Two ways of reacting to identical information.

This same man said he and his partner recently went to a bank to borrow money for the company.

"One of the bankers at the meeting started asking some personal questions. My partner immediately became defensive and said, 'You don't need to have that information.'

"I, on the other hand, probably would have given the banker all the information he asked for. And maybe I would have asked if there was anything else he needed."

A different way of thinking and then behaving.

Ask yourself: *Which of these two men would you be most likely to identify with? Do you know someone who would take the other man's way of seeing things?*

"Our organization has recently been reorganized," said Beth. "As a consequence, mail gets delivered to us that doesn't belong in our department. When I find a piece that isn't ours, I look up the person's name in our directory, find out what department it should go to, and send it on its way.

"The other people in our department think I'm silly for doing this. When they go through the mail and find a piece that doesn't belong to us, they send it back to the mailroom. They think it's the mailroom's job."

Who's right? It depends on the thoughts you choose to think.

———

A man and wife went to a wedding. During the ceremony the man commented to his wife, "My, this is a fancy wedding." After the wedding they went to the country club for the reception. When they arrived, he noticed that the bridesmaids were now in different dresses. He thought, "This *really is* a fancy wedding. They even changed their dresses." Once in the receiving line facing the bride and groom, the man realized he and his wife were at the wrong reception. The man had misread the situation but tried to make reality fit his thinking.

When my business partner, Serra, told people she joined the Peace Corps and was leaving for Romania, she got mixed reviews. Some said, "How wonderful. What an adventure you'll have." Others said, "I can't believe anybody would want to do such a thing." Again, same information presented, but different reactions based on different thinking.

If you want to live in peace with yourself and others, if you want your days to be calm, you must accept that your thoughts are only *your* thoughts. Others frequently see things differently and have different thoughts about the same event. Just as beauty is in the eye of the beholder, the "truth" is often in the thought of the thinker.

Now ask yourself: *When I'm in a discussion do I frequently act like my thoughts and opinions are the only right ones? If so, how do I do this?*

ARE YOU A POSITIVE OR A NEGATIVE THINKER?

You subconsciously weigh and evaluate, moment to moment, everything you attend to. If you put a neutral interpretation on the information or situation, you won't experience any particular feeling. If you put a positive interpretation on what you have attended to, you may experience a general sense of well-being or happiness. If your spin is negative, it's likely that you will generate within yourself negative feelings.

For example, the holidays were coming and a man invited for Christmas day a family who had just moved into his neighborhood. When the man's grown son learned about the invitation, he decided he and his family were not coming for Christmas. When the stunned father asked why, the son said he didn't like new people, Christmas was a time for families, and he wouldn't be able to relax. And how come his father had to go and spoil Christmas by inviting another family. Clearly the son had many negative thoughts.

What's interesting is that the son could just as easily have thought positively about the situation. He could have thought, "The more, the merrier." He could have looked for a common denominator. What did the man and woman do for a living? Did they have children? His children would probably enjoy having other children to play with. He might have put himself in the other family's shoes: How nice for them to have somewhere to go Christmas day.

Even if the son's past experience supported his present thinking, he chose to think negatively about the future, a future he had not yet experienced.

An Exercise: Think Negative, Think Positive

I asked a manager to take an incident that had happened at work recently and look at it in both a positive and a negative way. The situation she chose involved receiving a memo about a seminar she was expected to attend.

Her negative thoughts: "I don't want to go. I've got too much to do. I can't give up a day. I've already taken a seminar on this subject."

Her positive thoughts: "Maybe a day thinking about something else will energize me. In truth, I always learn something. Maybe I'll get some tips on handling people who don't get to work on time."

It's easy to see that the way the manager chose to think, first negatively and then positively, would have a bearing on her feelings. If she stayed with her positive thoughts, she might feel some anticipation, curiosity, and maybe even some enthusiasm as the seminar day approached.

If she went with her negative thoughts, probably she would have felt an on-again, off-again annoyance as the seminar day approached. On the actual day she may have felt somewhat helpless because attendance was required. And if she felt victimized, how much of the seminar information would she process?

———

Now it's your turn. Take a moment and think about an incident that's happened to you recently.

Come up with three negative thoughts about the incident:

1. _____
2. _____
3. _____

Come up with three positive thoughts:

1. _____
2. _____
3. _____

This exercise illustrates that you can cause yourself to feel a particular way simply based on the thoughts you choose to think.

JUMPING TO NEGATIVE CONCLUSIONS

Jumping to a negative conclusion is another way of thinking that invites bad feelings. You take one incident, add a number of assumptions, and come to a negative conclusion that frequently has no real basis. For example:

- Your husband turns on the radio when the two of you get into the car, and you jump to the conclusion that he doesn't want to talk to you.
- You see your supervisor talking and laughing with a co-worker, and you think she must like her better than you.
- You have fun with a new date, but because he doesn't call you the following day, you're sure he didn't enjoy himself.
- Your boss says she wants to talk with you, and you think she's going to call you on the carpet for something.

———

My mother and I were sitting in the hospital lobby waiting until we could see my father after some surgery. We were talking and laughing and enjoying ourselves for the first time in days because we felt Dad was going to be okay.

Across the lobby was a young woman with two small children. As Mom and I talked, I noticed that the younger child was giving his mother a hard time, fussing and tugging to get away from her grip. The mother was holding on to the child's sleeve with one hand and trying to balance a plate of cookies in the other.

I was looking at my mother, listening to her talk, when suddenly the young woman was standing in front of us. She leaned forward and demanded in a loud voice, "Are you having a good time?"

I was baffled. I looked around, thinking the woman must be chastising someone behind me. But no one was there. The woman then stormed past with her children and disappeared down the hall.

Mom and I concluded that the woman must have decided that we were enjoying her predicament. She saw us laughing and looking in her direction, then jumped to the conclusion that we were talking about her.

Can you recall the last time you jumped to a conclusion?

Stop, Step Back, Gather Facts

To stop yourself from jumping to a negative conclusion, use your feelings to monitor your thoughts. Any time you feel yourself becoming agitated or annoyed over an incident, stop, step back, and ask yourself, "What are the facts—only the facts? And what additional information do I need before making a decision?" Answering these two questions will keep you from acting impulsively.

Let's suppose the woman in the hospital had asked herself,

"What are the facts? Two women are sitting in the lobby carrying on a conversation, laughing, and looking my way. Those are the facts. Nothing more." This information would more than likely have stopped the woman from jumping to the conclusion that we were talking about her.

———

If you tend to jump to conclusions, perhaps the following story will be helpful to you.

Once upon a time a Chinese man owned the only horse in the village where he lived. Because he had a horse, he was able to plow more fields and make more money. Everyone in the village thought, "What a fortunate, lucky man."

When the villagers told the man how fortunate he was, he replied, "Maybe so, maybe not."

One day the man's horse ran away. On hearing the news, the villagers said, "How very unfortunate." The man responded, "Maybe so, maybe not."

A few days later the man's horse returned, bringing a wild horse with him. "Oh, how very fortunate for you," said the villagers. "Maybe so, maybe not," the man replied. Soon thereafter the man's son was riding the new horse, fell off, and broke his leg. "Oh, how unfortunate," said the villagers. "Maybe so, maybe not," shrugged the man.

Then a war broke out, and the king's men came to the town to press all young men into the service of the king. But because the boy had a broken leg, he was left behind.[5]

The story goes on, but the point is clear.

OVERGENERALIZING

Overgeneralizing is another way of thinking that causes problems. When you overgeneralize, you take the results of one experience or event, then apply those results to all similar experiences or events.

For example, I know an architect who missed out on a job;

he was the company's second choice. The last time I talked to him, he was miserable. He kept saying, "I'll never get a job in my field."

The architect leaped from one event—not being hired by one company—to the extreme generalization of never being hired by anyone. It's bad enough that he was rejected, but look at the way his thinking is inviting him to feel worse. Thinking that this is the end of his career is overgeneralizing.

It's normal to have some bad feelings when things don't work out as planned, but overgeneralizing gives too much weight to an incident.

Here are three more examples:

Judy thinks that when she finds a man and gets married, everything in her life is going to be perfect. Of course it won't. What Judy is doing is taking one event, marriage, and making it the be-all and end-all for her happiness.

A woman says to her husband, "You never listen to me." Now it's probably true that on some occasions her husband has not listened. But never listens? This is an overgeneralization. Anytime you catch yourself using the words *never, always, everyone,* and *everybody,* take it as your cue: You are probably overgeneralizing.

I know a wife who uses absolutes frequently. She says, "You always do this, you never do that." Her husband, instead of fighting and defending, says, "I never?" or "I always?" These comments act as a stop sign and help her see how she's overgeneralizing.

As David Reynolds writes, "We can build in unnecessary pain in our lives by creating tragedies when there are only events."[6]

Now ask yourself: *When have I built in unnecessary pain in my life? If I could relive the event, how would I do it differently?*

OBSESSING

You can create additional needless suffering for yourself by obsessing—replaying an incident over and over and over. For example, Walter confronted his supervisor at a meeting several weeks ago. Now all he can think about is the argument that ensued. He rehashes what he said and what the supervisor said. He thinks of things he might have said. And sometimes he thinks, "Why on earth didn't I keep my mouth shut?"

A friend told me that she obsesses about her mother, who died when she was six years old.

"It will be around Mother's Day and I'll go to the store to buy my mother-in-law a card. As I'm reading the cards, I think about which card I would have sent to my mother. Then I think, 'I don't have a mother.'

"After I leave the store, I go over and over this thought and feel awful.

"If something happens with my children, good or bad, I flip to the loss-of-my-mother channel. I think, 'I don't have a mother to share this event with.'

"After I run all this out in my head, I'm miserable. When I've had enough misery, I get busy. I clean a drawer. I call a friend and listen to her problems. I get into my life. I stop obsessing."

Sometimes people obsess on how clean the house is, what dress to wear to a party, who makes the most money, a car they want to buy, or how something isn't fair.

Are you causing yourself needless pain by obsessing?

———

One way to control your thoughts instead of allowing them to control you is to give them a focus. Get busy with a project, pay bills, clean out the refrigerator, help straighten up your child's room, read a book, refinish a piece of furniture. Chances are you'll stay focused, and your thoughts won't be all over the place.

If you feel you can't stop your thoughts from racing, one thing you can hold on to is a prayer. One woman reads the psalms, another prays her rosary to help focus and calm those internal churnings.

Repeating a phrase or affirmation can quell racing thoughts. If you can't stop thinking about how a relative or friend hurt you, you might say, *"I choose to forgive and move on with my life,"* over, and over, and over. If you're going through a divorce and you can't seem to stop fighting in your head with your soon-to-be ex-spouse, repeating an affirmation such as, *"I choose to grow from this experience and become a better person,"* will help you center yourself and get control of your runaway thoughts.

———

Author and spiritual teacher Sri Eknath Easwaran relates the following:

In the Hindu tradition, we often compare the mind to the trunk of an elephant—restless, inquisitive, and always straying. . . . In our towns and villages, elephants are often taken in religious processions through the streets. The streets are crooked and narrow, lined on either side with fruit and vegetable stalls. Along comes the elephant with his restless trunk, and in one sinuous motion it grabs a whole bunch of bananas. . . . He takes the whole bunch, opens his cavernous mouth, and tosses the bananas in stalk and all. Then from the next stall he picks up a coconut and tosses it in after the bananas. There is a loud crack and the elephant moves on to the next stall. No threats or promises can make this restless trunk settle down.

But the wise mahout, if he knows his elephant well, will just give that trunk a small bamboo stick to hold on to before the procession starts. Then the elephant will walk along proudly with his head up high, holding the bamboo stick in front of him like a drum major with a baton. He is not interested in bananas or coconuts anymore; his trunk has something to hold on to.[7]

Mindful Breathing

Another technique to stop yourself from obsessing is what Buddhists call Mindful Breathing. Every time you start to obsess about a particular issue, stop and switch to Mindful Breathing, which immediately moves you to the present moment.

When you do Mindful Breathing, you focus on your breath: breathing in and breathing out, breathing in and breathing out. Right now, why not try it?

Slowly, slowly pull the air in, allowing it to fill your belly.
Slowly, slowly let it out.
Slowly, slowly pull the air in, allowing it to fill your belly.
Slowly, slowly let it out.

It's impossible to have a fight in your head when you focus on your breathing. Sometimes saying an affirmation along with your breathing is also helpful.

——

Thich Nhat Hanh offers the following *gatha* (short poem) to help you quell obsessional thoughts and help you stay in the present moment. As you read the first line, you breathe in; the second line, you breathe out; the third, you breathe in. Slowly, slowly breathe along:

Breathing in, I know I'm breathing in.
Breathing out, I know
as the in-breath grows deep,
the out-breath grows slow.
Breathing in makes me calm.
Breathing out brings me ease.
With the in-breath, I smile.
With the out-breath, I release.

Breathing in, there is only the present moment.
Breathing out, it is a wonderful moment.[8]

Now reread this *gatha*, and breathe along with the words again.

What did you discover? If you felt relaxed after doing this exercise, perhaps you'll decide to memorize this poem and use it in your daily life.

Sometimes, after I suggest that someone do Mindful Breathing, that person later tells me, "Doris, it makes me too anxious. I feel like I'm wasting time sitting and focusing on my breathing." This often indicates that the person is already doing too many things and probably needs to slow down his or her life. You also might not be ready for a particular technique. That's okay. You can come back to it next month or next year.

Another variation: Try Mindful Breathing as you walk. For westerners, this sometimes works better, since we tend to believe that we need to be accomplishing several things at once.

IS YOUR THINKING PAST, PRESENT, OR FUTURE FOCUSED?

When you wake up in the morning, what are your first thoughts? Do you think about yesterday's disappointments? Are you already on the job talking to a colleague? Or do you think how wonderful the bed feels and how nice your pillow is?

As you're brushing your teeth, are you thinking about last night's television show? Are you making out your list of what you want to accomplish that day? Or do you feel the bristles of the brush and see the toothpaste foam in your mouth?

How much time do you spend thinking of the past? The present? The future?

Caught in the Past

I read a story about a man, Jimmie G., that I will never forget. The story was in the book *The Man Who Mistook His Wife for a Hat* by Oliver Sacks.

Jimmie G., age forty-five, had a neurological problem. Because of his problem, he had no recent memory. His doctor would talk with him and walk out of the room. When the doctor returned a few minutes later, Jimmie had no memory of ever having seen the doctor. "Whatever was said or shown to him was apt to be forgotten in a few seconds' time. . . . He is a man without a past (or future), stuck in a constantly changing, meaningless moment."[9]

———

Memory helps make you who you are. You build on the past. You call on it continually in the present. You use it to plan for the future. You can call forth the previous day. You use your memory to have a conversation with a friend. You can see your children, your mate, and your work environment in your mind's eye. You can recall a disappointment or a vacation you took long ago. You remember how it feels to bite into an apple, a lemon, or a piece of watermelon.

———

When I started working with Denise, she told me her most happy times were in high school. She was a cheerleader, had a date for every occasion, and had many good friends. Although not particularly interested in academics, she made good grades. Shortly after high school she married, had a son, and moved out of state. That's when her husband started abusing her. After a year, Denise divorced and moved home. For the past eight years she has been supporting herself and her son.

She came to see me because her boyfriend had left her and she was feeling depressed and lonely. She was having trouble getting up in the morning to help her son off to school. She had lost a considerable amount of weight. Her friends and family were worried. As we talked, Denise would tell me again and again, "The best part of my life is over. If only I could be back in high school."

Is it possible that you are hurting yourself by dwelling too much in the past?

When I see someone who focuses too much on the past, I often relate the following passage:

"A rushing stream of water flows around the obstacles that stand in its way. It doesn't stop to dwell on the injuries sustained by a projecting rock or a submerged log. It keeps moving toward its goal, encountering each difficulty as it appears, responding actively, then moving downstream. The stream has no imagination to create unchanging stories of its existence. It washes away its own wounds in its present purposefulness. The water bears no scars."[10]

Trapped in the Future

The antithesis of those who are caught in the past are those who think only of the future. It's always the next paycheck, the next deal, the next sexual experience, the next purchase, the next golf game. They're so caught up in what they think is going to happen that they miss out on the present.

The husband of a couple we used to socialize with was always thinking of the future. We'd go to dinner before a play. Before we ordered, he would announce the time we had to leave. On leaving the restaurant, we had to drive fast to the theater so we could get a good parking space. Before the curtain came down, this fellow wanted to be out the door so we could beat the traffic, so he could hurry home, so he could get to sleep, so he could jump out of bed in the morning and race to the gym.

It's important to think about the future some of the time. If you want to change jobs, you have to prepare a résumé. If your daughter's getting married, you have to plan the wedding. If you're running a company, you need to think five or ten years ahead. At the same time, you can miss the present because your thinking is too much in the future.

Often one of my students will say, "I'm taking five courses this semester. I want to get them out of the way so I can get on with my life." What he forgets is that his life is going on *now*. If he can see his education as a process instead of something to be "gotten over," he'll have more enjoyment along the way.

Advice for Worriers

Worriers are future-oriented people. They think, "I wonder if the plane will be on time? I wonder if they'll give us our loan? I wonder if he'll call?"

Some friends of ours who live on a farm have one answer for worriers. They learned it from an old farmer who lived down the road. They asked his advice about a calf. "Do you think it'll live?" they queried anxiously. After studying the calf, the farmer said, "Either it will or it won't."

Later in the year the woman was worrying about how dry everything was and wondered when it would rain, so she asked the farmer, "Do you think it's going to rain?" He again replied, "Either it will or it won't."

If you're caught worrying about the future, you can make use of this either-or sentence.

———

Here are some additional suggestions for worriers.

- Make a list of worries that never happened. Such a list works every time because it puts things in perspective.
- Bounce your worries off your friends. When one doctor friend said he had been dragged into a lawsuit, several of his friends shared similar experiences. Hearing what others had been through helped.
- Talk to God—and listen as he talks back.

- Get busy; get involved in a project. Clean out a file cabinet; sort through your toolbox. When you're in the process of doing something, your worries are in the background.
- Seek the help of your minister, rabbi, or priest, or go to a therapist. Read books on how other people quell their worries, such as *Worry* by Edward Hallowell.

THE PRESENT IS REALLY ALL YOU HAVE

Past, present, and future are all part of your life. It's best, however, to focus most of your thoughts on what you're doing in the present, because the present is really all you have. The past is gone, and the future hasn't occurred.

For example, while you're planting daisies, don't think about what happened yesterday at work or what you're going to do on vacation six weeks from now. Think about the plant you're putting in the soil. Notice how its roots cling to the container as you try to remove it. Feel the trowel in your hand as you dig into the dirt. Feel the temperature of the dirt as you place your plant in the ground. Observe the way the plant stands as you tap the dirt around its base. Step back and look at it in your garden. Enjoy. This is what it means to live in the present, in the now.

———

Ken Keyes Jr. in his book *Handbook to Higher Consciousness* suggests, "It is best not to hang out discussing the past, or to let your consciousness dwell on the past, for the constant churning of your mind (and the torrent of words that issues from it) keeps you from fully experiencing the now moment in your life.

"Nor will you generate the best future for yourself by being constantly preoccupied with thoughts of the future. . . . The real solutions to the problems in your life will come to you when you . . . become fully tuned in to the people and things that are around you."

Living in the present means you allow yourself to "experience everything in an accepting, relaxed and conscious way."[11]

DO YOUR THOUGHTS DETERMINE WHO YOU ARE?

Your identity, who you are, generally starts with the way you think about yourself and about situations and events in your life. Your thoughts mainly determine how you feel, and your behavior is driven by how you think and feel. Your thoughts, feelings, and behavior are all uniquely important and uniquely you.

Sometimes you have a thought, or someone says something to you, and you attach no particular feeling to the thought. Other times you have an instantaneous response and feelings explode within you. If your interpretation of the situation is positive, you'll experience a sense of well-being, perhaps even joy. If your interpretation of the event is negative, you're likely to feel frustrated, annoyed, and angry, or you may feel sad, defeated, and helpless. You may or may not choose to act on these thoughts and feelings.

Suppose you have the thought, "I haven't heard from Sandra in a while." Your next thoughts might be, "I wonder if she's irritated with me? Did I do something to offend her? I've called her the last three times. Maybe she calls only when she wants my help. She doesn't really care about me and my life. Well, I don't need her as a friend. I have plenty of other people who want to be my friends."

As you're thinking these thoughts that took less than a few seconds, feelings are also being generated. In this case you're probably going to feel hurt and angry. You may choose to act on your thoughts and feelings by deciding never to call Sandra or by calling her and picking a fight. Or you could decide that you'll stop this obsessing and focus on something else, perhaps your breathing or sorting out a clothes drawer, and your feelings will dissipate.

You can hurt yourself and others by the way you think, the negative feelings that you generate from your thoughts, and behaviors that sometimes follow.

I am not a therapist who thinks feelings are the most important part of you. I don't hold feelings up for admiration. I don't ask a client how she feels when she reports losing a job or has a fight with her mate. I can see how she feels. I hear her feelings in her voice, see her feelings in her eyes, her face, her body posture. I usually know when she is sad, annoyed, frustrated, worried, embarrassed, disgusted, guilty, pleased, content, or happy.

Feelings are integral to our humanness. Feeling sadness shows that you are vulnerable. Feeling fear warns, protects, and somtimes exposes your insecurities. Feeling anger indicates your desire to control and sometimes your strength. Feeling guilt helps you police your actions. Feeling loneliness shows your hunger for attachment to another human. Feeling disgust helps you avoid offensive situations and sometimes motivates you. Feeling happiness, joy, and awe indicates your capacity for pleasure, love, intimacy, and oneness.

It is your thinking, however, that drives almost every feeling. It is your thinking that directs your actions and keeps your behavior in check. It is your thinking that generates the feelings that allow you to tend to your wants and needs and to transcend your own wants and needs for those of others. It is your thinking that primarily determines your life.

Watch your thoughts, monitor them, reign them in, teach yourself to slow them down, and learn to step back from them. In the process you will gain freedom, and you will be using and expanding your sense ability.

ARE YOU A CRITICAL PERSON?

There is little room for wisdom when one is full of judgment.

Anonymous

For holidays and birthdays a group of us routinely gets together to celebrate. We talk, laugh, tell jokes, ride horses,
and solve world problems. These celebrations always include a sit-down dinner. After dinner we play a funny little
game. We've been doing it for years.

Someone moves his or her plate and glass and announces,
"Look how clean my place is."

Not to be outdone, others at the table move their dishes and
inspect the tablecloth in front of them. When a spill is spotted,
everyone hoots and hollers.

One particular gentleman almost always is declared the mess-
iest. We tease him unmercifully about his spatters and spills, and
he laughs good-naturedly.

At our last gathering this very gentleman started the game. He
said, "Look at me. Look at my place. Not a single spill. I win."

We all carefully compared his place to ours, and sure enough,
we declared him the winner. As we sat cheering and toasting
him, his wife sarcastically said, "Now, if you could only do that
at home." Some of us who heard the woman's comment were

embarrassed for the husband and, needless to say, we did not feel as loving toward her.

Did this man's wife intend to be critical of her husband at the moment of his triumph? Was her comment a ploy to shift the attention away from her husband and to herself? What was she thinking and feeling? What drove her remark?

Unfortunately, this woman is not alone in her behavior. Wives and husbands freely make critical comments to each other. Many parents criticize their children twenty or thirty times a day. Co-workers and bosses fire off disparaging remarks. Friends take potshots and laugh, or they try to hide their criticisms under the guise of helpful suggestions.

Why are so many people critical? Don't people understand how criticism affects others? Criticism separates, alienates, and invites resentment. Criticism blocks intimacy and closes out love. Criticism limits and stifles your sense of awareness.

In the following stories you will meet a number of critical people. As you read, ask yourself: *Am I like this person?*

———

Every year the Baker family—Mom, Dad, three grown daughters, and a grown son—go to Aunt Marie's house to help her with spring cleaning. This is the family's gift to Aunt Marie.

This year one of the tasks was to drag out the patio furniture and wash it. Afterward as everyone was sitting around admiring their efforts, Mom said, "Look at that dirt at the bottom of that chair. I bet it's the one your father washed."

No one made a comment. But eyes rolled knowingly, as if to say, "Here she goes again."

Later in the day, one of the daughters realized that her dad had been out in the heat too long trimming bushes. So the daughter went to the door and called out, "Dad, come on in and take a rest. You're working too hard." Before her dad had a chance to respond, Mom piped up and said, "He won't come in. You know your father. He's afraid he'll miss something."

Toward evening, as the family gathered at the table and everyone was filling his or her plate, Mom took yet another swipe at Dad. This time she said, "Well, are you going to pass those pork chops, dear, or are you going to hog them all for yourself?"

This woman fails to realize that her negative comments are a turnoff. She is certainly doing a good deed, helping her sister, but she loses her family's love and respect because of her critical comments. She doesn't understand that the children do not want to hear their father being put down.

Ask yourself: *Do I make critical comments to my children about their father or mother? If so, how do these comments affect my relationship with them?*

———

As you read this story, you'll see how Ralph inadvertently set the stage for an unpleasant evening. It all started when Janet asked Ralph to go to the movies.

"Ralph," said Janet, "let's go to a movie tonight."

Ralph's response: "That doesn't sound good to me."

Disappointed, Janet said, "Well, I think I'll go anyway." As she was getting her things together, Ralph suddenly clicked off the television and announced he would be joining her.

Janet, who had already switched plans in her head, asked, "Are you sure you want to go?"

Ralph assured her that he did.

As they drove into the theater parking lot, Ralph mumbled that the last movie must not have let out yet. So where did they expect everybody to park? Certainly the theater could do a better job of scheduling.

As they waited in line to buy tickets, Ralph said that everybody and their brother must have decided to see this movie, judging by the length of the line. Janet, sensing Ralph's annoyance, made small talk, hoping to divert him from making any more critical observations.

When they got into the lobby, Janet suggested Ralph get seats and she would get the popcorn.

Ralph said, "You're going to stand in that line just for popcorn?" Janet nodded.

With her popcorn in hand, Janet made her way to where Ralph was seated. His comment on seeing her: "You didn't get anything to drink?"

"No," she said. But she offered to go back to get him a drink.

"Never mind," said Ralph.

"Really, I'll go back," Janet said. "I just didn't think you'd want anything."

"I don't now," said Ralph.

As they sat in silence waiting for the show to start, Janet struggled with feelings of guilt over the drink and irritation over Ralph's negativism.

Once Ralph commented that the popcorn tasted stale.

At the end of the movie Janet asked, "What did you think?"

Ralph shrugged and said, "It was okay."

They drove home in silence.

———

Even in biblical times, criticism was a problem.

"In the desert the whole community grumbled against Moses and Aaron. The Israelites said to them, 'If only we had died by the Lord's hand in Egypt! There we sat around pots of meat and ate all the food we wanted, but you have brought us out into this desert to starve this entire assembly to death.'" (Exod. 16:2–3)

"'Why did you bring us up out of Egypt to make us and our children and livestock die of thirst?'

"Then Moses cried out to the Lord. 'What am I to do with these people? They are almost ready to stone me.'" (Exod. 17:3–4)

CRITICISM HURTS!

Criticism hurts everyone. It hurts the person who's on the receiving end of the comment, and it ultimately comes back to hurt the one who made the comment. If you criticize someone, I guarantee he or she is going to pull away from you emotionally. If you continually make critical comments, other people are not going to share their hopes and dreams because they don't feel close or safe with you. Your criticism, even though you may see it as helpful, alienates people.

When I ask couples in marriage counseling, "What are some of the problems in your marriage?" I'll often get the answer, "She's too critical" or "He's always criticizing me." Criticism is right up there with affairs, anger, the inability to solve problems, and not doing what you say you will do—the most frequent issues reported in marriage counseling.

I tell mates who are critical, "Others were not put on this earth to meet your expectations. When you got married, your partner did not sign up to be criticized or told what to do. Stop!"

I'm seeing a man in therapy who has cheated on his wife. His wife is in a rage. At this point they are separated. Every time they get together to see if they can work things out, she lets him have it. Her criticisms and anger are understandable and justified, but they won't help her save the marriage. His cheating has caused her great pain, and now, because of him, she must deal with this pain. However, being critical is not dealing with her pain, it is only intensifying it.

———

One morning when I arrived at my office, a man I had seen in therapy some years back was waiting outside. He looked terrible. He hadn't shaved. His clothes were disheveled.

When I brought him into my office, he started crying. He said he had slept in his car because he just couldn't face another night with his critical wife. He wanted to stay married, but he couldn't stand her constantly telling him what to do. He realized he needed to make some changes, but her criticisms were relentless.

His wife agreed to come to marriage counseling. He worked on taking more responsibility around the house and doing more chores. He also started recognizing his wife more, giving her hugs and I-love-yous, and saying thank you. She worked on recognizing the chores her husband actually did and on making *no critical comments*.

———

Many women come to therapy with the specific goal of getting help dealing with their critical mothers. Almost always they say they love their mothers, but they can't stand to be around them because they're so critical. Their complaints all have a familiar ring. Listen:

"My mother tells me she's lonely and has no friends. At the same time all she does is criticize her friends. Nothing they do is right."

"My mom is always complaining about my dad. I know he's difficult to live with, but I don't want to keep hearing about it."

"Mom never has anything nice to say about anyone. All she does is complain. I can hardly stand to be around her."

These daughters want to be a part of their mothers' lives, but the mothers are constantly pushing their daughters away with their negative comments.

Most parents want to be around their grown children and their grandchildren. It's one of their joys. And yet so many parents alienate their grown children because they criticize them. Unless asked, don't make suggestions to your grown children. Those "helpful suggestions" are hurting you. They are alienating you. If you have noticed your grown child avoiding you, take inventory and start using your sense ability.

ARE YOU A FAULTFINDER?

Critical people are always finding fault with someone or something. They simply can't resist pointing out the problem. With critical people, nothing is good enough, right enough. If you go out to dinner with someone who is critical, the food is overcooked or undercooked. The restaurant is too expensive, or the service is poor. If you listen to a critical person talk politics, you'd swear the country was going to hell in a handbasket. To be in an automobile with a critical person is torture. Nobody on the road knows how to drive. When critical people read the newspaper, listen to the news, or watch television, what is wrong with the world becomes the focus of their attention.

Faultfinders tend to have other characteristics in common. Almost always they expect perfection of themselves as well as others. Rarely are they satisfied. Their internal dialogue is often about what hasn't been done and what needs to get done. They are driven by a lot of *oughts* and *shoulds*. Critical people are usually responsible and can be counted on to get the job done. And if they say they will do something, chances are they will do it.

Some of their favorite phrases include "You should do this," "You need to do that," "Why don't you," "How come you don't," and "I think you should." I've also noticed that critical people do a lot of wagging of their index finger to get their messages across. In therapy I'm always saying, "Stop wagging your pointer."

HOW DID YOU BECOME SO CRITICAL?

Many roads lead to negativity.

Critical people seem to have a genetic predisposition—they have inherited emotionality, so they react more intently to stimuli. More things bother them. And they tend to be more pessimistic. Along with these tendencies, critical people often were raised in a competitive environment where comparisons were frequently made.

For example, Mom says to Jane, "I know if you try, you can get grades as good as your brother's," or "Your brother never leaves messes. Why can't you keep your stuff picked up?" Eventually Jane starts viewing the world from a competitive frame of reference. As a result she thinks about people, events, and situations in a comparative and often critical way.

Some people become critical because one or both parents were critical. They heard many critical remarks day in, day out. Taking a critical view of things was modeled for them.

People can become critical if they have critical mates or work closely with other critical people. Each day you are subtly influenced by those around you—their body language, their vocabulary, the way they express themselves and address issues, their opinions and values. If those around you are critical, it's going to start affecting the way you think and behave.

Sometimes people will become more critical because life has been hard on them. They are married to a selfish mate; they've had terrible financial problems; they've had to deal with a chronic illness.

I saw a man in therapy who had lost a child, and as a result he was critical with everyone. He felt it was *his right* to be critical and mean because of what he had to go through. His attitude was that others should suffer as he had to suffer.

Sometimes as people get older they become more critical because life isn't as they had imagined it would be. Their children haven't turned out the way they expected. They have little financial security. Some of their friends have moved away or died, their world is growing smaller, they're limited by health problems, and they can't do what they once could.

CRITICAL TACTICS

There are a variety of ways people are critical. The most common is simply to make a critical comment about someone's character, looks, ideas, or how she runs her life. Some critical comments are verbal and some nonverbal.

Here are a few critical comments I've heard throughout the years:

"Getting a little thick around the middle, eh Pete?"

"Man, those are some ears you have."

"Sam, what happened to your hair? Guess we're going to have to start calling you Old Baldy."

"I can't believe what an idiot you are."

"Larry, what's that on your nose?"

"That's the dumbest idea I ever heard."

———

Not only do people make comments that are critical, they also ask questions that are critical.

A mother dislikes the outfit her twelve-year-old has chosen to wear to school, so she asks, "Why are you wearing that outfit to school?" And because she doesn't think much of her daughter's hair style, she says, "Is there some reason you didn't comb your hair today?"

I was telling a friend about a new computer I was going to buy, and she said, "Why would you ever buy that kind?" Needless to say, I got her message.

I worked with one man who constantly asked questions with a critical agenda. We were at a business meeting, and he said to one woman, "How old are you anyway?" He had an incredible way of throwing people off balance. He had little understanding of himself or how much people disliked him for this behavior.

It's interesting that some people use criticism as a ploy to try to get closer to someone. For example, every time I saw Kevin, he seemed compelled to tell me some negative story about his wife. Perhaps he thought these tales brought us closer, sort of like the two of us against her. In reality his behavior caused me to avoid him.

Another maneuver people use is to give a compliment and then negate it with a critical remark.

A man who is an accomplished musician was taking a saxophone lesson. After he finished playing a particularly difficult piece, his teacher said, "You played that rather well. I'm amazed."

This man said he felt terrible and wished the teacher had made no comment at all.

A grandmother took her granddaughter shopping. When they got home, the woman said to her daughter, "What a nice time we had." Then she added, "But your daughter sure doesn't understand the value of a dollar."

This comment criticized not only the granddaughter, but the

daughter as well. Again, why make such a comment? What purpose does it serve?

People who make critical comments would do well to ask themselves the question that Luke posed: "Why do you observe the splinter in your brother's eye and never notice the great log in your own?" (Luke 6:41)

Nonverbal Criticism

I'm always amazed when I do marriage counseling at how adept couples are at criticizing each other without saying a word. Their mouths fly open, they thrust their heads back and their chins forward, they dramatically raise their eyebrows, they cross their arms across their chests. The messages they're sending with these actions: You're stupid, you're a liar, you don't know what you're talking about.

When I see this kind of nonverbal behavior, I often throw a Nerf ball at them. This is my way to say, "Stop that," as well as to call attention to their behavior. At the beginning of a couple's therapy, I may throw fifteen or twenty Nerfs in one session for negative nonverbal behavior. As people work with me and change this behavior, they often joke about how few Nerfs they got that day.

Right now take a moment and think about what you do with your body to indicate disapproval. Do you squint your eyes, purse your lips, stick out your chin like a disagreeable four-year-old?

Being impatient is another way people are nonverbally critical. You stand in line waiting with a disgusted look on your face. You shift your weight from one foot to another. You dramatically fold your arms in front of you. You open your eyes wide, lean your head back, slightly tilting to the right or left, as if to say, "Can you believe this clerk? I'm faster, smarter, and more efficient."

———

Another thing to keep in mind: Criticism does not get people to change, even if your criticism is valid.

For example, your husband is forever coming home late. You've asked him repeatedly to please call if he's going to be late. He says he will, but he never does. You confront, you criticize, you lecture.

Does he change? No.

A child brings home poor grades. The parent's response is constant badgering. "If you would only study. Can't you see how you're ruining your life?"

Does this criticism bring in better grades? No. But it does create a home filled with tension and resentment.

IS IT EVER APPROPRIATE TO BE CRITICAL?

Sometimes people ask, "Is it ever appropriate to be critical?" Yes, it's expected that a parent correct a child who is misbehaving. It's appropriate for an employer to tell a worker when he's not performing. And sometimes it's necessary for a therapist, teacher, minister, or friend to confront a person on his or her destructive behavior. Anytime an evaluation is required or requested, there's a chance someone is going to be criticized. But if the comment is critical, it should be constructive.

Constructive criticism has three components: (1) There is a contract between the people involved. The person who is making the critical comment is a parent, teacher, editor, supervisor, or very good friend. (2) The negative feedback addresses a specific issue. (3) There is direction for change. If your criticism is truly constructive criticism, all three components must be present.

Inappropriate criticism, on the other hand, is negative feedback that is uninvited (there is no contract). The feedback is nonspecific or broad based, or it is without direction for change.

For example, an engineer writes a proposal. The supervisor says, "This is terrible. Miserable. Don't they teach you guys to write in school?" This is not constructive criticism. This is inappropriate criticism. In this case there is a contract. The supervisor's job is to monitor proposals, but the feedback attacks the engineer generally (people in his profession can't write), and there is no direction for change.

Another example: A father says to his daughter, "Stop that whining. You are such a crybaby!" Here there is a contract (parents correct children), the feedback is specific (stop that whining), but the feedback attacks the daughter generally (she's a crybaby). This qualifies as inappropriate criticism.

A woman says to her husband, "You're so messy. Why can't you pick up after yourself?" Here there is no contract, the feedback attacks the person, and it is not specific.

Think of something you've said and ask whether it was constructive or inappropriate criticism. Run it through the formula. This is making use of your sense ability.

PUTTING AWAY YOUR CRITICISM

The first step to become less critical is to make a decision: "I'm going to stop being critical and I resolve to work at it."

The next step is to write down for one week every critical comment you make. Recording your statements increases awareness and helps make you accountable.

I used this technique with a mother and her twenty-four-year-old daughter, who had to move back home because of financial problems. Both mother and daughter knew how critical each could be. They were concerned that living together wasn't going to work because of their inclination to criticize.

Here are some of the criticisms the mother thought, but fortunately did not verbalize:

- Don't you brush your teeth first thing in the morning?
- Are you going to wear that shirt again without washing it?
- Would you please get your car fixed before your engine blows up?
- Isn't that the fourth shower you've taken today?
- There's a button missing on that blouse.
- Do you have your glasses?

- Stop watching television and go do something constructive.
- Your room is starting to look like a pigpen. Where is your pride?
- Don't forget to call your friend back.

And now the daughter's list of complaints:

- Those shoes look ridiculous.
- Why are you wearing nylons with shorts and sandals? If you could just see yourself.
- Can't you drive a little faster?
- Get those curlers out of your hair!
- Don't you ever shave your legs?
- Are you going to stand there and listen to my entire conversation?
- Are you going to wear that? It has got to be one hundred years old.
- Why don't you just chill out, relax, calm down?

Only a few days had gone by when they decided to share their lists. Although this was not part of the therapy plan, both of them had a good laugh when they shared what they had written about each other. It seemed that the mother had a preoccupation with cleanliness, and the daughter was preoccupied with Mom's appearance. After hearing each other's list, mother and daughter decided that they definitely needed to keep their criticisms to themselves.

Some of the items the mother noted about her daughter were valid according to her perception, just as some of the daughter's items were valid according to how she thinks. But remember, mother and daughter do not have an agreement to tell each other what they think is wrong with the other. Their agreement is to live peaceably.

If Mom starts with, "Don't forget to call your friend back," and "Your room is starting to look like a pigpen," the daughter is going to feel resentful. She may play out her resentment by finding fault with Mom or pulling back emotionally and refusing to share details of her life. And what chance will the two of them have if the daughter tells her mother to shave her legs and drive faster?

Writing down your critical comments is work, but it makes you aware. Once aware, you can change.

Sometimes I'll ask a person to write down not only all the critical comments she makes, but also all the ones she would have liked to have made.

This exercise has the added benefit of helping you feel a sense of accomplishment each time you see that you have refrained from making a critical comment. You have controlled yourself. You have used your sense ability.

WHAT IS YOUR HIGHER VALUE?

Another technique for change is to ask yourself, *"What is my higher value?"* Your higher value is your ultimate goal, the thing you want most to accomplish.

For example, before making a critical comment about her husband's tennis racket sitting in the entry hall, a wife might ask herself this question: *"What is my higher value?"* If her higher value is to have a close relationship with her husband, she may decide to forgo making a comment about his tennis racket. She may even decide to put it away.

Suppose you telephone your aging mom every few days to check on her well-being. While talking, you find yourself annoyed because she always seems to find something to complain about. Instead of becoming exasperated and negative, ask yourself, *"What is my higher value?"* If you answer, "My higher value is to check on Mom," you won't be thinking critical thoughts.

This question will also serve you well at work. Suppose you're in a disagreement at the office about how something should be handled. You see it one way; your co-worker sees it another. Instead of digging in your heels with a my-way-or-the-highway attitude, ask yourself, *"What is my higher value?"* This question will help you refocus on your goal, come to a compromise, and get the project finished.

———

Sometimes I will ask a critical person, "What epitaph would you like on your tombstone?" Will it be "Here lies Lucy: a highly critical woman," or will it be, "Here lies Lucy—a woman who knew how to love."

Most people do not want to be remembered for their critical comments.

———

Another suggestion: Focus on the positives in life. When you're thinking positive thoughts, it's not possible to think negative thoughts. You can't think two thoughts at once.

I also suggest that for every critical comment you catch yourself making, make three positive comments. Eventually, positive thoughts will become more frequent, and negative thoughts will not pop into your head as often.

Listen to what Saint Paul tells us: "Whatever is true, whatever is worthy of reverence and is honorable and seemly, whatever is just, whatever is pure, whatever is lovely, whatever is kind and winsome and gracious, if there is anything worthy of praise, think on and weigh and take account of these things, fix your mind on them." (Phil. 4:8–9)

———

In the early 1920s, Emile Coué, a French therapist, proposed the idea that repeating a positive phrase over and over would affect how you perceive yourself and would have a positive impact on your belief system. The technique was called "conscious auto-suggestion." Coué chose the phrase, *"Every day in every way, I'm getting better and better."* His suggestion was to repeat this phrase twenty times on awakening and twenty times before falling asleep. For years people in France and Great Britain walked around saying, *"Every day in every way, I'm getting better and better."* As with other tried and true techniques, this idea was eventually discarded.[1]

In the last twenty years, extensive research has been done on the efficacy of repeating a positive phrase, an affirmation, over and over. The results are in: This technique works. Repeating a positive phrase has a positive impact on one's belief system and subsequent behavior.

The affirmation I suggest for people working to become less critical is: *"I choose to be accepting. I choose to be loving."* Slowly say this statement as you're driving, riding the subway, walking across the parking lot to get to your building.

Another thing you might do is practice lovingkindness. You simply repeat several lines of a lovingkindness poem, which softens one's thoughts and calms one mind. One such poem is

May I be happy, may I be peaceful:
May you be happy, may you be peaceful.[2]

Again, constant repetition of an affirmation, a poem, or a prayer calms the mind, relaxes the body, and helps one be more accepting of imperfections.

DEALING WITH A CRITICAL PERSON

Some people are not critical themselves, but they must deal with critical people on a regular basis.

If your mate is critical, tell her that her critical comments are driving you away. They are inviting you to close off emotionally. They are chipping away at your self-esteem and the marriage.

If she defends herself by saying that she wouldn't be critical if you would do what you had promised, you can say, "You're right. I need to keep my promises. But criticizing is not going to help me keep them. Criticizing only invites me to run away."

To a mate or a family member who seems bent on making critical comments, you might say in a respectful tone, "That remark was hurtful." If the critical person counters with some remark such as, "Well, look who's talking," don't fight back. Say nothing in response. But each time you are hit with a critical comment say, "That was hurtful." Eventually the critical person will get the message.

Another tactic: Write down all critical comments the person makes for one week. Tell him you're doing this as a way to heighten his awareness. At the end of the week, give him the list, not in a mean-spirited fashion, but as a way to inform. Most critical people become defensive with this tactic, but it's interesting that they often clean up their act.

Another approach is to say, "Ouch," when someone makes a critical statement. This is a way to deflect the hurt while calling attention to the problem.

————

Critical bosses and co-workers also chip away at one's self-esteem. Depending on your relationship with the person, when a critical comment is leveled, you might moan and hold your stomach.

Another option is to talk to the person who is being critical, not at the moment when it's happening, but when the relationship is running smoothly. Chances are that when the critical person is called on his behavior, he will become defensive and start attacking you and your behavior. But you can hold the line by saying, "I know I could make some changes, but I really wish you would be more careful with your criticisms."

Remember: Having a relationship with someone does not mean the person holds an all-encompassing license to be critical.

CRITICIZING YOURSELF

Studies show that people who are critical of others are frequently very hard on themselves. If you are one of these people and know that you should be kinder in your self-talk, start by asking the question, "Why am I critical of myself?"

Asking this question of herself, one woman said, "My mom was very critical of me. I could never do anything quite right. I guess that's how I learned to be critical. Also, I often have the feeling that I'm not okay, like I'm not worthy."

Now ask, "How am I critical of myself?" Answering this question the woman said, "I don't allow myself enough sleep and I always push myself to do more."

This woman continues to carry the burden of having a critical mother and the notion that she must do it right and that she never quite measures up. Thus she drives herself with too many projects and too little sleep.

Using these two questions, first the *why* and then the *how*, is making use of your sense ability.

———

A man goes to weed his garden. He starts by pulling the biggest and most obvious weeds. Then he goes after the smaller ones. As he stands to survey his work, he sees more weeds.

After an hour more of weeding, with the sun shifting in the sky, the man stands again to see what he has accomplished. There, under the foliage of the eggplants, he notices still more weeds. But this time instead of bending down to pull the hidden weeds, he says, "It's quite good enough."[3]

Every once in a while when I've worked and reworked something, I'll hear myself say in my head, "Okay, Doris, stop, it's quite good enough." It's amazing the calming effect this tiny sentence has on me. Why not try it for yourself in the next few days?

It's quite good enough the way my daughter cleaned her room or my son picked up his toys. *It's quite good enough* the way I made the bed or cleaned the grout. *It's quite good enough* the way I conducted the meeting.

NOT MAKING CRITICAL COMMENTS
HAS MANY REWARDS

Because I've struggled with being critical, I'd like to share the following story with you.

It was Easter Sunday. We were in the car on our way to our friends' farm. As we were driving along, my husband said, "Easter just doesn't seem like that big of a deal anymore."

What I immediately wanted to say was, "I can't believe you. You may not think it's a big deal, but I made a sweet potato casserole. I got the wine. I bought a gift for our friends. I made an Easter basket for my parents. I stayed up until midnight helping Anna-Mary make two lamb cakes, and I packed the car before church this morning."

Instead I was silent. I was quiet. I said nothing.

As we drove, I started to think. I guess for my husband, Easter probably isn't that big a deal since our children are older. He no longer has to hide Easter eggs at the crack of dawn. There are no little wagons or wheelbarrows to put together. No tiny children to chase around and get dressed for church.

If I had chosen to run out my litany of everything I had done in preparation for Easter, my husband would surely have felt attacked. After the attack, I would have felt guilty and then remorseful. And I would have spoiled a nice ride to the farm.

That night, as we were driving home, my husband reached over, took my hand, and said, "It was sure nice, all the things you did for everyone."

———

An Eastern proverb says that each word we say, every comment we make, should be required to pass through three gates before it is spoken. "At the first gate the gatekeeper asks, 'Is it true?' At the second gate, he asks, 'Is it necessary?' And at the third gate, 'Is it kind?' "[4] As you use your sense ability, you wisely become your own gatekeeper.

8
ARE YOU AWARE OF YOUR PSYCHOLOGICAL BOUNDARY LINES?

Accept that some days you're the pigeon and some days you're the statue.

Roger Anderson in *The Rotarian*

Recently I was having dinner at a restaurant with a few friends and decided to order dessert. When my dessert came, one of my friends said, "Oh, let me taste." She then reached over with her fork and took a bite. Although I said, "Sure, fine," I didn't like that she had stuck her fork in my food. I'm very territorial. Of course, someone taking an unexpected bite of my dessert is not going to ruin a friendship. However, many psychological boundaries get crossed each day, which can leave you feeling uneasy, tense, and sometimes downright hostile.

YOU'RE INVADING MY SPACE

As a newborn, you don't recognize any margins or boundaries between yourself and the world. You don't distinguish between your hands, the bars of your crib, and your mother's body. The merging between yourself and others is seamless. By the time you're six months old, you have a basic awareness of your hand versus your mother's hand. You are beginning to understand your separateness.

By age two, a sense of self starts to emerge. You look into the mirror and you recognize yourself. You are becoming aware of your own abilities. As you climb the stairs, you say, "Go up." You start to realize that you have some power to influence others. You look at your mother and say, "Sit."

As your sense of self grows, your sense of ownership—what is yours and what is yours to control—is also growing. By age three, you are starting to define your psychological boundaries.

If another youngster comes along and plops down next to you, you may start pushing and shoving him away. By your actions you're saying, "My space, my territory. Move over, Buster." You not only define your territory, you also protect it, much as a country protects its borders.

As you move into grade school, you continue to define your psychological boundaries. Because boundaries are largely a matter of interpretation, your rights versus another person's rights, you are most influenced by the people around you, mainly family. For example, in some families, people drink out of each other's glasses and use each other's hairbrushes and bath towels without a thought. In other families the members are more territorial: "That's my chair"; "I told you I don't want you using my washcloth"; "Get out of my purse"; "Do not go in my toolbox"; "Stay out of my room."

As an adult, you may continue to follow the lines of demarcation you drew as a child or you may adjust or change them. This changeability depends on two things: your relationship with the person who has crossed the invisible line you've drawn and your level of acceptance that particular day.

For example, you may start out not using anyone else's hairbrush and not allowing anyone to use yours. Then one day you can't find your brush, and your good friend says, "Here. Use mine." Chances are you will feel uncomfortable, but you use her brush. If you use her brush a number of times, you may come to the point where you do not experience any negative thoughts or anxious feelings. In essence, you have changed this psychological boundary with this person. The boundary is still there, but not with her at this particular time.

Certainly your boundary lines are less rigid with family than with friends and less rigid with friends than with co-workers. If your wife or best friend reads one of your letters without asking, it might not bother you. If you catch an acquaintance doing the same thing, it may be a whole different story.

Your mood, how you think and feel on a particular day, also affects your response. Some days your acceptance level is high; other days it's low. If you and your friend are having a pleasant day, it may be no problem when she helps herself to some food in your refrigerator. If you're aggravated with her or you're having a bad day for some other reason, your response to her invasion of your refrigerator might be negative.

You might not mind your daughter going into your closet and rummaging around for something to wear. You might even be pleased that the two of you share clothes. However, if you're annoyed at her for leaving a messy kitchen, you may redraw a line around your things. Now if she walks into your closet, you might say in an irritated voice, "Get out of my closet. Those are my clothes."

Your daughter may think of you as someone who can't make up her mind. One day it's fine that she goes through your things. The next day you're all hot and bothered. Neither of you understands that you are always readjusting your psychological boundary lines.

I can't recall anyone coming to therapy to tell me they're having problems with boundary lines. But I have had someone tell me she has no time for herself, or her adolescent is driving her crazy because he keeps helping himself to whatever he wants no matter whose it is, or she's angry with her husband because he always has the television blaring. Underlying these issues— boundary lines are being crossed. Once your sense of awareness is heightened, boundary lines will give you less trouble.

A QUIZ: DISCOVERING YOUR BOUNDARY LINES

To discover some of your psychological boundaries, take a moment and answer the following twenty questions. There are no right or wrong answers. Your answers may surprise you, however, and most certainly will give you important information about yourself and your relationships.

1. Do you have a problem with someone going into your desk drawer to get a pair of scissors or a stapler?

    _____

    _____

2. Does it bother you if your mate opens your mail or someone at your office reads your faxes?

    _____

    _____

3. Are you annoyed if a friend comes to your home and turns on the television or goes in the refrigerator without asking?

    _____

    _____

4. Would you have a problem if someone wrote in the margin of one of your books?

    _____

    _____

5. Have you ever been irritated with a friend for forming a friendship with someone who was initially your friend?

    _____

    _____

6. Would you feel annoyed if someone stood over your shoulder and watched what you were writing on your PC or picked up a folder on your desk and flipped through it?

_____

_____

7. Would you have negative feelings if you left your sweatshirt at a friend's home, and when she returned it, she said she'd worn it?

_____

_____

8. When someone telephones, do you feel forced to keep talking long after you want to end the conversation?

_____

_____

9. When paying bills, working, or reading, do you prefer quiet?

_____

_____

10. Would it be a problem if a friend shared your medical diagnosis with others?

_____

_____

11. Would it bother you if a co-worker used your idea at a meeting without acknowledging that the idea was yours?

_____

_____

12. Do you feel comfortable sharing a dressing room with a friend to try on clothes?

_____

_____

13. Do you have a problem with using a unisex bathroom or shower?

_____

_____

14. Would you have a problem if you gave a neighbor a key for safety reasons, and he let himself into your home to borrow a ladder?

_____

_____

15. Would you have a problem if a friend bought a house on the same street as your house?

_____

_____

16. Do you have a problem when someone asks you if she can borrow a piece of clothing or jewelry or sports equipment?

_____

_____

17. Do you have a problem if a friend takes up one of your hobbies?

_____

_____

18. Does it offend you when someone asks you how much you make or why you don't have more children?

_____

_____

19. Would it be okay if your friend announced that your son had been accepted at Harvard before you had a chance to tell everyone?

_____

_____

20. Would you be upset if your mate unexpectedly shared with friends at a party the news that one of your children was having difficulty in school or had gotten in trouble with the law?

_____

_____

As you can see from this exercise, there are many invisible boundaries that surround you and help define how you think, feel, and behave.

Here's how I would answer the first five questions. As you read over my answers, compare them to yours.

1. I have no problem with someone going into my desk drawer for a pair of scissors. I would feel slightly annoyed if he ate all my cookies, which I also keep in my desk. Helping himself to a few would be fine.

2. I would be bothered if my husband opened my mail without asking. When I'm away on a trip and he asks if he should open something, I often say yes, but I feel a twinge of uncertainty, a little intruded upon. Reading my fax? I don't like it when people read my faxes, especially before I get a chance to read them.

3. If a friend came to my home and turned on the television or went in the refrigerator without asking, I'd be annoyed. If she asked, no problem.

4. If a person wrote in my book in pencil, my sense of nosiness, wanting to see what he had written, would override my an-

noyance. If the person wrote in pen, I definitely would feel a boundary had been crossed.

5. I have felt somewhat unsettled when a good friend of mine has befriended another friend and I've been left out in some way. I don't like that I feel this way, but I do.

Reading only a few of my answers, you can see that I'm fairly territorial. I don't like people invading what I define as my space, my territory. You may also be territorial. Or you may be more fluid and less possessive.

If you are territorial, you will experience discomfort when someone inadvertently crosses the line. Your response will more than likely be a negative thought such as, "Hey you, what's the deal?" or, "I can't believe she did that." These thoughts may be accompanied by a rush of adrenalin, culminating in feelings of anxiety or annoyance. When someone steps over one of your boundary lines, it takes only a second to react.

If you are more fluid, you simply have weaker and fewer boundary lines. You have less difficulty if one of them is crossed. You're not going to feel as strongly about the incident. In therapy I continually see people who inadvertently step over other people's boundary lines. More often than not, this lack of awareness leads to misunderstandings.

HIDDEN BOUNDARIES

In the following case, the information boundary line had been crossed: which information is okay to share and with whom.

A couple learned that their son had ADD, attention deficit disorder. On learning the diagnosis, the wife told several of her friends. When her husband found out that she had told other people, he was furious. He felt as if she had no right.

When the wife asked the son what he thought, the son had no problem with sharing. In fact, he had already told several of his high school buddies.

A few weeks later the man came to the realization that perhaps he was having trouble with other people knowing his son's diagnosis because someone might think it was his fault, based on his genes. I also think this man is simply more private than his wife. His information boundary line is tighter around himself and his family.

———

A husband may see no problem in telling his best friend that he and his wife have been trying to have a baby, while his wife thinks revealing this information is a betrayal of her and the marriage. On the other hand, the wife believes it's perfectly acceptable to tell her parents her husband's income, whereas he thinks it's nobody's business but his and his wife's.

This same information boundary line can be inadvertently crossed at the office. You're at a meeting and you casually share some findings with another company. Your partner becomes perturbed and thinks you've divulged too much information. You interpret his response as being ridiculous and a little paranoid, whereas he thinks you're a blabbermouth.

The unhealthy consequences that occur after the information boundary line has been crossed are unfortunate. One of the parties usually feels exposed and betrayed. Then comes the issue of trust: "If she shares this kind of information, what else does she share?"

———

A boundary line that frequently gets crossed is your *psychological noise boundary*. How much noise and how much silence are you comfortable with?

One spouse likes the television on and the volume high. The other prefers the television off, but if it is on, she prefers the volume low. When the volume is up, she feels intruded on; when it's down, he's uncomfortable.

If a husband enjoys quiet and his wife likes to talk, her talking may make him uneasy. On some level he feels as though he's being invaded. He may address his discomfort by walking out of the room or tuning his wife out.

The wife, on the other hand, may feel anxious when her husband doesn't talk. One might say that her psychological noise boundary has been invaded by his silence. She may address her uneasiness by chasing after him to talk or by picking a fight to get him talking.

One couple I worked with had trouble when the husband watched sporting events on television, particularly football. His wife said she could not bear the announcer's continual talking and the crowd's constant roar. It made her so anxious that she felt like going over to the television and clicking it off or running out of the house, both of which she actually had done. Once she was aware of her noise boundary and was able to talk about it, her agitation lessened when her husband watched football. He, on the other hand, has attempted to keep the volume turned down in deference to his wife.

———

Another way to think about one's psychological noise boundary is to understand the phenomenon called the "Bowery El effect."

"An elevated railroad once ran along Third Avenue in New York City. At a certain time, late each night, a noisy train ran. The train line was torn down some time ago, with some interesting after-effects. Many people in the neighborhood called the police to report 'something strange' occurring late at night— noises, thieves, burglars, etc. The police determined that these calls took place around the time of the former late-night train. What these people were 'hearing,' of course, was the absence of the familiar noise of the train. . . ."[1]

The Bowery El effect indicates that you have a model of the world in your nervous system. Although you continually revise and reprogram your model, if the input you receive and your model of the world agree, you are not conscious of anything different occurring. If the input becomes louder or softer, faster or slower, or it ceases, you become immediately aware because a familiar noise boundary has been crossed.[2]

As Sherlock Holmes commented to Watson, "The world is full of obvious things which nobody by any chance ever observes."[3]

———

Sometimes you may feel that a boundary has been crossed if a friend dresses in a similar manner, chooses the same hair style, buys an identical automobile, or starts wearing the same perfume. When you have a thought such as, "Stop copying me," or "Stop trying to act like me," it indicates that you are feeling invaded. In other words, a psychological boundary has been crossed.

———

Another boundary that has the potential to cause a good deal of emotional pain is the *boundary line of friendship*. For example, you introduce Sue and Mary. Soon you learn that the two of them are getting together without you. You feel not only that you are odd person out, but also that a line has been crossed. Do you have a right to feel this way? There is no right or wrong regarding how you feel. It's how you decide to deal with the feeling that's significant.

If you decide to say something to your friends, they may see you as petty and pull away from you, or they may resent you trying to control their time together even though they acquiesce to your wishes. A third possibility would be for you to let nature take its course and focus on some of your other friendships. The one thing you don't want to do is cause yourself more pain by obsessing.

———

The *boundary line of time* is another one that is problematic for many people. Most people feel that they have too little time. If you're home in the evening and having a good time with family, and a friend or co-worker calls, you may feel your time boundary has been crossed. You can regain territory by saying, "Can't talk now, but if it's important, I'll call you back later tonight." More and more people are screening their telephone calls as a way to protect their territory.

A THINKING EXERCISE

Now that you have become aware of a number of your psychological boundaries, think about one of them that may cause you distress (for example, your mate sharing information that you wish she hadn't, someone wanting to share a dressing room with you), and answer the following questions:

1. When I feel intruded on, what do I say to myself that causes me to feel a negative response?

_____

_____

2. Is my reaction linked to my childhood? Does it have anything to do with certain standards I've set for myself?

_____

_____

3. Would my mate or best friend feel the same if this happened to him or her?

_____

_____

4. Is this a boundary that I want to erase? Is this an issue I want to address, and if so, what will I say to get my point across?

_____

_____

The first question demonstrates how you feed yourself negative thoughts when someone crosses a boundary.

The second question shows that your boundary is linked to your upbringing or certain standards you have set for yourself and others along the way.

The third question indicates that people under similar circumstances often react differently. There is no right or wrong here.

The fourth question invites you to reassess your thinking as well as how you might address a touchy situation without escalating it.

A SENSE OF ME, A SENSE OF YOU

Make no mistake, psychological boundary lines are important. Your boundaries are a part of you. They help define you and your space. But they can be a source of trouble because you don't know they exist until one gets crossed.

When one is inadvertently crossed, the important thing is not to jump to an automatic response pattern of anger or criticism or obsessing. Rather, think about what's happening and decide how you want to handle the situation. Some situations you'll decide to let go. Others you'll want to discuss.

If, on the other hand, you step over someone else's line, you may find yourself in hot water. If your mate becomes upset because you shared something with a friend that he thought inappropriate to share, don't defend yourself and tell him why you shared the information. Focus on him and his feelings first. Apologize for stepping on his toes. Then bring up the issue of boundaries and how your lines are different. A discussion about how things might be handled in the future would be appropriate.

Remember, boundary lines are part and parcel of each person. Sometimes they are inadvertently stepped on. Using your sense ability means being aware of what's happening in a particular situation and being able to deal with it appropriately.

ARE YOU A CONTROLLING PERSON?

Count no day lost in which you waited your turn, took only your share and sought advantage over no one.

Anonymous

When I asked Gretchen how things were going in her marriage, she said, "It's the same. Sam's still trying to run my life.

"When we go to the grocery store, I like to read the labels, check out the fat grams. He says, 'Hurry up. Let's get going. You don't need to read that stuff. You're thin enough.'

"I tell Sam my thinness has nothing to do with reading the labels. I'm reading them for other health reasons."

———

Gretchen also told me this story: "Sam came in the house and said, 'Your lilies of the valley are blooming. Did you forget to pick them?'

"I told him no, I hadn't forgotten. I was just busy. I'd get to them.

"It wasn't more than a few hours later that he's in my sewing room telling me again that the lilies are blooming.

"I said, 'Yes. I know.' In my head I thought, 'Stop trying to tell me what to do!'

"The following morning when I came into the kitchen there was a note from Sam on the table. It read, 'Pick lilies of the valley. Sam.' "

Gretchen said she was so annoyed by the note that she decided she was *not* going to pick the flowers.

Neither of these people realizes they have a control issue. Gretchen could have given up the fight by picking the flowers, which she had originally intended to do. She likes to have the sweet smell of lilies of the valley in her house. Or, she could have told Sam lovingly to go ahead and pick them. On the other hand, Sam didn't need to keep reminding Gretchen about the flowers. He could have asked Gretchen if she minded if he picked them. Neither of these people is using his or her sense ability.

Gretchen controls by digging in her heels and becoming passive. Nobody is going to tell her what to do. Sam is more active in his desire to control. He directs and reminds and tells his wife what to do.

TELLING PEOPLE WHAT TO DO

One of the most common ways a person tries to control others is by telling them what to do. A parent gets to instruct a child because the parent is responsible for teaching the child and the child is supported by the parent. A boss gets to direct a worker because the worker gets a paycheck, and that's part of the agreement. Ministers, priests, rabbis, police officers, therapists, doctors, nurses, lawyers, and editors also get to tell people what to do on occasion. These people have a contract implied by the nature of the relationship, tacitly agreed to or written. For the most part, however, unless a person asks your opinion, you should proceed carefully.

There are occasions, however, when you want to tell someone something because you think you know best. On these occasions, try making a suggestion and posing it in the form of a

question. Both of these tactics give the other person more ma-
neuvering room.

Here are a few examples.

Suppose you want your husband to cut the grass. You might
state, "Bill, you need to get the grass cut before Saturday night,"
whereas you might ask, "Bill, is it possible that you could cut
the grass before Saturday night?" Asking a question instead of
making a statement, as well as using the word *possible*, gives Bill
a choice.

Suppose you think your friend has developed a drinking problem. You might state, "Susan, I think you're drinking too much."
Or you might suggest, "Susan, sometimes I think you . . . well
. . . maybe . . . drink a little too much." Clearly the second message, which contains some discounting words (*well, maybe, a little
too much*) helps make the message more receivable.

Pretend your secretary says to you, "I'm going to lunch." Now
pretend she says, "I'm going to lunch, if that's not a problem."
With the first comment she tells you. With the second comment
she gives you a choice. She includes you in the decision.

Suppose your seventy-two-year-old neighbor is out shoveling
snow. You know she's already had one heart attack. Do you tell
her what to do? You have no contract. It's really not your right.
On the other hand, perhaps walking out and saying, "Margaret,
come into the house, rest a bit, and I'll make you some hot
chocolate," would be the loving thing to do.

Suppose your brother-in-law looks sick and has had a cough
for a few months. Suggesting to him that he see a doctor might
be the most loving thing to do. Suggesting to your niece that
she consider staying in school and finishing her education might
be the most loving thing to do.

But telling someone where to park the car, or to drive faster,
or how to wear her hair, or how to handle her children may or
may not be loving.

Before telling or suggesting, review your motives. Ask of yourself: "Who am I serving? Am I being loving? Or is this comment
self-serving and designed to help me get my way?"

Temper Tantrums, Mumbling, Pouting,
Not Answering Questions

Temper tantrums are a favorite means of trying to gain control over another. You don't like something that's been said or done, so you get angry to force the other person into agreeing with you, into doing it your way.

Do you have temper tantrums to get your way?

Incessant talkers are controllers. As long as you keep talking, you are controlling the topic of conversation.

Do you insist on continuing to talk after the other person has made it clear it's time to change subjects, get off the telephone, move on?

Mumblers are also controllers. Have you ever noticed how others have to lean forward to hear a mumbler? Even when a mumbler is asked to please speak up, he doesn't.

Do people often ask you to speak up?

I have a friend who pouts. When someone disagrees with him, his first response is to get aggressive by raising his voice and telling the other person he's wrong. If the person doesn't back down, my friend then closes up like a clam and refuses to talk. Refusing to talk is a way to control others.

Do you pout? How many hours or days do you pout before you are willing to start talking and solve the problem?

If you pout, try this: No more than two hours of pouting without coming back and telling the person you're ready to start talking. Or, come back and tell the person you need to pout a few more hours. Remember, no problem ever gets solved when people pout. And pouting limits your sense of awareness.

————

I saw a man in group therapy who would never answer a question. You'd ask him something, and he'd go into some long dissertation. The other group members would say, "Answer the question," five or six times before he actually answered. He wasn't searching for an answer; he just liked to make you wait. While we waited, he was in control.

One woman I worked with wouldn't make a decision. She wouldn't decide where she wanted to go on vacation, what kind of a car to buy, what movie to see, or what restaurant she wanted to go to. While she hemmed and hawed, her husband and everyone else waited. If someone else made a suggestion, she found fault with it. Her behavior was self-serving and controlling.

THE "RIGHT" TO CONTROL

Why do people think it's their right to try to control others? Sometimes it stems from being outer-focused and a perfectionist. The person thinks she knows best. Because of this, she tries to get others to do things her way.

Do you often think you know best?

Sometimes a controlling person has low self-esteem. She hides her insecurity by frequently telling others what to do. In the telling she bolsters her opinion of herself. If the other person takes her advice, she gives herself a pat on the back for being "helpful."

An individual may try to control others because she lacks control of her own life. She dislikes her job, her house is in disarray, and her marriage is in shambles.

Have you ever noticed that when your life is out of whack, your desire to tell others what to do increases?

Pride is often a factor. The person is so arrogant that he presumes it's his right to instruct and tell others what's best for them.

Before telling a person what to do, always ask yourself if you have a contract, if you're being self-serving or loving. Discovering why you want to control, how you try to control, and what you might do differently is part of using your sense ability.

A QUIZ: HOW CONTROLLING ARE YOU?

Unfortunately, most people who are controlling don't think of themselves as controllers. They may see others as controlling, but not themselves. Take the following test to see how controlling you are. Check off each item that applies. Mark your answers because I refer to the individual items at the end of the test, and the results may surprise you.

_____ 1. Have you often been accused of not contributing to a conversation or giving only one- or two-word answers when asked a question?

_____ 2. Do you frequently talk too much?

_____ 3. Do you offer unsolicited advice, telling people how to solve their problems, which restaurants to go to, what to order, where to shop, what kind of cars to buy?

_____ 4. Do you have trouble apologizing, or are you the last to apologize after an argument?

_____ 5. Do you pout and refuse to talk when you get angry?

_____ 6. Do you tell people you'll call or do something by a certain date and then not get it done?

_____ 7. When you want something, docs it have to be done *now*?

_____ 8. Do you run late, making others wait?

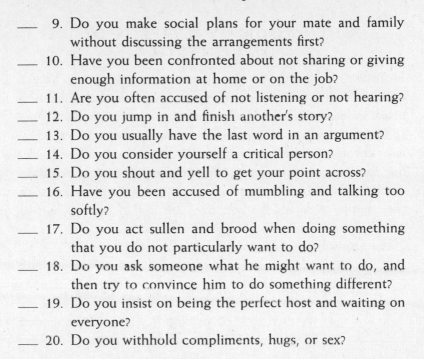

___ 9. Do you make social plans for your mate and family without discussing the arrangements first?

___ 10. Have you been confronted about not sharing or giving enough information at home or on the job?

___ 11. Are you often accused of not listening or not hearing?

___ 12. Do you jump in and finish another's story?

___ 13. Do you usually have the last word in an argument?

___ 14. Do you consider yourself a critical person?

___ 15. Do you shout and yell to get your point across?

___ 16. Have you been accused of mumbling and talking too softly?

___ 17. Do you act sullen and brood when doing something that you do not particularly want to do?

___ 18. Do you ask someone what he might want to do, and then try to convince him to do something different?

___ 19. Do you insist on being the perfect host and waiting on everyone?

___ 20. Do you withhold compliments, hugs, or sex?

Every check mark indicates controlling behavior. More than three checks means you're trying to run too many shows.

If you checked numbers 3, 7, 12, 13, 14, 15, and 18, you actively try to take control by offering advice, expecting people to meet your schedule, finishing people's stories, having the last word, and escalating your anger.

If you checked numbers 1, 2, 4, 5, 6, 8, 9, 10, 11, 16, 17, 19, and 20, you are more subtle in your desire for control. Your behavior, however, can be just as upsetting, annoying, and provocative as that of an active controller.

You may find after taking this test that you have both active and passive controlling behaviors. This indicates that you like to control and have subconsciously figured out a number of ways to do it.

Of the behaviors you checked, which ones are you willing to change?

WHEN YOUR OWN LIFE IS OUT OF CONTROL

In addition to trying to control others, many people have a problem with trying to control themselves. They may spend too much money, work too many hours, or spend too much time shopping, watching television, or being on the Internet. They may devote too much time to socializing, biking, fishing, golfing, running, or working out. They may eat too much, drink too much, or be too concerned with their weight, their looks, or their house. As a result, their lives are out of balance, out of whack, out of control.

Now answer the following five questions.

1. What is one area in my life that is out of control?

_____

2. How does this behavior interfere with my life?

_____

3. How does this behavior hurt me?

_____

4. How does it hurt my relationships with others?

_____

5. Am I willing to change this behavior? Yes or no?

_____

If you answered yes to number five, you are already halfway through the process of controlling yourself because you recognize you have a problem.

GETTING YOURSELF IN CONTROL

Recognition and awareness are the first step to change.

The next step to gaining control is the behavioral component of change. Start by recording how often you gamble, work, over-spend, drink, shop, use the Internet, etc. If you are overweight, keep a diary. Every day write down everything you eat. If you can't pay your charges because of your spending, write down every purchase you make.

Research shows that keeping a written record of how often you give into your craving or obsession has two benefits. It makes you aware, and it helps you stop that particular behavior.

Another important fact: There is a time lag between grabbing something to eat and eating it, between thinking about going shopping and handing someone your charge card. There is a time lag between thinking about stopping to buy a six-pack and buying one, between being besieged by thoughts of gambling and going to the casino.

It is in this time lag that you use your sense of awareness and make the decision whether or not to spend, drink, gamble, whether or not to give into your craving.

———

"I went gambling one weekend with my wife and friends," said Bruce. "Had a good time. Lost a little money. Found it to be an escape. Three weeks later, went again. Then a month later I was going every week. Then I went once a day, sometimes twice a day. It took me twenty minutes to get to the boat from my office. I was able to go whenever I wanted because I own my own company. So I went on my lunch hour, but I'd be gone two or three hours.

"I would leave the casino and feel horrible after losing, say three or four hundred dollars. Sometimes I'd lose a thousand. But by the time I got back to the office, I had rationalized that it was a small amount of money and I could win it back.

"One day I went to get more money at the casino—I had lost

five hundred dollars—and they wouldn't let me use my credit card. I was so mad. I also was lying to my wife as to where I was. I kept this behavior up for about six months. I finally told my wife I needed to see someone about my gambling, and I made an appointment with a therapist.

"The first time I saw the therapist, I made a contract. We agreed I could go gambling once a day, five days out of seven, but I had to hold the line. This was good, because if she had told me that I had to give up gambling all together, I would not have gone back to see her.

"The first few weeks I did fine, but then I cheated. When I saw my therapist again, I remade my contract, but again I found I could not stick to it. I really did not want to give up gambling, and the time period between when I thought about gambling and when I could actually get to the casino was only twenty minutes. I needed a longer time lapse. Again I talked to my therapist, and I decided to take voluntary banishment. I went to the casino and filled out a form. I would no longer be able to gamble in Missouri. Three days later I took voluntary banishment in Illinois. I had to make it more difficult to get to the casinos if I was going to break the habit.

"I still gamble about every six weeks. My wife and I drive to Mississippi, which takes about four hours. We make a weekend of it, but it's more normal. I'm focusing more on my business again, and I feel good about myself."

What Bruce found was that a twenty-minute time lag was not enough to stop him from gambling. So he extended the time lag between thinking about gambling and being able to get to the casino. He made it longer, he put up a barrier, which kept him in check. He used his sense ability.

Even if you have a genetic inclination or there is a biological component to your craving, as in alcoholism, you still have the ability to think and decide not to act on your craving.

In *Shadow Syndromes*, John Ratey and Catherine Johnson write, "The self's decision then feeds back into biology. When we make a decision not to act on the impulse our biology has sent, we weaken the circuitry sending the message ever so slightly, while strengthening the vital circuitry of resistance. This is the biological mechanism through which cognitive-behavioral therapy alters the brain."[1]

Working with a Cognitive-Behavioral Therapist

Another option to get in control of your destructive behavior is to work with a cognitive-behavioral therapist, either in a one-on-one situation or in group therapy.

Here's what you can expect. During the first session, the therapist will collect some information about your problem. She'll want to know when the problem started and what you've done to try to solve it. She'll also ask how this problem is causing difficulties in other areas of your life, such as in your marriage, with your children, on the job.

If you have an issue with spending, she'll want to know how money was handled in your family of origin. If you're wrestling with a drinking problem, she'll want to know if your parents or grandparents had a problem with alcohol. From this information, she'll make some educated guesses as to how your present problem is related to your past. Finding out why you have the problem or where it came from, however, is not the focus of therapy. The main focus is to solve the problem so you can lead a more effective life.

She'll take some history along the way, usually spending a session or two on your childhood, adolescence, early adult life, married life. This is her way to gather information not only about your past, but also about how you communicate, your philosophy, your values. Also, as you talk, you will be developing a relationship with her.

In the beginning, usually the first session, specific goals are established. For example, if you say you have a communication problem, your therapist will want to know what having a communication problem means. Does it mean that you and your wife never talk? Does it mean that when you talk, you end up fighting? Or does it mean that you have little in common to talk about?

In order for you to have better communication, she'll help you make some concrete goals. Your goals may be to initiate two conversations per day with your wife, to find out one new thing about her each day, and to start playing golf with her on the weekends.

Your therapist may do some role playing with you in order to learn how you talk to your wife, what you do to move the conversation along or to block it. She'll be checking to see if you have the skills to accomplish the goals you set.

If you want to cut down on your drinking, you may have the goal of no drinking during the week and no more than two drinks a day on the weekend. If you overspend, you may make a contract that you'll stay out of all department stores for a month and you'll write down everything you spend.

It is also the therapist's job to help you develop new patterns of behavior. If your goal is to stop spending, she will talk about what benefits you may get from shopping.

If she learns that shopping is your way to relax and reduce stress, she will suggest other ways you might reduce stress, such as walking three days a week, getting a massage once a month, and listening to a radio station that plays classical music on your drive home each night. She'll also ask for your input, how you think you might reduce your stress. Then the two of you will set specific goals—you will walk three days a week and listen to classical music in the car.

Your therapist will help you evaluate the ways you think about issues. If you are angry with someone, she may ask what negative thoughts you have about the situation that drive your anger. She may suggest you take a look at your *cognitive triad*. These are negative thoughts you have about yourself, about others, and about your future. You may be given a homework assignment to write down these thoughts during the week and read them at your next session.

She will also ask you to take a look at some of the distorted thinking she hears, such as, "Parties are no fun unless I can drink," or "I know I'll never amount to anything."

In addition, I almost always give my clients affirmations to say. I have standard affirmations, and sometimes the client and I develop one to address his specific problem. Clients often kick and fuss when I tell them they have to say their affirmation two or three thousand times a day. At the same time, I know that this works and that my clients usually reach their goals.

I assign people articles and books to read regarding the latest research on their particular problems.

If I think a person needs medication, I'll have her see a psychiatrist or her internist for an evaluation. I might also suggest a full medical checkup, depending on the symptoms she reports.

I have some adages that I frequently use. I tell people: "It doesn't matter if you're scared or shy or anxious or depressed, do it anyway." I tell them, "You play the hand you're dealt," and "Life's not fair," "Keep on truckin'," "Fix the mistake, not the blame," and "One step at a time."

I suggest movies that I think would be helpful to their specific problems. I also suggest people rent the movies *What About Bob?* and *As Good As It Gets*. Both movies show that change is really all about "baby steps," determination, and taking one day at a time.

———

Another reinforcer to change behavior and get in control is to attend a weekly therapy group. Groups usually consist of a therapist, a co-therapist, and eight or nine clients who are working on a variety of issues, such as relationship problems, parenting issues, job problems, depression, anxiety, and eating disorders. Generally, therapy groups meet once a week for two hours.

In a group, it's easy to see how an individual keeps himself from getting what he wants in life. He doesn't listen when someone is talking, he blocks out the suggestions of others, he doesn't answer questions and he changes the subject, or he gets sarcastic, critical, or rapidly moves to anger. What's also helpful is that he is getting a good deal of feedback, not only from the therapists, but from his peers. He's getting the feedback in the present, in real time, about how his behavior gets in the way of his accomplishing his goals.

Groups are helpful because members can see how others

tackle their issues, and it gives them hope. No therapist, no matter how smart, can compete with eight people who have lived life and found answers along the way.

Also, a feeling of camaraderie comes with participation in a therapy group. Members see that they're not alone in their difficulties, everyone has problems, we're all in this together, and we can do it, we can solve our problems.

Support groups designed to deal with specific issues are also helpful because they reinforce your resolve to change your behavior. There are Alcoholics Anonymous and Rational Recovery for people with drinking problems, Gamblers Anonymous for people with gambling problems, and Weight Watchers for people who are overweight, to name a few.

Quiet Therapies

Another therapy that is helpful in diminishing your craving comes from Japan. The idea is to learn to focus your mind on something other than the craving.

As you read the following two paragraphs, follow the instructions. As you do the brief exercise, you'll see its potential.

Sit on a chair in an erect position with your head level and your feet separated slightly and planted firmly on the floor. Place your hands on your lap and fold them in front of you. Now "belly-breathe." Slowly pull in air, filling your belly. Your shoulders should not rise, and your chest should not expand. As you fill your solar plexus with air, it will push forward. After filling your belly slowly, exhale. Fill your belly slowly again, now exhale.

How slowly should you exhale? "One should exhale so lightly that if a rabbit's hair were placed on the tip of one's nose it would not blow away."[2]

As you do this exercise, you will find thoughts coming and going. Don't get rid of them or try to close them out. Just notice them as you would a snowflake falling on your windshield. The snowflake appears and then disappears. Simply focus on your breathing and sit. Sitting and focusing on your breathing is a way to help you learn control.

When you do this exercise in its entirety, close your eyes. Start with ten minutes, and gradually over the next few weeks, increase your sitting to twenty minutes. I suggest you put on a timer so you won't be distracted by thinking of the time.

———

Another technique to gain more control over yourself is to take a tai chi class. Tai chi is both exercise and therapy. Although tai chi is one of the martial arts, it's considered a soft form because your muscles are relaxed when doing it. The movements of tai chi are based on the movements of various animals, particularly the crane and the snake. Doing these movements feels as though you are performing a very slow ballet. The movements take concentration and physical discipline. Because of this, and because you are constantly learning new movements, it isn't possible to think about your craving.

When practicing tai chi, one develops a mind-body integration, focused attention, balance, and self-discipline. Many people also report that when they do tai chi, they experience a wonderful sense of calm and connectedness.

Merely Changing a Word

You can also reprogram yourself by thinking of your craving as a mere *preference*.

For example, suppose you have become hooked on catalogue shopping. You could decide that when you receive a catalogue you will not even open it. To the trash it goes. Or you could decide that when you look through a catalogue, instead of saying, "I want that jacket," or "I want those earrings," or "I have to have that lamp," you say, "I *prefer* to have that jacket," "I *prefer* to have those earrings," or "I *prefer* to have that lamp." When people have a preference instead of a want, there is more of a feeling that it's a choice, they have latitude to act either way.

William Glasser, the father of *Reality Therapy*, believes that changing a word often reduces the emotional intensity of your craving. This is why you may feel instant relief by changing merely a word.

In therapy, I frequently ask people to substitute one word for another. For example, suppose I have a hard-driving person who rarely lets herself relax. Her life is filled with a lot of *shoulds* and *oughts*. If instead of her saying, "I *should* get this project completed," she says, "I *want* to get this project completed," she feels less pressure.

If she then changes "I *want* to get this project completed" to "I *prefer* to get this project completed," she feels even less pressure. A simple switch in words can help diminish a desire.

————

I recently had an antique cupboard shipped to our home. During the shipping it was damaged. Knowing how upset I can get when things don't go the way I think they should, I had already talked to myself about the possibility that the piece could be damaged. When I saw that one of the panes of old glass was broken and the door was sprung, I said in my head, "My preference is that the cabinet had not been damaged." Once I said this, I left the past and was able to move to the present and check out the Yellow Pages for a cabinetmaker. Even my daughter said, "Mom, you're so calm. Aren't you mad about your cabinet?" I said, "No, I just have to find someone to fix it."

Try it. It's amazing how it works. Take something you're desirous of, something you feel driven to have, and turn it into a preference. I *prefer* to get the living room painted by next Saturday. I *prefer* to be married. I *prefer* that my company win the contract. I *prefer* to make my quota. I *prefer* that the house stay clean.

————

Eastern philosophy teaches that unhappiness comes from desires. If you learn to quell and control your desires instead of always trying to satisfy them, you will find new meaning and freedom in your life.

CAN YOU OVERRIDE GENES AND OTHER INFLUENCES?

What you hear repeatedly you will eventually believe.

Mike Murdock,
author-composer

Have you ever heard the story of the scorpion who wanted to cross the river?

Once upon a time a horse was grazing by a riverbank when a scorpion walked up to him and said, "Kind horse, will you take me on your back across the river?"

Thinking it over, the horse said, "If I give you a ride, you'll bite me."

"Oh, no," said the scorpion, "Never. Why would I do that?" So the horse agreed to take the scorpion across.

When the horse had reached the middle of the river, he turned his head to look at the scorpion. Just at that moment the scorpion lifted his tail and stung the horse.

Astonished, the horse said, "Why did you bite me? Now both of us will drown."

The scorpion replied: "It's my nature."

IT'S YOUR NATURE

As it is the scorpion's nature to sting, research shows that it is your nature, in your genetic makeup, to be pessimistic, hostile, cheerful, aggressive, depressed, extroverted, cynical, religious, danger seeking, and self-accepting. Your genes are also *partly* responsible for IQ and for alcohol and drug abuse. But simply because you have a genetic trait or biological inclination, you are not so hard wired that you are doomed to behave in a particular fashion.

"At most, personality is only partly genetic. The degree of heritability hovers below .50 for all personality traits (except for IQ, which may be around .75). Even by the most extreme estimates . . . at most, half of personality is fixed. The other half of personality comes from what you do and from what happens to you—and this opens the door for therapy and self-improvement."[1]

Suppose you are more pessimistic and cynical because of your particular genetic makeup. You still have a brain, and you have your sense ability. Because of these, you have the ability to decide which thoughts to focus on. You have the ability to decide how you will behave. You can decide how you will or won't express your pessimism, cynicism, or aggressiveness. You will have to work harder if you have a genetic inclination that is not conducive to feeling content within yourself or having good relationships, but the door is open if you use your sense ability.

IT'S YOUR NURTURE

As I was growing up, being busy and working was always something you just did. Working is part of my automatic response pattern. In my family, you put your feet on the floor in the morning and started. When your workday ended, you went home and cut the grass, worked on the car, painted the fence, repaired the lawn mower, sewed and embroidered, made jelly, or planted bulbs that you were lucky enough to get from the neighbors.

Every summer our family took a two-week vacation. We'd drive to Michigan, where my parents' best friends had a farm. The first night my parents and their friends would sit around and talk. We children would play and get reacquainted. The following morning, we were up doing chores. My dad milked cows, combined, repaired machinery, and filled the barn with hay. My mom helped feed fifteen to twenty farmhands a hot lunch and hot dinner. The women made roasts, hams, fried chicken, fresh vegetables, mashed potatoes, and lots of fruit pies. I can still see Mom and her friend Dorothy mashing potatoes in a huge pot on the outside steps.

In addition to all the food preparation, they had seven kids to watch. I was one of them. Since I was the oldest, my job was to keep an eye on the little ones, help peel potatoes, set the table, and dry the dishes. Because no one complained about work and everyone did it, I grew up thinking that this is the way you live.

If money was short, as it frequently was, one of my parents took an extra job. When I was about seven and had to have my tonsils taken out, my dad took a second job working at the post office during Christmas rush to pay for the operation. When my mother wanted a new kitchen sink, she took a job on Saturday selling chickens.

One of my earliest memories is of standing in a cold garage at night listening to my parents talk and work. It was right after World War II. Dad had come home from the army. He had a day job, but that didn't quite cut the mustard since my parents were also helping support my grandma and great aunt. At night, to earn extra money, Mom and Dad scraped paint from used cars with a razor blade. They'd take the car down to bare metal. They were paid twenty-five dollars per car.

Since my husband also came from worker bees (his mother worked a full-time job until she was seventy-six), neither of us knew how to live life differently. I would hear friends say, "Sit down, Doris, relax." I'd say, "I am relaxed." I didn't understand what they meant until one of my clients confronted me.

I was giving him trouble about not getting up and going to work, and he said, "The problem is, you like to work, and I don't." That stopped me in my tracks. Some people don't enjoy working, being busy, accomplishing?

I'm rather high energy. That's genetic, that's nature. I have a bias toward working and accomplishing. That's what I was taught. It was modeled for me. That's nurture. I am also subtly influenced every day by my environment—how others around me behave, how much they work, what I hear and read, the thoughts I choose to focus on, and how I'm applauded for accomplishing.

In the process of discovering who you are and expanding your sense of awareness, it's helpful to understand the various ways you have been and presently are being influenced.

AN EXERCISE:
INFLUENCES FROM CHILDHOOD

Take a few moments now to answer the following questions. This exercise will give you more insight into why you think, feel, and behave as you do.

1. Thinking back on your childhood, what is the best memory that stands out in your mind? Has this event in any way affected your life today?

_____

_____

2. What is the worst memory you have? How do you think this event has affected your life?

_____

_____

3. When you think about your mother, how are you like her?

_____

_____

4. What about your father? How are you like him?

_____

_____

5. What feelings did your mother and father generally express when something didn't go their way? What feelings are you most likely to have when a situation doesn't go your way?

_____

_____

6. How did your parents view work? Was it something that they enjoyed, dreaded, avoided? How has their work ethic affected your life?

_____

_____

7. Did your parents take time for fun? What did they do? Do you have similar interests?

_____

_____

8. What did your parents tell you about education, religion, and God? How has this affected your life?

_____

_____

9. Can you name one gesture or habit, such as standing with your hands on your hips or running your hands through your hair, that is identical to the way your mother or father acted?

_____

_____

10. As a child, if you could have changed anything about each of your parents, what might that have been? Do you have similar issues?

_____

_____

11. How did your parents treat you when you were sick? How do you treat yourself, your mate, and your children when ill?

_____

_____

12. What was your parents' view of money, and what part did it play in their life? How do you view money?

_____

_____

13. Were your parents generous with others in the family? Outside the family? How? Have you patterned yourself after them?

_____

_____

14. Were you compared to your siblings or other family members? Do you frequently compare yourself to others?

_____

_____

15. What did your parents tease you about? A habit, a physical characteristic, a particular lack of talent? How do you view this issue today?

_____

_____

16. Did your parents have a favorite motto or saying? What was it? Has that saying in any way affected your life?

_____

_____

17. What did your parents want you to be when you grew up?

_____

_____

18. Did your parents think you would amount to anything?

_____

_____

19. Have you met their expectations? How?

_____

_____

20. Name one positive value you learned from each of the following: mother, father, brothers, sisters, each grandparent, and a favorite aunt or uncle.

_____

_____

After answering these questions, it's easy to see how you were influenced, how your upbringing is reflected in your thinking, feelings, and behaviors. It's also interesting to see in which ways you're different and in which ways you've changed.

———

Often people want to blame their parents for their problems. "I've never done anything with my life because I wasn't encouraged as a child," or "I can't make a decision because my parents made all my decisions for me," or "I beat my kids because my folks beat me."

A person may blame his parents for his present life to avoid taking responsibility. It's his way to stem feelings of failure. It's also easier to be a victim and blame your failure on someone else because when you're a victim, people are more compassionate. If you say, "It's my fault my life is in such a mess," people aren't as understanding.

Blaming others also raises your self-esteem because the failure is not your responsibility. It's easier to say, "It's my parents' fault that I have a lousy marriage," than to say, "I was too quick to marry, I married the wrong man, I'm a difficult person to live with, and I have an anger problem."

Parents have a strong influence on their children's lives. How could they not have? Nevertheless, now that you are an adult, it's your responsibility to change. For instance, if you weren't encouraged to study or get an education, okay, but now you can get an education. If you saw your father pout when things didn't go his way, okay, but you don't have to be a pouter. More effective ways are available to show your disapproval.

Ask yourself: *What do I blame my parents for? And what am I doing to correct the situation?*

HIDDEN RULES OF INFLUENCE

Many people look at how they were influenced by parents; more are starting to see how genetic makeup plays a part; but few examine how their behavior is being influenced by the people they relate to each day, the media, and their internal self-talk. And yet these influences can be as powerful and sometimes more powerful than genetics or upbringing.

The Werther Effect

In the late seventeenth century the German writer Johann von Goethe wrote *The Sorrows of Young Werther*. In the book young Werther shoots himself rather than face life without his true love. Soon after the book's publication, countless young people across Europe committed suicide in emulation of young Werther. The book's effect was so powerful that various countries banned its sale.

In the early 1970s, David Phillips, a social psychologist, researched what he defined as "the Werther Effect." Phillips found that after the appearance of a front-page story on suicide, the incidence of suicide significantly increased in the areas where the newspaper was published. Since then, Phillips and other researchers have demonstrated repeatedly, in some fascinating experiments, that (1) people decide how to behave based on how others around them are behaving, (2) they are more likely to follow the lead of individuals whom they view as similar to themselves, and (3) when people are unsure of how to act in a given situation, they are *especially* likely to behave as everyone else does.

Let's suppose your son starts a new school. You note that most of the parents at this school are very involved, planning activities, participating in the parent-teacher organization, and acting as guest lecturers. Within several months you find yourself following this norm by offering to teach an art class after school, something you would never have thought of doing three months ago.

You start a new job. You're immediately susceptible to behaving like the other people in your department. Their behavior tells you whether to come in early or stay late, how you should dress, how many breaks to take, and how much of your personal life to share.

These norms are helpful because they allow you to know what's expected. They help you feel that you are a part of the group, that you fit in. Although not written, these norms are as influential as, or in some cases more influential than, the written word.

After working several months with one company, Brad kept hearing from various people about how they padded their expense accounts. Brad thought this was morally wrong, and he reported only his true expenses. Then one month he had some extra bills, so he decided to turn in a few expenses that he hadn't really incurred. Several months later Brad was regularly padding his expense account. He still thought it was wrong, but his behavior had changed. He had allowed his behavior to be adversely affected by those around him. The Werther Effect in action.

"In this way it was possible to decoy a herd toward a precipice and cause it to plunge over en masse, the leaders being thrust over by their followers, and all the rest following of their own free will, like the sheep who cheerfully leaped, one after another, through a hole in the side of a high bridge because their bell-wether did so."[2]

This passage from "The Extermination of the American Bison," referring to a herd of buffalo, was written in 1887. It could just as easily be written today referring to individuals who allow themselves to be swept along because "everyone else is doing it."

Ask yourself: *Is there something I'm doing because everyone else does it? Is there something I'm doing even though I know that it is ethically wrong?*

The Rule of Reciprocation

Another way you may be influenced without knowing it is by the Reciprocation Rule. This unwritten rule says that you should repay in kind what another person has given you. Someone does you a favor, and in return you should do that person a favor. It's the old you-scratch-my-back, I'll-scratch-yours philosophy. Sounds reasonable and innocent enough and it's part of societal expectations, but look at the possible consequences.

For example, Joe decides he wants you for a friend. He knows you're interested in tennis, so he invites you to play at his club. You accept. Because of the Reciprocation Rule, you feel on some level obliged to pay Joe back. So you take Joe to a football game. Before you know it, you're socializing with Joe, someone you may or may not want to have as a friend.

———

Janice is always telling me how much she hates going to lunch with a particular woman. I say, "Why do you keep going when you know you don't have a good time? You don't even like her."

Janice shrugs helplessly and says, "But she keeps calling. She keeps inviting me." Because Janice thinks she is getting something, an invitation, she feels obliged to give back. She gives back by spending time with a woman she dislikes.

In this situation it would be best if Janice declined the woman's invitations. Eventually the woman would stop calling and more than likely find a friend who did appreciate her.

———

Suppose you're in charge of a department. Everyone knows you love hockey. Someone in the department gives you hockey tickets. You are now indebted. How will you pay this person back? Maybe he'll get a slightly better evaluation. With enough hockey tickets, maybe he'll become the supervisor.

———

If you have a child, he or she probably puts the Reciprocation Rule to work every day. For example, four-year-old Joannie says, "I gave you a kiss. Will you buy me a puzzle?" Ten-year-old Jason says, "Cleaned my room, Mom. Can I go to Marty's house?" And sixteen-year-old Sherrill says, "Got my homework done. Can I have the car?"

This is the way a lot of businesses get themselves in trouble. They follow the Reciprocation Rule. They give their business to people who have done them favors in the past, rather than to the company who has the best product. The United States Congress is a good example. Often votes are cast not on the basis of the integrity of a bill, but on the basis of a favor.

Ask yourself: *Have I done someone a favor recently when I really didn't want to? Why did I do it?*

If your answer is "I felt obligated," you were being influenced by the Reciprocation Rule.

It's important that a society have unwritten rules and maintain protocol, and reciprocation is part of societal expectations. At the same time, as you develop your sense ability, you will come to understand not only how these unwritten rules are influencing your life, but also the ways in which you will no longer allow yourself to be influenced.

The Reciprocal Concession Rule

Another factor that subconsciously influences you is the Reciprocal Concession Rule. This rule says you're obliged to make a concession to someone who's made a concession to you.

For example, you ask your boss if you can take off next Friday. He says, "Fine." He has granted you a concession. He then asks you to work the following weekend. It's your turn to grant him a concession. Seems fair enough. But here, too, you can be unknowingly manipulated.

Suppose your son wants a car. You think he doesn't need a car. Also, buying him a car would place a strain on your family's finances. In talking about a car, your son says, "I'll take a part-time job. I'll pay for the insurance and my gas." With this offer, he's made a concession. Now it's your turn to concede. On Saturday you find yourself looking at cars even though it's not the best thing for your family's financial situation.

I wonder how many families get dogs because of the Reciprocal Concession Rule. Can't you hear it now? "Mom, I promise, I'll take care of the dog. I'll feed it. I'll take it for a walk. You'll never have to do anything!"

An engineer says to his boss, "This car's not ready to go into production. It shimmies between forty and fifty miles an hour." The supervisor says, "Tell you what. We'll slide the schedule. We'll delay production six months, and you work things out."

What's happened? The boss has granted a concession—a delay. Now it's the engineer's turn to grant a concession. Six months later he signs off on the car even though it still shimmies.

That's often how defective products get on the market. Everyone is granting concessions without thinking about the consequences.

Use your sense ability to watch for those who are willing to grant you a concession. Then see if you grant one back. Also, check to see if the reciprocal concession you granted is really in everyone's best interests.

The Consistency Principle

Another rule that continually influences you is the Consistency Principle. Deep within you is a desire to appear consistent or to act consistently. It's part of everyone's response pattern. Once you've made a decision, you tend to hold to that decision so people view you as well grounded in your opinions and strong enough to stick to them.

I have a friend who's very overweight. He tells me he's never been thin. His view of himself is that he's fat. He tells me he has always been fat and he will always be fat.

I convinced him to go on a low-fat diet a few years ago. I even prepared a few meals to show him how tasty they could be. He immediately lost weight. Then he went back to his old ways of eating, and his weight went right back up. As long as his view of himself is that he's fat, he'll stay that way. He has bought into the Consistency Principle.

You go to buy a new car. Before buying it, you're uncertain as to the type of car you want and not sure if you should spend the money. As you leave the dealer's showroom two hours later, you're telling yourself that you chose the best make of car and got the best price. It's not that you have that much more information about the various models on the market, it's that you signed the deal. As soon as you put your John Hancock on the contract committing to a certain make and price, you had to bring your thoughts in line with your behavior. So you tell yourself repeatedly that the model you chose was the best your money could buy. The Consistency Principle has taken effect.

———

Suppose a boss promotes someone, but within weeks it's clear that he's made the wrong choice. Instead of moving the person to a different position, however, the boss holds to his original decision. Within him is an overwhelming desire to see himself as consistent as well as to have others view him as consistent.

Why? Because consistency is considered a valuable trait in a person. If someone is consistent, he is seen as intelligent, logical, honest, and stable. You see him as a person you can count on. To be inconsistent is to be seen as weak, confused, and not knowing one's own mind. So once a person makes a decision, right or wrong, she usually stands by it because of an unconscious drive to be consistent.

Consistency is valuable and necessary in society. But not being able to change your mind because of a need to appear consistent can have negative and far-reaching consequences.

I often think of Gene Roddenberry, the creator of *Star Trek*, and how the first pilot episode didn't work, which almost always guarantees the demise of the idea. But several executives at NBC decided to let Roddenberry do a second pilot. Today *Star Trek* and its spin-offs are among the longest-running syndicated and continuing shows in television history.

Random Acts of Kindness

In the last few years the random acts of kindness movement has been spreading. The idea is to do random acts of kindness for others, especially strangers. For example, give up your seat on the subway. Let someone go in front of you in a checkout line. Carry someone's grocery bag. Hold open the door for a group of people. Buy movie tickets and give them to the people standing behind you in line. It is hoped that by your doing random acts of kindness, others will follow suit.

If this movement really catches on, it will be because people decide how to behave based on how others around them are behaving. Also, if you think of yourself as a kind person who does good deeds, you will be kind and do good deeds. If you do good deeds for others, they in turn will do good deeds. And soon there will be acts of kindness everywhere.

Ask yourself: *Do I do one random act of kindness per day? Is this something I would consider doing?*

The Power of Positive Self-Talk

Studies done since the early 1940s have shown that the best way to get people to do a good job, after they have their basic needs met, is to give them positive strokes. People who accomplish a good deal and enjoy the process know this secret. They have running dialogues of what they want to accomplish on any given day, and then they give themselves positive strokes for their accomplishments. They might say, "I really accomplished a lot today," or "I think I did a good job explaining things to that group." Because of these strokes, they keep performing. Positive self-talk reinforces their desire to accomplish and do a good job.

Have you ever noticed how a person becomes attached to her to-do list? She loses it, and, instead of making another, she searches to find it because she wants that particular list. The reason is not because she can't reproduce her list, or remember what's on her list, but because she has been using her list to give herself positive strokes.

Some people, after completing a task, run a straight or squiggly line through the item or make a check mark. These lines and checks not only indicate that the job is complete, but also say, "Good job. Well done."

I can remember finding a list of my daughter's when she was in kindergarten. It said, "Brush teeth. Dress. Pet cat. Go to school. Go to bed." She was following her parents' habit of list making. As she crossed off items on her list, she felt a sense of accomplishment.

If your self-talk is positive and filled with "Way to go!" and "Nice job," you are going to have a sense of well-being.

Right now why not reach over your shoulder and give yourself a pat on the back for reading this book, for learning to use your sense ability, for caring enough about yourself and others to make a difference in this world.

Now reach around again and give yourself a pat on the back just for being you.

DANCING WITH NATURE, NURTURE, AND PRESENT INFLUENCES

You are influenced by many things: genetics, upbringing, parents, grandparents, teachers, sermons, books, the way people around you behave, television, movies. You can't do anything about your genetics. You can't relive your childhood. But you can be aware of the unwritten laws of influence, how others may be influencing you today. You can decide which movies you will attend, which books you will read, who you will listen to on the radio, and who you will have as friends. You can monitor your self-talk.

Fully developing and using your sense ability calls for a realization of how you are being influenced.

HOW ENVIOUS AND
JEALOUS ARE YOU?

Character is what you have when nobody is looking.

Marie Dressler,
actress

Imagine saying to someone, "I don't like you because you're prettier than I am, or a better athlete, or smarter, or taller, or better off financially." Or, "I don't like you because you have the bigger office, or you drive a better car, or your children are so successful. I only like you when you don't do as well as I do." But that's the way you think when you envy another.

Envy is a feeling that results when you want what someone else has, be it fame, fortune, friends, looks, education, money, or lifestyle. Whenever a comparison is made, you can feel envious.

Of all feelings you generate with your thoughts, envy is a special kind of meanness. You feel happy when someone suffers and has a bad time of it. And you feel sad when things go well for the person. This is one reason people like to hear about the troubles of others. If someone else is in difficulty, they get to feel one up and smug and think, "They're not so hot after all."

Whenever you feel envy, you restrict your sense ability, block love, and stop the possibility of experiencing closeness and connectedness with another. And you ultimately lower your self-esteem because it's hard to respect yourself when you know that deep down you feel envious.

THE ENVIOUS WOMAN

Colleen and her husband had just put a down payment on a house. The day before, she had learned they were going to have a baby boy. Colleen was ecstatic. Life couldn't get any better, she thought. Then she ran into her friend Marge, who was also feeling happy. Marge had been promoted to one of the television networks and would be moving to New York, and her boyfriend had been able to find a job with a good firm there.

When Colleen left Marge, she didn't feel as content and happy as she had before. She wanted to continue to feel good, but she couldn't.

That night with her husband she was more quiet than usual. When he asked what was wrong, she said, "Nothing. I'm just tired."

Colleen knew, but was too embarrassed and guilty to admit, that she was feeling envious of Marge. Colleen knew that she didn't want her friend's life. She wanted to be married and have this child. She understood that she was allowing the news of her friend's good fortune to ruin the evening with her husband, but she couldn't seem to stop herself.

TRUE CONFESSIONS: ENVIOUS FEELINGS

Because envy is something that most people have difficulty acknowledging, I prevailed on some people to talk about their envious feelings. As you read their stories, think about yourself and if you do something similar.

"When we are with our friends, I'm always comparing myself to other women," said Louise. "If I think someone looks better than I look, I can't have a good time. I try, but my evening is a little ruined."

"My business is pretty cutthroat," said a stockbroker. "When a guy tells me he's had a bad day, I find myself feeling a little happy. Stupid, huh?"

"Our son and daughter have done very well. They both have nice homes, nicer than ours. They take expensive trips. I'm glad for them. But sometimes I'm envious. We provided them with their education, paid for all of it, and now they live better than we do. You're not going to use my name, are you?"

"I can be driving in my car, feeling quite peaceful and listening to the radio," said Sandra, "when I hear that someone else has been honored with an award. All of a sudden I don't feel good. I start ruminating about why I haven't been honored. My whole mood changes."

In the eighteenth century, Moshe Luzzatto had great insight on envy when he wrote: "Envy, too, is nothing but want of reason and foolishness, for the one who envies gains nothing for himself and deprives the one he envies of nothing. . . . There are those who are so foolish that if they perceive their neighbor to possess a certain good, they brood and worry and suffer to the point that their neighbor's good prevents them from enjoying their own."[1]

BEHAVIORS THAT REVEAL ENVY

Often people think they are hiding their envy, but it's more noticeable than they think. For example, you envy how much money a friend makes, so you talk about how little time he gives to his family. You envy a co-worker's good looks, so you make disparaging comments about how she cheated on her first husband. When I meet people who talk against others, I wonder if their motivation is envy.

Writing on envy, Saint Basil said, "Envious persons are skilled in making what is praiseworthy seem despicable by means of unflattering distortions. . . . The courageous man they call reckless; the temperate man, callous; the just man, severe; the clever man, cunning."[2]

———

Holding back and not applauding someone else's achievements is a way envy shows itself.

I still remember years ago when I got my first book contract. I called a fellow writer I had admired and praised many times through the years. When I told him about the contract and the publisher, he said, "They're a bad publisher."

My stomach knotted and I felt terrible. I wanted so much for him to share in my happiness. Our relationship worked when he got the attention, but it didn't work as well when I expected attention.

Our friendship waned after this incident. He probably continued to feel envious and didn't want to see me, and I felt uncared for. Then a year later we ran into each other on the street, and he apologized. He said he was struggling with his writing and had felt envious when I told him of my good fortune.

———

Envy also shows itself when people don't share the credit. Jean is a wonderful gardener. Her specialty is herbs. Her friend Barb asked for advice on putting in an herb garden. A few months later we were at a party at Barb's house. She took us to her herb garden and all of us oohed and ahed. Jean was also there. Not once did Barb mention how helpful Jean had been.

How much nicer if Barb had said, "Jean helped me select the plants and place them." Sharing the applause would not have taken away from Barb. In fact, she would have received more praise, for surely Jean would have said thank you, and others would have noticed that Barb had shared the applause.

Taking all the credit has reached epidemic proportions in the business world. Tom comes up with an idea, and the project is assigned to another person. The project goes well, and everyone congratulates the person who did the job. Rightly so. But wouldn't it be nice if the man who was being congratulated could say, "Tom also deserves some congratulations. It was his idea."

Sharing the spotlight is an act of generosity on your part, and the other person feels good. The more you use your sense ability, the more willing you'll be to give credit and share the spotlight.

Now ask yourself: *Do I share the credit?*

WHERE DOES YOUR ENVY COME FROM?

If you suffer from envy, look inside yourself for the reason. The answer is there.

If as a child you were always compared, whether favorably or unfavorably, to a sibling, classmate, or relative, chances are you operate from a *competitive frame of reference.* This means you continually compare, measure, and evaluate yourself against others. If you fall short, your response is likely to be envy. You desire what another person has.

Sometimes envy arises from never feeling secure within yourself. Perhaps your parents never felt comfortable about themselves, and you picked up on their discomfort and longings to possess what others seemed to have. For example, maybe your parents were embarrassed about their educational level, the house they lived in, or being the least successful of their brothers and sisters.

Perhaps your days in school were not particularly happy or fulfilling. Maybe you had difficulty with your classes, had few friends, were a poor athlete, or had a body type that our society does not define as attractive. Maybe you noted that others who did better academically or athletically or seemed to have a better figure were happier and had more friends. As an adult you continue to watch others and compare yourself. When you fall short or feel "less than," you experience envy.

As a child you may have received far more attention than most. As an adult you continue to have this same expectation.

I'm working with a woman in therapy who rarely feels she receives enough attention. She's always comparing what her husband does for her to what her friends' husbands do for them. At her job she compares how much praise her boss gives her with how much praise he gives others in the department. She was an only child and an only grandchild. She admits, "The world revolved around me." Now, when she doesn't have the attention, she feels envious. Today her struggle is to learn to be satisfied with less attention, to stop comparing herself to others, to shut out these thoughts, and to build her own self-esteem.

Maybe your self-doubt started as an adult. You are not able to accomplish what you had hoped, your children are not turning out as you expected, your partner left you for someone else, or your job is less than satisfactory. You look at your friends or people in general and feel envious of those whose lives seem easier, less painful, more desirable.

HOW TO QUELL YOUR ENVY

To stop feeling envious, you must stop operating from a competitive frame of reference. Do not allow yourself to compare. If someone tells you she just got a great job offer, keep your thoughts focused on the other person. Ask her questions about the new job. Think about how hard she works. Keep yourself out of the equation. If you don't compare, you won't feed your envy.

Appeal to your reason. Tell yourself over and over: "Every time I compare myself to someone else, one of us wins and one of us loses. Do I really want to set myself up to have bad feelings?" Also ask yourself, "Why shouldn't he reap what he has sown?"

Another question to ask: "Am I willing to put in the time and energy it took that person to reach her goal?" For example, you may be envious of the way your friend plays the piano. Are you willing to put in as many hours taking lessons and practicing?

Another question: "Would I trade my life for his life, knowing I must accept his disappointments, sufferings, and flaws along with what I desire?"

Sometimes envy will appear when you least expect it. For example, someone tells you he just received a large inheritance. Instantly you think negative thoughts about his windfall and feel envious. Instead of showing your envy, make an appropriate comment such as, "That's great." If a man says his son made varsity basketball, congratulate him. You may feel envy, but you don't have to act on this feeling. You don't have to behave poorly.

JEALOUSY—THE GREEN-EYED MONSTER

Jealousy, closely linked to envy, also creates needless suffering, closes out love, and limits your sense ability. Whereas envy arises in reaction to what others have, jealousy is fear and apprehension of losing something you have or think you have.

"I have a good job," explained Kim, "lots of contacts. Because of this, people are always asking me to do them favors, to use my influence to get them interviews with the company. I tell them okay, sure, but then I don't do it. I worked hard to get where I am. The way I figure it, why should I help someone else? I'm not saying I'm proud of myself for feeling this way, but no one made it easy for me."

Kim is jealous. She is fearful of losing something if someone else gets a job in her company. So she does nothing to help others get an interview.

Ask yourself: *Have I told people I would help them out and then not followed through because I didn't want them to get ahead?*

———

Here are several examples of jealousy in the making.

Some of your friends are going to lunch. They invite you, but you need to get a few phone calls made, so you decline. Later, as you think about your friends at lunch, you wonder if they are having a good time. You wonder if they are going to exclude you in the future. You feel jealous of the time they are spending together.

You're working on a big project, and the boss tells you that she thinks you need help. You start to worry and feel jealous. Will she wind up giving someone else a major portion of your project?

You may feel jealous over your child liking her father more than you. You may feel jealous if you're not invited to a party. You may feel jealous when you hear that someone has recently been recognized in your field.

In reality, you probably want your child to have a good relationship with her father. You might not want to go to the party. You might not really care if you're recognized in your field. But you are fearful that others no longer hold you in high esteem. Others no longer admire you. This is what drives your jealousy.

———

Jealous feelings over your mate's family, friends, and activities can cause you as well as him a great deal of pain. If you're suspicious when he talks to someone of the opposite sex, if you demand a report of how he spent every moment of his time, if you periodically check his odometer, listen in on his telephone conversations, check his E-mail and phone records, and make comments concerning how he must be attracted to this person or that person, your jealousy is consuming you.

If this is you, take care of yourself and seek the help of a professional. No one, neither you nor your mate, should have to live under the shadow of jealousy.

BETTER SELF-ESTEEM

The way to put an end to jealousy is to stop focusing on others and keep improving your self-esteem. Think about what would make you more secure within yourself. Becoming proficient at bridge? Getting more education? Losing weight?

A woman I know just lost a considerable amount of weight.

"Physically I feel better," she said. "I have more energy. I can put on my nylons without difficulty. People compliment me and tell me how good I look. I got a new hairdo. I've started an exercise program. I bought some new clothes. I go more places. Visit my friends more. Sometimes I put on something that's way too big, and I think, 'Look at me. Look at what I did.' I feel I can accomplish what I set out to do. I like myself. My self-esteem has skyrocketed."

People who are loved and admired usually have high self-esteem because when you are loved, it's easy to view yourself in a favorable light. Having friends to confide in and go places with is an excellent way to increase your self-esteem.

Another technique to increase self-esteem is to write down twenty or thirty things you like about yourself. Then read what you've written periodically throughout the day. This exercise helps you to focus on yourself, your attributes, and your inherent talents. Also, make a pact with yourself. Learn to do three new things each year. This will keep your self-esteem high.

COMPETING FOR ATTENTION

Sometimes feelings of envy and jealousy are expressed by competing with others for attention. This is called being *attention-competitive*. For example, if you talk too much, you are competing for attention. As long as you keep talking, you have everyone's attention. What you convey by your constant chatter is, "Recognize me. Pay attention to me."

Attention-competitive people do not listen. When someone else is talking, you allow your mind to wander. You may think of a call you want to make or an item you want to pick up from the store. Also, as the other person is talking, you rarely ask questions or make a comment, which again conveys lack of interest.

Interrupting is another attention-competitive behavior. Someone is telling a story, and you butt in and take over. You may continue the story or tell an entirely different one.

Another way of competing is to start a side conversation. A person is talking, and you start a conversation with someone else. This maneuver shifts some of the attention away from the person who has the floor.

Every time you interrupt or start a side conversation, you're indirectly saying, "What I have to say is more important than what others have to say. I count more."

Acting unenthusiastic or unappreciative is another subtle form of keeping the attention on yourself. A friend gives you a sweater, and you don't even take it out of the box. You say, "Oh, that's nice," close the box, and say nothing more.

———

Here are additional examples of shifting the attention away from another:

A woman says to her friend, "I think I'm coming down with a cold." His response: "Oh no, now I'll get it." Notice how rapidly he diverts the attention away from her and onto himself.

A wife comes down with the flu, and her husband gets angry. He doesn't want his life disrupted, and he doesn't want to take care of her. He wants her to be focusing on him.

A woman was working in her office at home when her husband walked in and said, "I've been running all over the house trying to tell you goodbye." Notice how his focus was on himself, even though he was trying to be thoughtful of his wife.

Now ask yourself: *Do I talk too much? Do I pretend to listen while not listening at all? Do I have a habit of interrupting? Do I act unappreciative of what others do for me?*

USING YOUR SENSE ABILITY

Everyone needs to be center stage some of the time. However, always trying to grab attention by talking too much, not listening, interrupting, or shifting the attention will not bring you success or happiness or make you closer to other people. If anything, it will drive others away.

Many people have told me, "I know I talk too much." If you

are aware that you talk too much, talk less. Don't keep up this nonproductive behavior. A good rule of thumb is not to talk longer than two minutes before you stop and let the other person make a comment, ask a question, or change the topic of conversation. Remember also, silence is golden. Allow yourself and others golden silence.

———

If you frequently interrupt, make a decision to be more conscious of not interrupting. Some years ago I interviewed many people about their marriages. I would ask questions, and they would talk. Over and over people told me how much they enjoyed the interviews. I think it was because I was respectful of their stories and I listened with little interruption.

LISTEN TO LIFE

Life is sometimes very hard. Why make it harder on yourself by feeling sad or angry or disappointed at another's good fortune? Why continually compete with others to be center stage? Wouldn't it be nice to feel good when you hear of someone else's success? Wouldn't it be nice to sit back and relax, not always having to grab the spotlight? Wouldn't it be nice to feel happy about your good fortune and achievements as well as others'? Think of how much more joy you would have in your life. Your joy would increase exponentially. All because you choose to give up being envious and jealous and competitive. All because you chose to use your sense ability.

DO YOU SUFFER
FROM ANXIETY OR
DEPRESSION?

Sometimes even to live is an act of courage.

Seneca

If you are an anxious or a depressed person, you are among the 8 to 15 percent of the population who must face these additional obstacles in life. If you're anxious, you often experience intense fear, worry, irritability, and difficulty concentrating. If you're depressed, you suffer from feelings of worthlessness and sadness and an inability to think and concentrate.

When you are suffering from either anxiety or depression or a combination, it is more difficult to explore who you really are and to fully use your sense of awareness. You're simply too caught up in your emotions.

Today much is known about anxiety and depression, and if you suffer from either, your job is to help yourself and engage others to help you. You can then embrace life, look outside of yourself, and use your sense ability. But getting help for your anxiety or depression becomes one of your first tasks.

"I had my first anxiety attack at thirty-two. My heart started racing and I thought I was dying. I went to the hospital, and they said I was fine. Soon I was having attacks on a regular basis. Everywhere I went I had an anxiety attack. My heart would pound, and I'd feel as though I was going to pass out. I seemed to have more attacks at work, so I quit my job. I started staying home. I didn't want to go to the grocery store. I couldn't go to a mall. I became homebound.

"I saw a therapist. She taught me some tricks, how to get out of the house. I would drive one mile a day. Every day another mile. She also had me name my fear. I called my fear 'bear.' I got a stuffed bear and put it in the car with me. It may sound silly, but it helped me confront my fear. I got a job again but continued to feel very anxious.

"I live under a lot of 'what ifs.' 'What if it storms?' 'What if I lose my job?' 'What if I can't pay the bills?'

"My anxiety has hurt my husband and children. One of the girls would want to go to the mall to shop, and I couldn't stand it when I got there. I'd have to leave. I wouldn't go to the movies or restaurants with my family.

"I have trouble with taking medication, so it's not an answer for me. I pray a lot. I listen to relaxation tapes. Sometimes they help. I've seen three therapists over the past twenty years. Each has helped in some ways. Recently I have been using a tapping sequence that my present therapist taught me. The tapping immediately lowers my anxiety level. I do it anytime I feel anxious, on and off during the day.

"Successes help a lot—like when I drive across a bridge, or go to the movies, or go out to a restaurant for dinner.

"I think my anxiety button got stuck in the on position, and I can't get it off. I would not wish my anxiety on anyone. It's like a prison with no bars. But a prison term has an end."

ANXIETY CAN BE HEALTHY
OR DEBILITATING

Humans are programmed to feel some anxiety. Anxiety announces to you, "Danger, danger." It's time to be alert and figure out what might go wrong, what you need to change in your environment. Anxiety pushes you to plan, think ahead, and problem-solve.

For example, if you don't feel some anxiety when you notice the gas gauge registering empty and therefore don't do anything about it, you may find yourself needlessly inconvenienced. If you don't experience some anxiety when you notice a lump in your breast or neck, you may not seek medical help, which in the end could cost you your life.

The problem comes when you feel too much anxiety. When you always feel nervous, restless, tense, on edge, irritable. When you experience a constant stream of "what ifs" and "if onlys." When you know your worrying is irrational and out of proportion to what's going on, but you can't seem to control it. When you are too fearful to take a class, drive on the highway, run to the mall, take in a movie, or volunteer at your child's school.

Progressive Muscle Relaxation

One of the techniques I suggest to an anxious person is progressive muscle relaxation. You either sit or lie down, and then you tighten each major muscle group. As I explain the technique, do it with me now.

1. Make a fist with your right hand. Tense your fist and right arm. Breathe in slowly. Hold for the count of five. Breathe out and relax your arm and fist.
2. Do the same with your left arm. Make a fist, tense your fist and arm, breathe in slowly. Hold for the count of five. Breathe out and relax.

3. Tense your right leg. Breathe in slowly. Hold for the count of five. Breathe out and relax.

4. Tense your left leg. Breathe in slowly. Hold for the count of five. Breathe out and relax.

5. Tighten your buttocks. Breathe in slowly. Hold for the count of five. Breathe out and relax.

6. Open your mouth wide. Breathe in slowly. Give a big yawn. Breathe out and relax.

I ask clients who are extremely anxious to use this progressive muscle relaxation technique at least twice a day. The purpose is to help you experience the difference between being relaxed and being tense. It allows you to feel some control because *you* are tensing and relaxing. It also keeps you in the present moment.

For a fuller explanation, check out the books *Minding the Body, Mending the Mind* by Dr. Joan Borysenko and *The Relaxation Response* by Dr. Herbert Benson.

Thought Field Therapy

Another technique I use comes from Thought Field Therapy™ which was developed by Dr. Roger Callahan.[1] Thought Field Therapy integrates kinesiology, acupressure meridians, and psychotherapy. You tap on certain points on your body in a particular sequence depending on your particular problem.

The following tapping sequence is for generalized anxiety. I have made some minor adjustments to Dr. Callahan's technique. You might want to do this technique along with me as you read.

1. Think about your anxiety on a scale of 1 to 10, with 10 being the most anxious. Give your anxiety a number.

2. Now you are going to tap gently on certain points of your body called *energy points*. With one or two fingers tap on the bony ridge at the outer edge of either eye. Find it? Tap gently nine or ten times on this spot.

3. Now put your hand under one of your armpits. Slide it down

the side of your body about four inches. This is where you are to tap. Tap here nine or ten times.

4. Go to the area on your neck where you would normally tie your tie. Place your finger in the indentation of your collarbone. Now slide your finger straight down about one inch, and then over to the left about one or two inches. You should feel an indentation. Tap here nine or ten times.

Let's put it all together:

• Where on the scale is your anxiety?
• Now tap gently nine or ten times under your eye.
• Tap nine or ten times under your arm.
• Tap nine or ten times on your collarbone spot.
• Where on the scale is your anxiety now?

Most patients report feeling less anxious after using this tapping sequence. If your anxiety level does not drop by two points, another sequence is used.

This tapping sequence is good to use any time you start to feel too anxious. I also suggest the anxiety tapping sequence right before retiring if you have trouble sleeping.

Go Do Something

I ask people who have problems with anxiety to read books on the subject. I want you to know that you are not alone, that others face the same problems, and that numerous techniques exist to help quell anxiety.

I also ask you to push yourself to do one outside activity each day, such as going to watch your son play baseball, going to the supermarket, meeting someone for lunch, or arranging a tennis game. It doesn't matter how anxious you feel with these activities because research shows that 60 to 80 percent of people are helped significantly merely by changing their behavior. An imaging technique called PET (positron emission tomography) has shown that the effects of behavioral therapy are identical to those of medication in producing positive physical changes in the brain.

Other techniques already mentioned in this book—becoming an Impartial Observer, affirmations, staying in the present with Mindful Breathing, and prayer—will all help quell your anxiety. But you must do them and do them daily.

Medication

Frequently when people suffer from acute anxiety, an antianxiety or an antidepressant medication is prescribed. These medications are helpful in getting you over the initial phase. Even if you are taking medication for your anxiety, it is still important to use behavioral techniques on a daily basis.

"They Don't Get It"

Another difficulty when you suffer from anxiety is that other people don't seem to understand. They can't imagine why you simply can't get a grip and do what you need to do. So I tell someone who is overly anxious that here's one way to explain it to her family:

Suppose I tell you that each morning in order to leave your house you must walk a board three feet wide and fifty feet long. Would you walk the board? Probably so. Would you be anxious? Probably not.

But suppose I tell you that each morning in order to leave your house you must walk a board three feet wide and fifty feet long and the board is balanced between two office buildings twenty-six floors up. Could you walk this board? No matter how much you wanted to leave your house, go to work, see your child perform in the school play, or go to the movies with the family, could you walk this board?

This is what it feels like when you have too much anxiety, when your anxiety is out of control, when your "anxiety button is stuck in the on position."

After such an explanation, sometimes family members become more understanding.

DEPRESSED—WITH AND WITHOUT REASON

If you are depressed, you will probably experience feelings of sadness and hopelessness and have little joy. If you are severely depressed, you may think nothing is important and life doesn't matter. You may even question your existence. You may have difficulty making decisions and feel unmotivated and lethargic. You may not be able to get even the basic things done. You may suffer from sleep difficulties—either you can't go to sleep, or you can't stay asleep, or you can't seem to wake up. You often feel tired, may miss work, have little desire for sex, and show little interest in outside activities. Even answering the telephone involves too much effort.

If you suffer from *agitated depression*, you probably feel grumpy, irritable, and testy along with feeling sad and hopeless. You may also find yourself avoiding people because they irritate you.

In severe cases of depression, you may have suicidal thoughts, as you see no way out of your excruciatingly hopeless, helpless position.

Depression is also identified as major or minor. If you experience a major depression, you will have a number of symptoms, and your symptoms will be severe. If you experience a minor depression, you will have fewer and less severe symptoms.

Treatment for major depression involves medication and usually some form of psychotherapy. Minor depression may be treated with medication and psychotherapy or psychotherapy alone. In some instances of minor depression, you can get yourself out of your depression by exercising, reading self-help books, talking to friends, and staying active.

Depression is also divided into two categories: situational and clinical. *Situational depression* is a result of an event in your life that causes you to feel down, empty, blue. Job loss, loss of a friend, divorce, infertility problems, ongoing difficulties with in-laws, or a problem boss can lead to a situational depression.

If you are situationally depressed over a long period, a change in brain chemistry may occur, and a *clinical depression* may follow. Or a change in brain chemistry occurs without any identifiable stressors, and you slide into a clinical depression.

Some depression is genetically and biologically linked. However, anyone can fall prey to depression due to a change in brain chemistry or problems in his life.

"I Have Hope for the Future"

"On thinking back," said Rita, "I may have been depressed my entire life. I listen to my mother describe me as a child. She says I was an adult at the age of two—sober, sensible, compliant, quiet. At the time these were considered virtues. Now that I'm an adult and can look at my children and see how happy they can be, I wonder if I've always had some level of depression.

"I've always had periods of being blue and have been on medication on and off. I have also used work to help me cope. I filled hours and days with work.

"I could feel my depression growing. I felt stressed. Couldn't sleep. One of the things that clued me in to my depression was that I was sitting on the sofa and realized my cats were looking at me and I wasn't paying attention to them. I started to pet one and I didn't feel anything coming through my hand. There was no sensation, no pleasure, nothing. This was the first thing that made me wonder if there was something terrible going on.

"My life had been reduced to a treadmill, doing what needed to be done from moment to moment. I had diminished concentration, couldn't get anything finished. I would go to my office, close the door, and sit. The reason I could get away with it was that I was the boss, no one was checking up on me, challenging me.

"One day I called my husband from work and told him I was sick. Would he please meet me at home. He came home, held me, and got me an appointment with a psychiatrist who put me on medication. At first the medication didn't help, so the doctor increased my dose and then put me on a second medication.

"I also started exercising. I walked before work and at night I swam. The exercise helped with my agitation. I started getting some good relief in about three weeks. I was also told to see a therapist to work on behavioral issues.

"The therapist encouraged me to go out and play. I thought about how play has never held a legitimate place in my life. I started to develop a few friendships. I was told to smile at people, that people would react to me differently if I smiled. I found my sense of humor. I have laughed more in this year than I ever have in my entire life.

"I'm still on medication. I think I may be on it for the rest of my life. I now understand that getting better does not mean getting off my medication. It means how I feel, how I enjoy life. I have hope for the future. I can continue to be well."

Medication and Psychotherapy and Pulling Yourself Together

If you are clinically depressed, you have a chemical imbalance. Therefore drugs are prescribed to restore the balance. About 60 to 65 percent of people taking medication report feeling considerably better in two to three weeks. Those who do not respond to the medication in five or six weeks receive a different medication or a combination of several drugs.[2]

Studies show that psychotherapy coupled with medication often gives the best results. Therefore I usually recommend that you join a therapy group, because your progress can be monitored on a weekly basis. Also, you receive feedback from other group members as to how you might be contributing to your depression—negative thoughts, isolating yourself from others, not reaching out to friends, not returning phone calls. I also recommend several social activities each week, as well as a regular exercise program.

How About a Dog? A Cat? A Goldfish?

Another support for you is a pet, such as a dog or a cat. If these animals seem like too much work, how about a goldfish? Studies show that pets help reduce stress. Part of the reason is that a pet demands that you look outside yourself. A dog wags his tail at you. He plants himself at your feet. He says with his body language, "Hey, you, pay attention to me. Take me for a walk on this beautiful day."

A cat leaps up on your lap and nuzzles up against you. He shows his delight with you by purring. He bats a string hanging from your sweater. You have to make sure he has food and water and his litter box gets changed. These chores, no matter how mundane, keep you focused outside of yourself.

Even a goldfish can give you pleasure as you sit and watch him swim around. And as I tell my patients, "I've never heard a dog, or cat, or goldfish criticize anyone." So, no matter how you feel, you have one cheerleader in your corner.

You Are More Than Your Depression

Frequently, depressed or anxious people will say, "I'm depressed," or "I'm anxious," and indeed they are. This is one way to describe yourself. But in reality, you are much, much more than your depression or anxiety. You may be the mother of three children, a chemist, a daughter, a daughter-in-law, a sister, a tennis player, a Ping-Pong player, an ice skater, a cook, a baker, a gardener, a bridge player, a friend.

Right now, review who you are. Or if you prefer, write out a "Who Am I?" list. This technique gets you away from identifying yourself only with your depression or your anxiety, because you are so much more.

DRAGGING YOURSELF TO WELLNESS

No one wants to go through life anxious or depressed. Nor should you. You must use every means available to get beyond your anxiety and depression. Read, exercise, pray, listen to self-help tapes, become a volunteer, and consider taking medication (it helps). Drag yourself into wellness. You can do it. And in doing so, you will develop your sense ability.

DO YOU TALK TO GOD?

Among all God's creatures, only humanity receives the image of God, and that quality separates us from all else. We possess what no other animal does; we are linked in our essence to God.[1]

Paul Brand and Philip Yancy,
In His Image

Do you pray? Do you talk to God?

My earliest recollection of talking to God is of kneeling with my mother and sister before bedtime at the side of the bed. We'd start with the "Our Father," and then we'd pray for special intentions. One of us would say, "God, take care of Grandma," or "God, please help all the people who are hungry."

As I grew, I continued talking to God. I'd ask God to please, please have Sally invite me to her birthday party, or please let me be elected to student government. During grade school I realized that if Betsy asked God to help her be elected and I asked God to be elected to the same position, there was a problem. So I'd add, "If thy will be done." I was hoping, of course, that my will would be done.

Besides going to church on Sunday and special days during the year, our family also prayed together once a month. My dad would say, "We're going to pray today." My sister and I would roll our eyes at each other. Reluctantly we'd go into my parents' bedroom, where all four of us would kneel around the bed and Dad would lead the prayers. Despite my initial resistance to getting on the hard floor and praying, I must admit I always felt good afterward. Secretly I thought it was pretty neat that our family all knelt down together and prayed.

As I got older, I continued to keep up my relationship with God. I'd ask God to get me dates and help with tests. At that time I still had a take-care-of-me view of God. He was my Father in heaven, and he was supposed to take care of me as a good father does. At the same time, I had biblical backing: "And all things, whatever ye shall ask in prayer, believing, ye shall receive." (Matt. 21:22)

I also made regular bargains with God, such as, "If you help me pass algebra, I'll say a hundred prayers for the sick."

I think the first time I became angry with God was when I missed out on a modeling job. Silly, huh? That wasn't the last time, however. I'd get righteous about something I'd hear on the news, and I'd tell God to get busy and do something.

After our second child was born, I had complications and was near death. I was being wheeled to surgery and I remember thinking, "Well, God, if I don't wake up, I'll see you in heaven. Please take care of my family." Maybe I was naive, but, because I felt a connectedness with God, because talking to God has always been an integral part of my life, I was not afraid of death.

Today I still use formal prayer, usually before I go to sleep. But during the day I just talk to God. I ask him to help people who have difficult lives. I ask him to help people who have problems with their anger. If I'm annoyed at someone, I'll pray for the person. This helps me let go of my irritation.

I also say, "Thank you, God," many times each day. I give thanks for my gentle, loving husband and wonderful children. I thank God all the time for giving us our two boys and then a girl years later. I thank God for letting my parents live for so many years. I thank God for a soft rain, a sunny day, a beautiful sunset. Lately, I've been thanking God for helping me write this book.

In therapy, I never shared that I prayed. I'd give people all sorts of assignments, but never prayer. Then I started seeing people who were trying to cope with the death of a child. They were in unbearable pain.

They'd ask me if the pain would ever go away. I'd shake my head no, but tell them it would lessen in time. I'd listen to their stories. Sometimes I'd wrap a blanket around them and just hold them tightly as they cried. Sometimes I'd have a couple hold each other. I recall one woman who came every week to cry. She'd curl up like a baby and weep. I felt helpless seeing her pain. Then one day I suggested that perhaps if she prayed, talked to God, she would get some relief. And she did. I now routinely suggest prayer as a way to get through problems and regain hope.

———

"A story is told of a child who goes out to the woods each day. His mother asks where he is going, and he tells her he is going to be with God. Day after day this goes on until finally she says, 'You know, son. God is the same everywhere.' He responds, 'I know. But I'm not.'

"Prayer is where we go to feel our connection to God."[2]

THE BENEFITS OF PRAYER

I believe prayer has numerous benefits. If you have faith and believe in God, why not have a conversation with him? Certainly you carry on conversations regularly in your head with various people. Why not God? He's the most accepting and forgiving friend you could possibly have.

Prayer helps you feel safe. It's like when you were little and you ran to Mom because you were afraid, and she said, "It'll be all right." That's what prayer does.

I believe people who pray are more loving, compassionate, and forgiving. It's hard to hate when you've been talking to God.

When people pray, they often report feeling less anxious and more peaceful. The fact that the electricity goes off or a friend makes a hurtful remark seems less important.

Prayer has a calming effect. It gives you strength and courage to face an existing problem or a tough decision. Praying helps you close off past regrets and future wants. It quells your obsessional thoughts. Prayer is steadying and adds balance to your life. It empowers you to feel more in control of yourself. It gives you the courage to let go of those things you can't control. Prayer calls on you to be responsible to yourself and to others. Praying is good therapy.

Sometimes when I look at the mountains or think of my family, I swell with feelings of strength, warmth, and love. I take a deep breath, and it's as though everything is one with the world. At that moment I want to share that feeling. Who better to share it with than God? "What a great day, God. Thanks."

———

Spiritual leader Sri Eknath Easwaran writes, "There is a saying in India that when we take one step toward God, he takes seven steps toward us. The Lord is very eager to see us take the first step, but he knows us very well by now, and he watches carefully to see that we take that step and don't wobble back and forth. It is not enough just to put your foot forward or even to touch it lightly to the ground; we must put our weight on it completely. When you do take a sincere step towards the Lord, by bearing patiently with those around us, or changing some unhealthy habits, or repeating the Holy Name, we can be sure that the Lord will take seven steps towards us. But we must take the first step."[3]

Prayer is often the first step.

———

I talked to a number of people of various religious backgrounds about prayer. Here is what they had to say:

"When I pray, it makes me more accountable to myself. I feel more protected from making mistakes, from choosing things that are not good for me. I feel on the right path. I know God listens when I pray. The prayer I say the most is, 'Help me be who you would have me be.'"

A wife, mother, and student

"I pray because I can't make it without God. I think there are a lot of things in life that I can't control. I pray for strength, courage, wisdom, the gift of letting go and not trying to control people I love. A lot of times I feel anxious that a family member won't make the right decision, so I pray a lot about that. I turn that over to God. I ask that he take care of them and give me the grace to let it go. I pray for my boyfriend, who has a troubled relationship with his son. I pray for good health, and I pray that if my health fails, I'll have the strength to handle it. I pray for the gift to enjoy life.

"I go to church every Sunday and once during the week. I take a few moments in the day and put myself with God. I no longer use a lot of formal prayer. I just talk to God. When I see flowers or a blue sky, I say, 'This is God's goodness.'"

A social worker

"Prayer for me is usually making a request of God for other people or for me. If someone is sick, I ask that he get better. I pray for people to be safe on a trip. I pray that things work and will go well in my business. I usually pray in the morning or at night. I feel less anxious when I pray."

A company president

"I pray in my head, I pray at church, I pray in the car. I talk to God in the middle of the night about my family, my health. I belong to a prayer group. We meet once a week to say prayers and study the Bible. When I pray, I ask for patience, a good day at work. I thank God for all I have. I'm a very impatient, anxious person, and when I pray, I become calm. I have a horrible fear of flying, and sometimes I have to fly. The last time I flew, I was in the air praying like mad. My prayer group was on the ground praying for me. It was the easiest flight I've ever had."

An insurance adjuster

"Hi, God, It's Me"

There are many ways to pray to God. For some, prayer is simply sitting quietly and listening for God. Others find formal prayer more helpful. Some start with formal prayer and then listen. Some people read the Bible, the Siddur, or other inspirational material. Many people talk to God as they would any other friend.

Sometimes people think they're too busy to stop and pray. I always say that you can pray anywhere. You can pray sitting at a stop sign, brushing your teeth, or exercising on the floor. I read of a woman who would walk through her neighborhood and pray for the occupants of each house as she passed.

If you'd like to start praying, ask a friend for his or her favorite prayer. Some well-loved prayers are the Lord's Prayer; the Hail Mary; the Shema, which begins, "Hear, O Israel, the Lord our God, the Lord is One. . . . " (Deut. 6:4); the Serenity Prayer; and Psalm 23, which begins, "The Lord is my shepherd; I shall not want. . . . "

Start saying a prayer each morning, during the day, or at night. Start reading the Bible or a prayer book. Try talking to God in your head as you would anyone else—"Hi, God, it's me." Or sit quietly and listen for God.

In talking and listening to God, you will become more loving. You will strengthen your relationships. You will expand your sense ability.

DO YOU FEEL
ONENESS?

Independence? That's middle class blasphemy. We are all dependent on one another, every soul of us on earth.

George Bernard Shaw, playwright

When my dad was growing up, no one taught him to say, "I love you." It wasn't what people, particularly men, said seventy-five years ago.

Through the years I would put my arms around my dad and say, "I love you, Dad."

He'd pat me on the back and say, "That's nice."

I'd smile and say, "Dad, say, 'I love you' back to me."

He'd hem and haw and say, "You know I love you."

I'd say, "Yes, I know. But I want you to tell me."

Finally after years of nudging, my dad has come around and whenever he is leaving our house or ending a conversation on the telephone, he says, "I love you."

Recently, Dad's become hard of hearing.

This past spring he was helping me put in some new rose bushes, and I said something to him about mulching them. He looked at me, smiled, and said, "I love you, too."

What an incredible moment of oneness.

ONENESS—WHAT IS IT?

Oneness. You often hear the word, but what is it? It is a feeling of love. It is a feeling of connectedness and closeness that bonds, for a moment in time, one human to another, to a group, to nature, to all living things, to the world, to God.

When experiencing this feeling, you are absolutely free of anxiety, depression, and suffering. You have no yearnings, no expectations, no shoulds or oughts. You are completely involved in the present moment. You are totally aware.

The feeling of oneness can occur when you are alone—you feel one with another without the other person having any knowledge of your feelings. For example, I'm getting ready for work and I hear my husband singing in the shower, "Raindrops Keep Fallin' on My Head,"[1] and I smile and feel connected. Oneness.

You're shopping and notice a mother kissing her little boy all over while he giggles, twists, and wiggles in her arms. You experience a feeling of connectedness, of oneness, with both the mother and the child.

A woman told me she has the feeling of oneness when she looks at her husband and his hair is all rumpled. "He's a banker and almost always looks impeccable," she says. "His rumpled hair turns him into a little boy."

A hummingbird was caught under the roof of my front porch. I got a dust mop, put it under him, and very slowly edged him up to the roofline. When there was nowhere else for him to go, he settled onto the mop. I then took the mop out from under the porch and held it up in the air. After a few seconds he realized he had his freedom and off he hummed. As he left the dust mop, I felt a moment of oneness with that tiny bird.

Oneness can be experienced as you pet your cat. Oneness can be experienced as you listen to music, watch the sunset, stand by a roaring stream, or survey your garden.

Oneness can happen simultaneously between two people. You feel one with me, I feel one with you. You run into a good friend at the store. You smile, give each other a hug, and experience, for a moment in time, oneness.

You and your husband are in the delivery room. The doctor says, "Well, this time you've got yourselves a little girl." You look at each other and experience oneness.

You're fishing with a friend. He gets a strike. He flashes you a smile and says, "Did you see that?" You nod, and briefly the two of you experience intimacy, oneness.

You hear on the news about the death of a child, and you experience a connectedness, a oneness with her grieving parents.

I was having a cup of coffee on the second floor of a shopping mall, watching all the shoppers below. I saw a couple, who were probably in their seventies, standing by a fountain. They were both wearing navy blue berets. Suddenly they looked up and saw me looking at them. I waved, pointed to their berets, smiled, and nodded my head in approval. They smiled, and each of them blew me a kiss. I blew two kisses back. Oneness in progress.

Oneness can also be experienced in a crowd of strangers. You're at the stadium watching a basketball game and your team scores. You experience, for that moment in time, a feeling of connectedness to all the other people who are yelling and cheering. Then the moment is over. You get quiet. You sit down in your seat. And the experience is gone.

Someone once asked me, "Is this connectedness, this oneness, a form of love?" Yes, it is love. But I believe it goes beyond the bounds of love. I think this feeling is a moment of awareness that God is alive within us. It infuses us with peace and loving-kindness, charity, and goodness.

––––––

In April of 1934, when Rear Admiral Richard Byrd was manning a weather base in the Antarctic, he wrote: "Took my daily walk at 4 P.M. today, in 89' [feet] of frost. The sun had dropped below the horizon, and a blue—of the richness I've never seen anywhere else—flooded in, extinguishing all but the dying embers of the sunset. . . .

"I paused to listen to the silence. . . . The day was dying, the night was being born—but with great peace. Here were imponderable processes and forces of the cosmos, harmonious and soundless. Harmony, that was it! That was what came out of the silence—a gentle rhythm, the strain of a perfect chord. . . . In that instant I could feel no doubt of man's oneness with the universe."[2]

———

When my mother-in-law got to be in her seventies, her eyesight started failing. As the years went by, it became impossible for her to read or see television or even make out the faces of those around her. Whenever we had a celebration of some type and I'd invite her to be a part of it, she would ask how many people were going to be at the house. Because she could barely see, it was hard for her to sit at our dining room table with ten or twelve other people talking and laughing and figure out what was going on.

She didn't complain much about her failing eyesight, but I knew it was devastating. She started listening to the radio more and more. She rarely turned on the television. She stopped buying the newspaper and magazines. When she needed to pay her bills, my husband or I would sit down with her and put a finger on the checks where she should sign her name. We got her a microwave oven and glued Velcro on some of the buttons so she could heat up her coffee.

She still kept a few African violets on the windowsill, although I doubt if she could really see them. She would go to the window and hold one of her beloved violets to the light in the hopes of seeing its tiny pink or purple flowers. When our young daughter, Anna-Mary, visited her, she would give her a hug and ask, "How's my sweet little girl?" Then she'd take Anna-Mary to the window where perhaps, if the light were just right, she could make out her tiny face.

Coupled with these memories of my mother-in-law are thoughts of a woman in her late eighties who was losing her eyesight and feeling depressed. As I sat talking with her, she suddenly interrupted me and said, "I don't know if it's the light in this room, but I can sort of make out your face." Then she said, "Do you think my daughter could come in here and sit where you are sitting? Maybe I could see her."

I immediately went to the waiting room and got her daughter. The daughter sat down in the chair I had been sitting in, and her mother tried to see her face. The mother had her daughter shift the chair one way and then another. Sadly, no matter how the old woman strained to see, she could not see her daughter.

Every time I think of my mother-in-law's trying to see our daughter's face or her little violets, or I think of the old woman who so desperately wanted to be able to see her daughter, I feel a oneness with humanity.

Tears in the Snow

An organization called Retrouvaille (Rediscovery) helps couples in troubled marriages. When I'm working with couples in therapy, I'll frequently suggest they attend a Retrouvaille weekend. Last year I was invited to give a talk at their international meeting.

A friend and I flew to Detroit for the meeting and were to be picked up by one of the Retrouvaille couples. There was a breakdown in communication, and the couple went to the gate while my friend and I stood on the sidewalk.

When we finally connected some forty-five minutes later, I saw that the couple had four little ones with them. The dad had a child on his back and one in his arms. The mom also had a baby in her arms and a young child by her side. As we were driving to the hotel, I learned that the family had had to leave their house three hours earlier to get to the airport. Then they had to drive another hour to our hotel.

When I commented on how difficult it must have been to get the children up and going that morning, the young woman said, "Retrouvaille saved our marriage. We must do something to give back."

When I asked where she attended her first Retrouvaille week-end, she didn't know. She said that she and her husband were late for the weekend, which began on Friday evening. It had snowed heavily that day, and all she remembers was running across a big field of snow. She kept falling down and she was crying. But she had to get to the Retrouvaille weekend to save her marriage.

Each time I think of this woman, I feel a bonding, a oneness with a crying woman frantically running through the snow, try-ing to save her marriage.

A Chair by the Bedside

I'd like to share another story that I believe invites a feeling of connectedness and oneness.

A woman came to see a priest and she said, "Would you come and pray with my daddy? He's dying of cancer and he wants to die at home." The priest went to the house and, when he walked into the man's room, he saw the man lying on the bed with an empty chair beside the bed. The priest asked the man if someone had been visiting. The man replied, "Oh, let me tell you about that chair. I've never told anyone this—not even my daughter. I hope you don't think I'm weird, but all of my life I have never known how to pray. I've read books on prayer, heard talks on prayer, but nothing ever worked. Then, a friend told me that prayer was like a conversation with Jesus. He suggested that I put a chair in front of me, imagine Jesus sitting in the chair, and talk to him. Since that day, I've never had any dif-ficulty praying. I hope you don't think I am off-the-wall." The priest assured the man that there was nothing weird about pray-ing to Jesus in a chair. The priest anointed the man and left. Two days later, the daughter called to say that her father had just died. The priest asked, "Did he die peacefully?" She replied, "I left him at 2:00 this afternoon. He even told me one of his corny jokes. When I returned at 3:30, he was dead. One curious thing, though—his head was resting not on the bed, but on the empty chair beside his bed."[3]

––––––

With all the press about the discovery of the ship *Titanic*, as well as about the movie, many people have reflected and felt sad for those who lost their lives at sea and for the family members who were left behind. Feelings of oneness.

Perhaps at no other period in history has the world experienced such universal sadness as when Princess Diana was buried from Westminster Abbey. Were we mourning for Diana? For her children? For ourselves and our children? For each other? I believe that on that day and during that week following her death, many experienced a oneness with others. Then Mother Teresa died, and again many in the world felt one with another.

THWARTING ONENESS

It is believed by spiritual leaders the world over that criticism and anger are the two biggest ways to thwart feelings of oneness. If you are thinking negative thoughts or feeling angry, oneness will not happen. You cannot hate and feel close at the same time. In addition, once you've been critical or angry with someone, it's going to take time before your feelings dissipate and the other person lets down her guard, trusts you again, and opens herself up for closeness.

Being too busy also keeps you from feeling one with others. If you don't take time to listen to your inner feelings, if you don't take time for others and observe what's going on around you, oneness won't happen.

Too much talking also does not serve you well. If you're focused always on your story, you won't be able to focus on another. Envy and jealousy also rob you of any chance of oneness, for you are too busy comparing yourself to another.

Negative thoughts, negative feelings, and negative behavior all close out the possibility of oneness.

SETTING THE STAGE

I don't think you can make oneness happen, but by being aware of yourself and others, you will experience it more and more. Prayer and meditation set the stage for oneness. Laughter, acts of lovingkindness, celebrations, and being with friends also get us ready for oneness.

Other ways you might set the stage:

- Watch a funny movie with your family. Each time you all laugh, there's a possibility that one of you will look at the other and you'll feel oneness.
- Listen respectfully and quietly as someone talks.
- Look through an old family photo album.
- Take a walk with a friend.
- Stop by a church for a quiet visit.
- Tell a joke to a co-worker.
- Bring everyone at the office a flower.
- Confide a dream for the future.
- Look up and smile when someone comes into the room
- Sit quietly in a lawn chair and listen to the birds.
- Walk outside after a storm and smell the air.
- Take a drive in the country.
- Invite friends over for a chili dinner.
- Give someone a compliment, a present, a hug.

The more you open yourself up for oneness, the more you will experience it. It's plentiful and all around you. It's free. It makes you feel loved and loving. It's energizing and calming. It's miraculous. It's a gift you can give yourself fifty times a day. If you use your sense ability, you will attain oneness.

REACHING FOR
ENLIGHTENED
MATURITY

*To transform the world, we must begin with ourselves; and
what is important in beginning with ourselves is the intention.
The intention must be to understand ourselves and not to leave
it to others to transform themselves. . . . This is our responsibility, yours and mine; because, however small may be the
world we live in, if we can bring about a radically different
point of view in our daily existence, then perhaps we shall
affect the world at large.*[1]

Betty Edwards, artist-author

In your quest over these last few weeks and months, what
have you discovered, what have you learned?

How has being an Impartial Observer and using your
sense ability worked for you? Life becomes so much calmer,
easier, less upsetting, and more meaningful when you have the
ability to step back and watch yourself as you interact. You
simply don't get entangled in every negative comment or upsetting situation. You simply see it as an event, and then you
gracefully and with awareness move on.

Has your life become more balanced? Have you become more
aware of others, making thoughtful telephone calls, doing what

you have agreed to do? Have you carved out some special time for yourself?

Have you become more loving in your behavior? Have you tried to listen harder and be more understanding of your mate or one of your friends? Have you been able to forgive someone who previously you would not let yourself forgive? In your forgiveness, did you gain freedom?

What did you learn from the people in this book who shared their sufferings? What did Amanda, the woman who has had the headache for eleven years, teach you? What about the woman who broke a blood vessel in her eye from the tears she shed on learning of her husband's affair? And what did you learn from Tom, the man who held his dying seventeen-year-old son in his arms? The lives of others have so much to teach if we simply open our hearts and listen.

Traveling along on your journey, learning to use your sense ability, have you become less angry? Have you become less anxious, depressed, less critical, less needful to have things and more things? What has happened to you as you have moved through the pages of this book?

ENLIGHTENED MATURITY

Remember when you got your driver's license? Did you think you were all grown up?

How about when you moved away from home, got your own apartment, got married? Did you think you were grown up then?

What about after you had your first child? That's a wake-up call. Did this make you a grown-up person?

You lose a grandparent. One of your parents dies, your mate leaves, you lose a friend, a job. Is this what being grown up is all about?

You have children in high school. One of them comes home drunk. You don't like your daughter's boyfriend. Your kids won't get off the telephone. You can't sleep. Every time your teenager has the car, you pray, "God, please don't let anything happen."

You're starting to turn gray. Is this what it means to be mature?

Your children are out of the nest. You helped a good friend bury her brother. You're starting to notice that the world is changing. More and more people are younger. You look in the mirror and think, "I wonder how old people think I am?" You decide to start exercising again. You decide to start playing the piano, you once again take up your paints and easel. You're becoming more patient when you have to wait at the post office. You don't dwell on an insult. You're starting to become enlightened.

Somewhere along the way you've come to the realization that life is hard. People suffer. Not everyone thinks as you do. Fighting and bickering are ridiculous—there are better ways to get your point across. It's not important that you have a bad hair day. And so what if the cat throws up on your new carpet? You'll get a rag and clean it up. You are coming of age.

Does anyone reach *totally* enlightened maturity? I think probably not. I believe it's something you have to work toward each day, every day, for your entire life. But in the process, by using your sense ability, you awaken.

A CHECKLIST

For the last few years I've been taking notes on how someone who has reached enlightened maturity would live. I've thought about how the person would think and feel and behave. I've come up with a list that bespeaks enlightenment. If you can put a check mark by 95 percent of the items, you're almost there.

So get your pencil and start checking:

____ 1. You understand that life is hard, but you also realize that life provides satisfaction and pleasure and some miracles along the way.

____ 2. You know that life is not fair and sometimes bad things happen to good people.

___ 3. You do not make more than three critical comments per week.

___ 4. You do not lose your temper: no screaming, name calling, pouting. You have learned to manage your anger.

___ 5. You do not obsess about an old hurt or disappointment. You have come to understand that you can forgive almost anything.

___ 6. You do what you say you will do. Amen. Period.

___ 7. You always take others into account, as well as yourself, before making a decision.

___ 8. You give yourself time alone, some solitude each day.

___ 9. You allow yourself to laugh, notice the sunset, breathe in deeply, and enjoy the very sensation as air fills your lungs, each and every day.

___ 10. You can admit to three incidents in your life that you mishandled, causing yourself and others pain. Review those incidents now.

___ 11. You apologize when you've made a mistake and work hard not to repeat it.

___ 12. You do not have affairs or one-night stands.

___ 13. You know how to listen. You are attentive and responsive. You ask questions when appropriate, and you do not shift the conversation to what you want to talk about.

___ 14. You use a variety of options for dealing with emotional pain. You pray, call a friend, get busy on a project, do something for someone else, seek the help of a professional.

___ 15. You behave in a nonjealous way even though you sometimes think jealous thoughts and have jealous feelings.

___ 16. You have a goal of learning three new things each year—how to change the furnace filter, how to E-mail, how to fly-fish. Can you name three things you will accomplish this year?

___ 17. You don't cry over anything that can't shed a tear for you.

___ 18. You do not say yes to too many things and overextend yourself.

___ 19. You freely give compliments and credit to others.

___ 20. You never drink too much or abuse drugs.

___ 21. You work hard to keep the annoyance and irritation out of your voice.

___ 22. You have resolved your issues with your parents and have forgiven them for their flaws. You have moved to a give-and-take relationship with them.

___ 23. You do not do anything that is against the law, even a minor infraction.

___ 24. You work hard to overcome loneliness and depression and anxiety. You do not passively give in to them.

___ 25. You know how to enjoy life. You're as happy and fulfilled putting in a hard day's work as a hard day's play.

___ 26. Your waking hours are spent mostly in the present, living each moment in a relaxed and accepting way.

___ 27. You don't defend, get sarcastic, or immediately come up with an excuse when you are criticized. You think about the feedback, and only after contemplation decide to accept or reject it.

___ 28. You do an act of kindness each day—calling an aging parent, fixing someone a snack, slowing down to let someone move over into your lane.

___ 29. You have learned not to sweat the little aggravations—someone arriving late, a slow line at the checkout counter, no toilet tissue in the bathroom.

___ 30. You have realistic expectations. You fully understand that having expectations that are too high leads to anxiety and frustration and having expectations that are too low leads to boredom and lack of involvement in life.

___ 31. You understand that each belief you hold, each decision you make, and each behavior adds to or subtracts from your dignity and worth as a person.

___ 32. You live by the following: "Hurt not the earth, neither the sea, nor the trees." (Rev. 7:3)

___ 33. You live by the Golden Rule: "So always treat others as you would like them to treat you." (Matt. 7:12)

___ 34. You understand and live by the following words: "Let there be peace on earth and let it begin with me."[2]

___ 35. You never forget the true reason you are here on this earth: to have good relationships, to be one with others, to laugh, and to walk with God.

Well, how did you do? Are you 95 percent there? Eighty-five percent enlightened?

For every check mark give yourself a gold star and a pat on the back. Come on, take your hand, put it over your shoulder, and give yourself a pat. Funny how we like those pats and seldom give them to ourselves.

Now take a look at those items that in good conscience you could not check. Which of those items will you start working on?

JUST A FEW OTHER REQUIREMENTS

There are several other requirements for fully developing awareness and reaching enlightened maturity. One requirement is that you remember the Sabbath.

In our hurry-up, get-the-job-done, acquiring and accumulating, cell-ringing, fax-buzzing world, you often forget that you must stop and rest. In fact, you are commanded to stop and rest: "Remember to keep holy the sabbath day. Six days you may labor and do all your work, but the seventh day is the sabbath of your Lord, your God." (Exod. 20:8–10)

On the Sabbath, you are to go slowly, savor, take stock, and find out once again who you are and what your true purpose is on earth.

Years ago almost everything was closed on Sunday. The closings were a reminder that this day is not to be about busyness or doing. It is about rest. It is the Lord's day. Now we must remind ourselves.

If you buzz from one chore to the next, from one activity to the next, how can you enjoy your world? The sound of the wind, the rain splashing on the window, the warmth of the sun, the little bird at the feeder, the laughter of your children playing on the floor, your dog curling up at your feet. If you don't stop to take time for God, for church, for temple, how can you take note of yourself and review the last six days? If you don't stop now, when will you have time to stop?

God's Other Children

Life is not meant for us to be isolated or for us to try to handle our sufferings and joys by ourselves. Life is meant to be lived in communion with others. Intimate attachments give strength. They are part of our life as they evolve from infancy to grade school, through adolescence, early adulthood, middle age, and into old age. From our relationships we gain strength, acceptance, knowledge of ourselves, enjoyment, and love.

When someone in therapy tells me she has few friends, I give her a mission to find more friends. I have her pick out a potential friend from work, from her neighborhood, from her family. Sometimes I suggest she join a church group. Then she has to do one social activity a week. Making and keeping friends means giving of yourself. But in giving you will receive, in friendship you will discover love and oneness. I can't imagine life without friends.

Support Groups

Support groups can help you move closer to awareness: church groups, Bible study groups, therapy groups, AA groups, Make Today Count groups.

You may want to form a study group with some of your friends using the information and techniques in *Sense Ability*, working through a chapter each week or each month, because it is in repetition and rereading that the material will become a part of you. Set up an environment that celebrates responsibility, self-exploration, loving relationships, and community.

I had a friend write me a card catching me up on a tiny slice of her life. She said, "Tonight I'm having our Women's Journey meeting from church. I didn't want to do it, you know. Cleaning the house, getting the food, beverages, etc. Getting all psyched up to have a bunch of people here. But I'll be glad I did it afterwards."

Solitude

Solitude means putting aside time for yourself to walk, listen to nature, look at the sky, see the stars, read the psalms, enjoy a quiet lunch, and listen to Mozart, Johann Sebastian Bach, Beethoven, and Vivaldi. No one should leave this world without having steeped themselves in these experiences.

Solitude is a place for self-discovery. When you are alone a kind of sorting process occurs, as in dreaming, and you discover your deepest feelings, your innermost thoughts. It's the capacity to be alone, to have the inner security to be yourself, to decide not what the world wants or what you should be all about, but to decide what you want, what you are all about.

In solitude you do not need to be completely away from others; you may even be in the presence of another who is reading or puttering in the garden. In solitude you are fully absorbed in your world. Remember, Jesus spent forty days in the wilderness before proclaiming his message to the world. Buddha sat beneath the banyan tree meditating for years before he gave the world his Noble Truths and knowledge of the human condition.

Sleep

Sleep not only restores you but also helps you integrate your life. A reprogramming and reprocessing of materials occur and affect your entire being. It has been suggested that entering the chaotic, mad world of dreams each night promotes mental health in ways no one yet understands.

Sleep is also conducive to the creative process, as ideas expand, are sorted, organized, and compared. Insight and solutions that have long eluded you are now available. So take care and allow yourself to be renewed and refreshed. Allow yourself to get adequate sleep.

Selfless Service

Our world requires selfless service, and fully developing your sense ability demands it. We are all journeying together. Some are closer to the end of their journey, some in the middle, some just starting out.

Along the route many people need to be helped. Some require emotional support; some, physical care; others, financial help. Working in a literacy program, making casseroles or building homes for the homeless, becoming a driver for Meals on Wheels, babysitting your neighbor's children, taking a friend to the doctor, donating money to send a child to camp. It's not about rescuing, but about compassion, lovingkindness, reaching outward, giving back. It's the attitude that we're all in this together.

As author Diane Ackerman so beautifully writes, "We need to send into space a flurry of artists and naturalists, photographers and painters, who will turn the mirror upon ourselves and show us Earth as a single planet, a single organism that's buoyant, fragile, blooming, buzzing, full of spectacles, full of fascinating human beings, something to cherish. Learning our full address may not end all wars, but it will enrich our sense of wonder and pride. . . . It will persuade us that we are citizens of something larger and more profound than mere countries, that we are citizens of Earth, her joyriders and her caretakers, who would do well to work on her problems together."[3]

I believe selfless service is an acknowledgment of what you have been given. It is a thank-you for your life. A thank-you for the ability to *hear* a piano concerto, to *smell* the earth after a rainstorm, to *see* the stars, to *taste* fried chicken, mashed potatoes, string beans, and cold applesauce, to *sense*, to *intuit* that there is far more to life than you know.

Selfless service is a thank-you for your family, your children, your children's children, your friends, your religion, your community. It is a way to express gratitude for your education, for your possessions, for the ability to laugh out loud when something tickles you.

Giving to others helps you get away from thoughts of jealousy and envy and thoughts that there is a lack of people or goods in your life. It helps you recognize that you have enough. Selfless service helps you feel complete and allows you to experience your connectedness with others. Of all the things you can do to develop your sense ability, selfless service is one of your most important tasks.

If you think you are too burdened with small children, a busy schedule, poor health, or lack of financial assets—no matter. Make a pact right now. Decide to do one small selfless act each day for the rest of your life. Each day write down your selfless act or make a tiny star representing an act of giving. You can write your good deeds in a journal or make your stars in the margins of a favorite book—day after day, week after week, month after month. Making this decision and following through can be your special, unique gift to humanity.

YOU CAN MAKE A DIFFERENCE

A story is told of two birds sitting on the limb of a tree, quietly watching the snow as it fell ever so lightly. The young bird looked over at his companion and said, "How much does a snowflake weigh?" The older bird said, "Why, it weighs nothing more than nothing."

The snow continued to fall, and after some time the older bird flew away. The younger bird decided that he would count the snowflakes that fell on the limb below. He counted thousands and tens of thousands, and eventually he came to the number 3,700,001. He then counted 3,700,002. At that very moment, the branch broke.[4]

If one snowflake that weighs "Nothing more than nothing" can make a difference, think of the difference a parent, a child, a husband or wife, friend, teacher, salesperson, musician, engineer, or secretary can make. Think of the difference you can make.

––––

Live your life fully. Be all that you can. Understand yourself and know yourself. Recognize your weaknesses and have the courage to change. Love and be lovable. Laugh. Celebrate life. Feel your oneness with others, with nature, with God. And fully use your extraordinary, remarkable, wondrous sense ability.

POSTSCRIPT:
IT TAKES FOUR
SEASONS

After reading this book in manuscript form, a number of people said how much their lives had been affected by what they had read. They reported that they were much more cognizant of their thoughts and feelings and behavior. They liked the awareness of what they were experiencing. Furthermore, because they had changed some of their behaviors, they had more respect for themselves.

One woman said she was able to stop obsessing about a job she had lost. Another said she had stopped fighting with her teenage daughter. After years of being burdened with a bad temper, a man said he finally had a handle on his anger. A woman became more accepting of the little aggravations in life. Another man had started to pray twice a day, something he had never done in his life.

Then several months passed. Despite their best efforts, several of these people were again grappling with the same issues.

Why this slippage?

It's not because they didn't want to change, weren't motivated to change, or hadn't seen improvements in their lives after they first changed. They regressed because they did not keep the information in the forefront of their mind, and it takes time for life changes to become permanent. I tell people in therapy that it takes four seasons for changes to become a part of you. It takes four seasons of not being critical or keeping your temper in check before your new behavior actually becomes second nature.

Because it is difficult to maintain the changes you have made, I suggest that you keep this book by your bedside. Periodically pick it up and reread the sections that you're struggling with. You'll be encouraged to continue using your sense ability and keep up your new behavior.

As I stated earlier in this book, start your own Sense Ability Study Group. Meet with several of your friends every few weeks, set goals for yourselves, read and review various sections of the book, and share your struggles and triumphs. Or once a week over lunch, discuss the material with your co-workers.

If you take the time to be introspective and to be accountable to yourself, change will occur. And the changes you make will last a lifetime.

STARTING A SENSE ABILITY
STUDY GROUP

Visit me on the Web at www.doriswildhelmering.com, where you can view my weekly newspaper column and also get information on starting a study group.

You may write me at Doris Wild Helmering, P.O. Box 410222, St. Louis, MO 63141.

———

William Morrow & Company, Inc. is not responsible for contents of the material provided by the author. If you have any questions, please contact the author at the above address.

NOTES

1. Discovering Your Sense Ability

1. Arthur J. Deikman, *The Observing Self* (Boston: Beacon Press, 1982), 129.
2. Paul Brand and Philip Yancy, *In His Image* (Grand Rapids, MI: Zondervan Publishing House, 1984), 111–19.
3. Marius von Senden, *Space and Sight*, trans. Peter Heath (Glencoe, IL: The Free Press, 1960), 146.
4. Larry Kettelkamp, *Tricks of Eye and Mind* (New York: William Morrow & Company, Inc., 1974), 111.
5. Ibid., 108.
6. Ken Keyes Jr., *Handbook to Higher Consciousness*, 5th ed. (Berkeley, CA: Living Love Center, 1975), 31.
7. Thomas F. Crum, *The Magic of Conflict* (New York: Simon & Schuster, 1987), 223–24.
8. Lewis Carroll, *Alice in Wonderland* (New York: Grosset & Dunlap Publishers, 1994), 43–44.

2. Are You Outer-Directed or Inner-Directed?

1. Anthony de Mello, *The Song of the Bird* (New York: Doubleday & Company, Inc., 1982), 8.

3. Do You Know How to Love?

1. David K. Reynolds, *Constructive Living* (Honolulu: University of Hawaii Press, 1984), 94.
2. Joan Borysenko, *Guilt Is the Teacher, Love Is the Lesson* (New York: Warner Books, Inc., 1990), 51.
3. Merle Shain, *Hearts That We Broke Long Ago* (New York: Bantam Books, 1983), 71.
4. Thich Nhat Hanh, *Living Buddha, Living Christ* (New York: Riverhead Books, 1995), 94.
5. Lewis B. Smedes, *The Art of Forgiving* (New York: Ballantine Books, 1996), 8.

4. Do You Get Too Angry?

1. Daniel Goleman, *Emotional Intelligence* (New York: Bantam Books, 1995), 292–93.
2. Carol Tavris, *Anger: The Misunderstood Emotion* (New York: Simon & Schuster, 1989), 83.
3. Pema Chodron, *Awakening Loving-Kindness* (Boston: Shambhala Publications, Inc., 1991), 28.
4. Seymour Boorstein, ed., *Transpersonal Psychotherapy*, 2nd ed. (Albany: State University of New York Press, 1996), 416.
5. Solomon Schimmel, *The Seven Deadly Sins* (New York: The Free Press, 1992), 91, citing Saint Thomas Aquinas, *Summa Theologica* 44, 2a2ae (New York: McGraw Hill, 1964), 120–21.
6. Thich Nhat Hanh, *Present Moment Wonderful Moment* (Berkeley, CA: Parallax Press, 1990), 66.

5. How Do You Handle Suffering and Disappointment?

1. Charles S. Prebish, *The Historical Dictionary of Buddhism* (Metuchen, NJ: Scarecrow Press, 1993), 54.
2. Dennis Wholey, *The Miracle of Change* (New York: Pocket Books, 1997), 33.
3. Catherine Hoffman, Dorothy Rice, and Hai-Yen Sung, "Persons with Chronic Conditions: Their Prevalence and Costs," *Journal of the American Medical Association* 276 (13 November 1996), 1477.
4. Margery Williams, *The Velveteen Rabbit* (New York: Simon & Schuster Books for Young Readers, 1983).
5. David K. Reynolds, *Water Bears No Scars* (New York: William Morrow & Company, Inc., 1987), 68.

6. Do You Monitor and Direct Your Thoughts?

1. Edward M. Hallowell, *Worry* (New York: Pantheon Books, 1997), 57–58.
2. Betty Edwards, *Drawing on the Artist Within* (New York: Simon & Schuster, 1986), 173.
3. Gerald H. Fisher, "Measuring Ambiguity," *American Journal of Psychology*, 80 (December 1967), 543.
4. Arthur Conan Doyle, *The Complete Sherlock Holmes Treasury* (New York: Bramhall House, 1976), 184.
5. Seymour Boorstein, ed., *Transpersonal Psychotherapy*, 2nd ed. (Albany: State University of New York Press, 1996), 263.
6. David K. Reynolds, *Water Bears No Scars* (New York: William Morrow & Company, Inc., 1987), 52.
7. Eknath Easwaran, *The Mantram Handbook* (Tomales, CA: Nilgiri Press, 1998), 82–83.
8. Thich Nhat Hanh, *Present Moment Wonderful Moment* (Berkeley, CA: Parallax Press, 1990), 34.
9. Oliver Sacks, *The Man Who Mistook His Wife for a Hat and Other Clinical Tales* (New York: Harper & Row Publishers, Inc., 1987), 27, 29.
10. David K. Reynolds, *Water Bears No Scars* (New York: William Morrow & Company, Inc., 1987), 53.
11. Ken Keyes Jr., *Handbook to Higher Consciousness*, 5th ed. (Berkeley, CA: Living Love Center, 1975), 26, 52.

7. Are You a Critical Person?

1. Delroy L. Paulhus, "Bypassing the Will: The Automatization of Affirmations," in *Handbook of Mental Control*, ed. Daniel Wegner and James W. Pennebaker (Englewood Cliffs, NJ: Prentice-Hall, Inc., 1993), 573–87.
2. Seymour Boorstein, ed., *Transpersonal Psychotherapy*, 2nd ed. (Albany: State University of New York Press, 1996), 424.
3. David K. Reynolds, *Water Bears No Scars* (New York: William Morrow & Company, Inc., 1987), 17.
4. Eknath Easwaran, *The Mantram Handbook* (Tomales, CA: Nilgiri Press, 1998), 66.

8. Are You Aware of Your Psychological Boundary Lines?

1. Karl H. Pribram, "The Neurophysiology of Remembering," *Scientific American* 220 (January 1969), 73–86, 138. Paraphrased in Robert E.

Ornstein, *The Psychology of Consciousness* (New York: The Viking Press, 1972), 30.

2. Robert E. Ornstein, *The Psychology of Consciousness* (New York: The Viking Press, 1972), 31.

3. Arthur Conan Doyle, *The Complete Sherlock Holmes Treasury* (New York: Bramhall House, 1976), 206.

9. Are You a Controlling Person?

1. John J. Ratey and Catherine Johnson, *Shadow Syndromes* (New York: Bantam Books, 1997), 365.

2. David K. Reynolds, *The Quiet Therapies* (Honolulu: University of Hawaii Press, 1980), 84.

10. Can You Override Genes and Other Influences?

1. Martin E. P. Seligman, *What You Can Change and What You Can't* (New York: Alfred A. Knopf, Inc., 1994), 45.

2. William T. Hornaday, "The Extermination of the American Bison," *Report of National Museum*, 1887, 421.

11. How Envious and Jealous Are You?

1. Moshe C. Luzzatto, *The Path of the Just*, trans. Shraga Silverstein (New York: Feldheim Publishers, 1966), 165.

2. Saint Basil, *Ascetical Works*, trans. Sister M. Monica Wagner (New York: Fathers of the Church, 1950), 471.

12. Do You Suffer from Anxiety or Depression?

1. For information regarding Thought Field Therapy,™ contact Dr. Roger Callahan, The Callahan Techniques, 45350 Vista Santa Rosa, Indiana Wells, CA 92210, or Ms. Suzanne Connolly, 70 Payne Place, Suite #6, Sedona, AZ 86336.

2. Simeon Margolis and Peter Rabins, *The Johns Hopkins White Paper: Depression and Anxiety* (Baltimore: Johns Hopkins University Press, 1977), 24.

13. Do You Talk to God?

1. Paul Brand and Philip Yancy, *In His Image* (Grand Rapids, MI: Zondervan Publishing House, 1984), 21.

2. David J. Wolpe, *Teaching Your Children About God: A Modern Jewish Approach* (New York: HarperCollins Publishers, Inc., 1993), 44. Paraphrased in Rabbi Rona Shapiro, "Prayer," sermon on Yom Kippur 5755, 15 September 1994, Berkeley Hillel, Berkeley, CA.
3. Eknath Easwaran, *The Mantram Handbook* (Tomales, CA: Nilgiri Press, 1998), 200.

14. Do You Feel Oneness?

1. Hal David, "Raindrops Keep Fallin' on My Head." Music by Burt Bacharach.
2. Richard E. Byrd, *Alone* (New York: G. P. Putnam's Sons, 1938), 84–85.
3. Brennan Manning, *The Wittenburg Door* 93, (October–November 1986), 17.

15. Reaching for Enlightened Maturity

1. J. Krishnamurti, *The First and Last Freedom* (New York: Harper & Row Publishers, Inc., 1954), 42–49. Paraphrased in Betty Edwards, *Drawing on the Right Side of the Brain* (New York: J. P. Tarcher, Inc., 1979), 192.
2. Sy Miller and Jill Jackson, "Let There Be Peace on Earth" (Honokaa, HI: Jan-Lee Music, 1955 and 1983).
3. Diane Ackerman, *A Natural History of the Senses* (New York: Vintage Books, 1991), 285.
4. Kurt Kauter, "A Tale for All Seasons," New Fables: "Thus Spoke the Caribou," in Thomas F. Crum, *The Magic of Conflict* (New York: Simon & Schuster, 1987), 250.

BIBLIOGRAPHY

Ackerman, Diane. *A Natural History of the Senses*. New York: Vintage Books, 1991.

A Course in Miracles. New York: Penguin Group, 1975.

Averill, James R. *Anger and Aggression: An Essay on Emotion*. New York: Springer-Verlag, 1982.

Basil, Saint. *Ascetical Works*. Translated by Sister M. Monica Wagner. New York: Fathers of the Church, 1950.

Beck, Aaron T. *Love Is Never Enough*. New York: Harper & Row Publishers, Inc., 1988.

Beck, Judith S. *Cognitive Therapy: Basics and Beyond*. New York: The Guilford Press, 1995.

Benson, Herbert. *The Relaxation Response*. New York: William Morrow & Company, Inc., 1975.

Berkowitz, Leonard. "The Case for Bottling Up Rage." *Psychology Today* 7 (July 1973): 24.

Block, J. Richard, and Harold Yuker. *Can You Believe Your Eyes?* New York: Gardner Press, Inc., 1989.

Boorstein, Seymour, ed. *Transpersonal Psychotherapy*, 2nd ed. Albany: State University of New York Press, 1996.

Borysenko, Joan. *Guilt Is the Teacher, Love Is the Lesson*. New York: Warner Books, Inc., 1990.

———. *Minding the Body, Mending the Mind.* New York: Bantam Books, 1988.

Brand, Paul, and Philip Yancy. "And God Created Pain." *Christianity Today* 10 (January 1994): 18–23.

———. *In His Image.* Grand Rapids, MI: Zondervan Publishing House, 1984.

———. *Pain: The Gift Nobody Wants.* New York: HarperCollins Publishers Inc.; Grand Rapids, MI: Zondervan, 1993.

Burns, David D. *Feeling Good: The New Mood Therapy.* New York: William Morrow & Company, Inc., 1980.

Buss, Arnold H., and Robert A. Plomin. *A Temperament Theory of Personality Development.* London: John Wiley & Sons, 1975.

Canfield, Jack, and Mark Victor Hansen. *Chicken Soup for the Soul.* Deerfield Beach, FL: Health Communications, Inc., 1993.

Carlson, Richard. *Don't Sweat the Small Stuff.* New York: Hyperion, 1997.

Carroll, Lewis. *Alice in Wonderland.* New York: Grosset & Dunlap Publishers, 1994.

Chodron, Pema. *Awakening Loving-Kindness.* Boston: Shambhala Publications, Inc., 1991.

Chopra, Deepak. *The Seven Spiritual Laws of Success.* San Rafael, CA: Amber-Allen Publishing and New World Library, 1993.

Cialdini, Robert B. *Influence: Science & Practice.* New York: Harper & Row Publishers, Inc., 1988.

Colt, George Howe. "Were You Born That Way?" *Life,* April 1998, 46.

Copp, Jay. "What Are You Praying For?" *U.S. Catholic* 57 (July 1992): 34–38.

Crum, Thomas F. *The Magic of Conflict.* New York: Simon & Schuster, 1987.

Cunningham, Lawrence S. "Why People Still Put Their Body and Soul into Prayer." *U.S. Catholic* 58 (July 1993): 6–13.

Dass, Ram, and Paul Gorman. *How Can I Help?* New York: Alfred A. Knopf, Inc., 1985.

Deikman, Arthur J., *The Observing Self.* Boston: Beacon Press, 1982.

de Mello, Anthony. *The Song of the Bird.* New York: Doubleday & Company, Inc., 1982.

Dossey, Larry. *Healing Words: The Power of Prayer and the Practice of Medicine.* New York: HarperCollins Publishers, Inc., 1993.

———. *Prayer Is Good Medicine.* New York: HarperCollins Publishers, Inc., 1996.

Doyle, Arthur Conan. *The Complete Sherlock Holmes Treasury.* New York: Bramhall House, 1976.

Dyer, Wayne W. *Manifest Your Destiny*. New York: HarperCollins Publishers, Inc., 1997.

Eardley, Linda. "Drinking Students Suspended." *St. Louis Post-Dispatch*, 27 April 1994, B-1.

Easwaran, Eknath. *The Mantrum Handbook*. Tomales, CA: Nilgiri Press, 1998.

Edwards, Betty. *Drawing on the Artist Within*. New York: Simon & Schuster, 1986.

Ekman, Paul. "An Argument for the Basic Emotions." *Cognition and Emotions*, 6, 1992.

Evatt, Chris, and Bruce Feld. *The Givers and the Takers*. New York: Ballantine Books, 1983.

Fisher, Gerald H. "Measuring Ambiguity." *American Journal of Psychology* 80 (December 1967): 541–557.

Gilhooly, K. J. "Thinking." In *Encyclopedia of Human Biology*, edited by Renato Dulbecco. New York: Academic Press, Inc., 1991.

Glasser, William. *Choice Theory*. New York: HarperCollins Publishers, Inc., 1998.

———. *Take Effective Control of Your Life*. New York: Harper & Row Publishers, Inc., 1984.

God's Little Instruction Book. Tulsa, OK: Honor Books, Inc., 1993.

Goethe, Johann Wolfgang von. *The Sorrows of Young Werther*. New York: Penguin Books, 1962.

Goldman, Ari L. "Religion Notes." *New York Times*, 9 April 1994, A-10.

Goleman, Daniel. *Emotional Intelligence*. New York: Bantam Books, 1995.

Hales, Dianne, and Robert E. Hales. *Caring for the Mind*. New York: Bantam Books, 1995.

Haley, Alyssa. *Your 30-Day Journey to Kicking the Procrastination Habit*. Nashville, TN: Thomas Nelson Publishers, 1992.

Hallowell, Edward. *Worry*. New York: Pantheon Books, 1997.

Hanh, Thich Nhat. *Living Buddha, Living Christ*. New York: Riverhead Books, 1995.

———. *The Miracle of Mindfulness*. Boston: Beacon Press, 1987.

———. *Present Moment Wonderful Moment*. Berkeley, CA: Parallax Press, 1990.

Harris, P. L. "Infant Cognition." In *Handbook of Child Psychology*, edited by Paul H. Mussen. Vol. 2 of *Infancy and Developmental Psychobiology*, 4th ed. New York: John Wiley & Sons, 1983.

"Health After 50." *The Johns Hopkins Medical Letter*. Vol. 10, No. 1, March 1998.

Helmering, Doris Wild. *Being OK Just Isn't Enough.* Kansas City, KS: National Press Publications, 1996.

————. *Happily Ever After.* New York: Warner Books, Inc., 1986.

————. "At Last a Fancy for Felines." *St. Louis Post-Dispatch,* 4 April 1992.

————. "Controlling Behavior Can Be Active or Passive." *St. Louis Post-Dispatch,* 29 May 1991.

————. "Dad, Do You Remember When?" *St. Louis Post-Dispatch,* 15 June 1988.

————. "Differing Standards Are a Cause for Conflict." *St. Louis Post-Dispatch,* 12 July 1993.

————. "Don't Assume You Are Center of the Universe." *St. Louis Post-Dispatch,* 3 January 1994.

————. "Focus on the Past Reflects Changing Life." *St. Louis Post-Dispatch,* 8 November 1989.

————. "Foot-in-Mouth Types Often Trample on Others." *St. Louis Post-Dispatch,* 17 February 1988.

————. "Give Others Sunshine, Not Dreary Rain Shower." *St. Louis Post-Dispatch,* 28 March 1994.

————. "Maybe Might Be Best Answer of All." *St. Louis Post-Dispatch,* 11 July 1992.

————. "Memories of Mom on Her Birthday." *St. Louis Post-Dispatch,* 23 October 1995.

————. "Secret Spending Costs $35,000 in Savings." *St. Louis Post-Dispatch,* 2 May 1990.

————. "Tiff over Flowers Is Really About Control." *St. Louis Post-Dispatch,* 7 June 1989.

————. "Unkind Responses Fatal to Intimacy." *St. Louis Post-Dispatch,* 9 November 1991.

————. "When It's Time to Hang up the Keys." *St. Louis Post-Dispatch,* 7 March 1994.

Hoffman, Catherine, Dorothy Rice, and Hai-Yen Sung. "Persons with Chronic Conditions: Their Prevalence and Costs." *Journal of the American Medical Association* 276 (13 November 1996): 1473–79.

Hokanson, Jack E. "Psychophysiological Evaluation of the Catharsis Hypothesis." In *The Dynamics of Aggression,* edited by E. I. Megargee and J. E. Hokanson. New York: Harper & Row Publishers, Inc., 1970.

Hokanson, Jack E., and Michael Burgess. "The Effects of Status, Type of Frustration and Aggression on Vascular Processes." *Journal of Abnormal and Social Psychology* 65 (1962): 232–37.

Hornaday, William T. "The Extermination of the American Bison." *Report of National Museum*, 1887.

Houston, Jean. *The Possible Human*. New York: St. Martin's Press, 1982.

James, Jennifer. *Success Is the Quality of Your Journey*. Seattle: Jennifer James, Inc., 1983.

Jung, C. G. *Psychological Types*. Princeton, NJ: Princeton University Press, 1971.

Kettelkamp, Larry. *Tricks of the Eye*. New York: William Morrow & Company, Inc., 1974.

Keyes, Ken, Jr. *Handbook to Higher Consciousness*. 5th ed. Berkeley, CA: Living Love Center, 1975.

Kornfield, Jack. *A Path with Heart*. New York: Bantam Books, 1993.

Krishnamurti, J. *The First and Last Freedom*. New York: Harper & Row Publishers, Inc., 1954.

Kushner, Harold. *When Bad Things Happen to Good People*. New York: Schocken Books, 1981.

———. *Who Needs God*. New York: Simon & Schuster, Inc., 1989.

Luzzatto, Moshe C. *The Path of the Just*. Translated by Shraga Silverstein. New York: Feldheim Publishers, 1966.

McGinnis, Alan Loy. *Bringing Out the Best in People*. Minneapolis: Augsburg Publishing House, 1985.

Manning, Brennan. "The Wittenburg Door Interview: Brennan Manning." *The Wittenburg Door* 93, October–November 1986.

Margolis, Simeon, and Peter Rabins. *The Johns Hopkins White Paper: Depression and Anxiety*. Baltimore: Johns Hopkins University, 1977.

Martin, Julia Vituello-Martin, and J. Robert Moskin. *The Executive's Book of Quotations*. New York: Oxford University Press, 1994.

Mayer, Richard. *Thinking, Problem Solving, Cognition*. New York: W. H. Freeman and Company, 1983.

Muller, Wayne. *How Then Shall We Live?* New York: Bantam Books, 1996.

Murdock, Mike. *The Double Diamond Principle*. Dallas, TX: Wisdom International, Inc., 1990.

Mussen, Paul, John Conger, Jerome Kagan, and Aletha Huston. *Child Development and Personality*. New York: Harper & Row Publishers, Inc., 1990.

Muto, Susan. "The Threefold Path to Peaceful Intimacy." *Liguorian* 82 (January 1994): 18–24.

Ornstein, Robert E. *The Psychology of Consciousness*. New York: The Viking Press, 1972.

Osborn, Ian. *Tormenting Thoughts & Secret Rituals*. New York: Pantheon Books, 1998.

Paulhus, L. Delroy. "Bypassing the Will: The Automatization of Affirmations." In *Handbook of Mental Control*. Edited by Daniel M. Wegner and James W. Pennebaker. Englewood Cliffs, NJ: Prentice-Hall, Inc., 1993.

Peck, M. Scott. *The Road Less Traveled*. New York: Simon & Schuster, 1978.

Persons, Jacqueline B. "Cognitive Behavior Therapy," In *Encyclopedia of Human Behavior*, edited by V. S. Ramachandran. New York: Academic Press, 1994.

Plato. Translated by B. Jowett. New York: Walter J. Black, 1942.

Plebram, Karl H. "The Neuropsychology of Remembering." *Scientific American* 220, January 1969.

Prebish, Charles S. *The Historical Dictionary of Buddhism*. Metuchen, NJ: Scarecrow Press, 1993.

Random Acts of Kindness. Berkeley, CA: Conari Press, 1993.

Raskin, Valerie Davis. *When Words Are Not Enough*. New York: Broadway Books, 1997.

Ratey, John J., and Catherine Johnson. *Shadow Syndromes*. New York: Pantheon Books, 1997.

Reps, Paul. *Zen Flesh, Zen Bones*. Rutland, VT: Charles E. Tuttle Company, Inc., 1957.

Reynolds, David K. *Constructive Living*. Honolulu: University of Hawaii Press, 1984.

———. *The Quiet Therapies*. Honolulu: University of Hawaii Press, 1980.

———. *Water Bears No Scars*. New York: William Morrow & Company, Inc., 1987.

Ripple, Paula. *Growing Strong at Broken Places*. Notre Dame, IN: Ave Maria Press, 1986.

Sacks, Oliver. *The Man Who Mistook His Wife for a Hat and Other Clinical Tales*. New York: Harper & Row Publishers, Inc., 1987.

Sadker, Myra, and David Sadker. *Failing at Fairness*. New York: Charles Scribner's Sons, 1994.

Saklofshe, D. H., and H. J. Eysenck. "Extraversion-Introversion." In *Encyclopedia of Human Behavior*, edited by V. S. Ramachandran. New York: Academic Press, 1994.

Salovey, Peter, Christopher K. Hsee, and John D. Mayer. "Emotional Intelligence and the Self-Regulation of Affect." In *Handbook of Mental Control*, edited by Daniel M. Wegner and James W. Pennebaker. Englewood Cliffs, NJ: Prentice-Hall, Inc., 1993.

Schiff, Jacqui Lee. *Cathexis Reader*. New York: Harper & Row Publishers, Inc., 1975.

Schimmel, Solomon. *The Seven Deadly Sins*. New York: The Free Press, 1992.

Schlessinger, Laura. *How Could You Do That?!* HarperCollins Publishers, Inc., 1996.

———. *The Ten Commandments*. New York: HarperCollins Publishers, Inc., 1998.

Schmidt, Louis A., Airana Shahinfar, and Nathan A. Fox. "Individual Difference in Temperament." In *Encyclopedia of Human Behavior*, edited by V. S. Ramachandran. New York: Academic Press, 1994.

Seligman, Martin E.P. *What You Can Change and What You Can't*. New York: Alfred A. Knopf, Inc., 1994.

Shain, Merle. *Hearts That We Broke Long Ago*. New York: Bantam Books, 1983.

Shapiro, Rabbi Rona. "Prayer." Sermon preached on Yom Kippur 5755, 15 September 1994, Berkeley Hillel, Berkeley, CA.

Shirley, Debbie A., and Janice Langan-Fox. "Intuition: A Review of the Literature." *Psychological Reports*, 79, 1996.

Shor, Ronald E. "Three Dimensions of Hypnotic Depth." In *The Nature of Hypnosis: Selected Basic Readings*, edited by Ronald E. Shor and Martin Orne. New York: Holt, Rinehart & Winston, 1965.

Smedes, Lewis B. *The Art of Forgiving*. New York: Ballantine Books, 1996.

Spezzano, Charles. "What to Do Between Birth and Death." *Psychology Today* 25 (January–February 1992): 543–55.

Spielberger, Charles, Susan Krasner, and Eldra Solomon. "The Experience, Expression and Control of Anger." In *Individual Differences, Stress, and Health Psychology*, edited by M. P. Janisse. New York: Springer-Verlag, 1988.

Tavris, Carol. *Anger: The Misunderstood Emotion*. Rev. ed. New York: Simon & Schuster, 1989.

Thomas, John B. "How to Be Happier." *St. Louis Post-Dispatch*, 22 August 1993.

Thorne, B. M., "Intuition." In *Encyclopedia of Psychology*. 2nd ed. New York: John Wiley & Sons, 1994.

Tice, Dianne M., and Roy F. Baumeister. "Controlling Anger: Self-Induced Emotion Change." In *Handbook Of Mental Control*, edited by Daniel M. Wegner and James W. Pennebaker. Englewood Cliffs, NJ: Prentice-Hall, Inc., 1993.

Volland, Victor. "More Students Suspended for Drinking." *St. Louis Post-Dispatch*, 1 May 1994, D-1.

Von Senden, Marius. *Space and Sight: Perception of Space and Shape in the Congenitally Blind Before and After Operation.* Translated by Peter Heath. Glencoe, IL: The Free Press, 1960.

Weiss, Robert S. "Loneliness." *The Harvard Medical School Mental Health Letter* 4 (June 1988): 4–6.

Wellesley College Center for Research on Women. *The AAUW Report: How Schools Shortchange Girls.* Washington, D.C.: American Association of University Women Education Foundation, 1992.

Wholey, Dennis. *The Miracle of Change.* New York: Pocket Books, 1997.

Wilkins, Rich. *Going Beyond a Positive Mental Attitude.* Shepherdsville, KY: POS Publications, 1993.

Williams, Margery. *The Velveteen Rabbit.* New York: Simon & Schuster Books for Young Readers, 1983.

Williamson, Marianne. *Illuminata.* New York: The Berkley Publishing Group, 1994.

Wolpe, David J. *Teaching Your Children About God: A Modern Jewish Approach.* New York: HarperCollins Publishers, Inc., 1993.

Woodward, Kenneth L. "Talking To God." *Newsweek,* 6 January 1992, 38.

Zillmann, Dolf. "Mental Control of Angry Aggression." In *Handbook of Mental Control,* edited by Daniel M. Wegner and James W. Pennebaker. Englewood Cliffs, NJ: Prentice-Hall, Inc., 1993.

PERMISSIONS

Grateful acknowledgment is given to the following for permission to reprint previously published material:

Thomas Crum. Reprinted with the permission of Simon & Schuster from *The Magic of Conflict* by Thomas Crum. Copyright © 1987 by Thomas Crum. (Paraphrased)

Larry Kettelkamp. Reprinted with permission of Larry Kettelkamp from *Tricks of Eye and Mind*, published by Morrow Junior Books, a division of William Morrow & Company, Inc., 1974.

Anthony de Mello, S. J. Reprinted with permission of Doubleday, a division of Bantam Doubleday Dell Publishing Group, from *The Song of the Bird*, 1982. (Paraphrased)

© Gibson Greetings, Inc. Reprinted with permission of Gibson Greetings, Inc., Cincinnati, Ohio 45237. ALL RIGHTS RESERVED.

Joan Borysenko. From *Guilt Is the Teacher, Love Is the Lesson*. Copyright © 1990 by Joan Borysenko. By permission of Warner Books.

Merle Shain. Reprinted with permission of Bantam Books, a division of Bantam Doubleday Dell Publishing Group, Inc., from *Hearts That We Broke Long Ago* by Merle Shain. Copyright © 1983 by Merle Shain.

Thich Nhat Hanh. Reprinted by permision of Riverhead Books, a di-

INDEX

Ackerman, Diane, 232
adultery:
  anger about, 73, 87
  forgiveness for, 52–53
  pain and suffering caused by, 87, 88, 97
Adventure of Silver Blaze, The (Doyle), 107
affirmations, 9–10, 116, 205
  anger and, 76–79
  criticism and, 139–140
  self-control and, 168–169
aggressiveness, 174
aging:
  inner-directed vs. outer-directed responses
    to, 22–23
  love and, 39–40, 46–47
agitated depression, 206
airplane accidents, 94
Alcoholics Anonymous, 57, 170
Alice in Wonderland, 12
always, 114
Anderson, Roger, 144
anger, 1, 12–13, 59–82, 222
  acceptable, 73–74
  confronting and, 45, 87
  consequences of, 81–82
  as control, 2, 59, 60
  control of, 14, 73, 75–80
  Do I act like this person? and, 60–62
  exercise on, 68–69
  genetic basis of, 69–70
  Impartial Observer and, 7–8
  intensification of, 66–67
  as interpretation, 67–68
  -in vs. -out, 74–75
  main reasons for, 62–65

  as norm, 70–71
  of others, dealing with, 80–81
  research on, 71–72
antenuptial agreements, 39
anxiety, 2, 14, 107, 200–205, 209
  anger vs., 68
  awareness of, 9
  behavioral therapy for, 204–205
  getting sympathy for, 205
  healthy vs. debilitating, 202
  medication for, 205
  Mindful Breathing and, 118
  prayer and, 213
  progressive muscle relaxation and, 202–
    203
  Thought Field Therapy and, 203–204
apologizing, 1, 59, 98
Art of Forgiving, The (Smedes), 35
As Good As It Gets (movie), 169
attention:
  to boys vs. girls, 22
  competing for, 197–199
  envy and, 193–194
  focus of, 16–26; *see also* inner-directed;
    outer-directed
  giving of, 31
attention deficit disorder (ADD), 151–152
Augustine, Saint, 74
authenticity, 98–99
automatic response pattern, 2, 7
awareness, *see* sense ability

Balanced Self, 23–24
  hardiness and, 100
Basil, Saint, 191

behavior:
  attention-competitive, 197–198
  envy revealed by, 191–193
  see also specific topics
behavioral therapy, for anxiety, 204–205
Benson, Herbert, 203
best response, searching for, 10–11
Bible, 14, 27, 83, 134
  criticism in, 128
bicycles, as gifts, 37–38
birthdays:
  forgetting of, 29, 33
  remembering of, 34–36
blaming, 7–8
  of parents, 179–180
blood pressure:
  decrease in, 72
  increase in, 67, 68, 71
body language, 20, 60
  critical, 132, 134
  listening and, 31
book contracts, 192
Borysenko, Joan, 40, 203
bosses, 111
  as controlling, 158
  as critical, 126, 141
  as difficult, 86, 88
  love and, 37, 44–46
boundaries, psychological, 13, 145–156
  hidden, 151–155
  importance of, 156
  invasion of, 144–146
  quiz on, 147–151
  thinking exercise on, 155–156
Bowery El effect, 153–154
Boys from Syracuse, The (Hirschfeld), 106
brain, 3, 174, 205, 207
Brand, Paul, 210
breast cancer, 71, 101–102
Breathing, Mindful, 117–118, 205
Buddhism, 13, 54, 79, 83
Byrd, Richard, 218–219

Callahan, Roger, 203
calmness, 9, 10, 172, 213
cancer, 23, 37, 48
  anger and, 71
  resiliency and, 101–102
cards, thank-you, 34
cars:
  accidents with, 97
  purchase of, 186
  see also driving
change:
  baby steps to, 169
  capacity for, 11–12
  criticism and, 134–135
  inner-directed vs. outer-directed and, 20
chemotherapy, 100, 101, 102
children, childhood, 39, 152, 158, 190, 211
  confronting and disciplining of, 47–50
  death of, 93–95, 98, 100–101, 212
  exercise on influences from, 176–180

listening to, 3, 18
marriage of, 97–98
of outer-directed mothers, 24
parental anger toward, 63–64, 67–68, 72, 73
parental criticism of, 126, 130, 131, 133, 135–138, 142
parental envying of, 191
psychological boundaries of, 145
Reciprocation Rule and, 183
resiliency of, 100
Chinese horse story, 113
Chinese proverb, 59
Chodron, Pema, 70
Christianity, 13, 54, 74
  see also God; prayer
Christmas, 98, 109–110
closeness, 2, 189
clown figure, 5–6
cognitive-behavioral therapy, 167–170
cognitive triad, 168
communication:
  cognitive-behavioral therapy for, 167–168
  nonverbal, 20, 31, 60, 132, 134
  see also conversation; talk, talking
comparison, envy and, 190, 193–194
compassion, 95, 180
compliments:
  criticism and, 133
  giving, 26, 31, 38, 133, 223
  prickly, 38
conclusions, negative, jumping to, 111–113
confronting, 87
  love as, 45–50
Congress, U.S., 184
conscious autosuggestion, 139–140
Consistency Principle, 185–186
constructive criticism, 135–136
contentment, 4, 13
controlling behavior, 13, 157–172
  anger as, 2, 59, 60
  quiz on, 162–163
  as right, 161–162
  telling people what to do as, 158–159
  see also self-control
conversation:
  avoidance of, 28
  initiation of, 26
  side, 197–198
copying behavior, 154
Coué, Emile, 139–140
Course in Miracles, A, 74
credit, sharing of, 192–193
criticism, critical people, 13, 17, 28, 88, 125–143, 222
  causes of, 131–132
  change and, 134–135
  constructive, 135–136
  dealing with, 140–141
  faultfinding and, 130–131
  higher value technique and, 138–140
  nonverbal, 132, 134
  pain of, 128–130

criticism (*continued*)
  putting away, 14, 136–140
  self-, 141–142
  stories about, 126–128
  tactics of, 132–135
  writing down, 136–138, 141
crying, 17, 41, 72, 85
cultural factors, 22, 42
curfews, 49–50
cynicism, 174

dating, 111
death, the dead, 23
  of children, 93–95, 98, 100–101, 212
  love and, 37, 48–49
  of mother, 115
  talking to, 95
decision making, 25–28
  avoidance of, 161
  at work, 45–46
Deikman, Arthur, 1
depression, 91–92, 200, 206–209
  agitated, 206
  anger and, 71
  clinical, 207, 208
  coping with, 14, 206, 208–209
  pets and, 208–209
  quelling and controlling of, 14, 172
  situational, 206–207
Diana, Princess, 222
diaries, anger, 79–80
diet, 57
disciplining, love as, 45–50
divorce, 36, 39
  education and, 63, 64, 67
  obsessing about, 116
  suffering and disappointment caused by,
    87–88, 89
Do I act like this person?, 60–62
Dressler, Marie, 189
drinking problems:
  control of, 57, 159, 166, 167, 168, 170
  genetic factors in, 166, 174
driving, 46–47, 48, 223
  see also cars
"Drop the rock!," 90
drug abuse, 174

Easter, 143
Easwaran, Sri Eknath, 116–117, 213
education, 28
  anger about, 63, 64, 67
  criticism and, 135
  envy and, 193
  influences on, 181
Edwards, Betty, 224
emotions, *see* feelings and emotions
energy, 18
  of inner-directed vs. outer-directed, 20, 21
energy points, 203
enlightened maturity, 13, 224–234
  checklist for, 226–229
  friendship and, 230

Sabbath and, 229–230
selfless service and, 232–233
sleep and, 231–232
solitude and, 231
support groups and, 230–231
envy, 189–195, 222
  attention-competitive behavior and, 197–
    198
  coping with, 14, 194–195
  defined, 189
  examples of, 190–191
  in revealing behaviors, 191–193
  sources of, 193–194
epitaphs, 139
events:
  acceptance of, 8, 9–10
  negative interpretation of, 7–8
everybody, 114
everyone, 114
exaggeration, anger and, 66–67
exercise, 57, 85, 208
  tai chi, 171
expense accounts, padding of, 182
"Extermination of the American Bison, The,"
  182
extroversion, 21
eyesight, failing, 219–220

fathers:
  inner-directed, 18
  love and, 49–50, 57–58
faultfinders, 130–131
fear, 104
  anger and, 64–65, 67, 74, 82
  see also jealousy
feedback vs. listening, 31
feelings and emotions:
  intense, 65
  thoughts in creation of, 2, 62–70, 104
  see also specific feelings
finances, 28, 39, 55–56, 132
firings, 89–90
focus, *see* inner-directed; outer-directed
food, psychological boundaries and, 144, 146
forgetfulness, 18, 32, 33, 39
forgiving, forgiveness, 116
  love as, 48, 52–56
  of yourself, 48, 55–56, 57
friends, friendship, 2, 223
  criticism of, 126, 130
  enlightened maturity and, 230
  envy and, 190, 192
  jealousy in, 195
  listening and, 31–32
  psychological boundaries in, 144, 145–
    146, 154
  Reciprocation Rule in, 182–183
  remembering, 32–33, 34
  worries discussed with, 121
future, trapped in, 120–122

Gamblers Anonymous, 170
gambling, 165–166, 170

gardening, 122, 142, 192
gatha, 117–118
genetics, 21, 174
  anger and, 69–70
  control and, 166
  criticism and, 131
giving:
  of gifts, 34, 37–38, 42, 223
  love as, 36–40, 57, 58
  receiving vs., 41–44
  see also selfless service, acts of
Glasser, William, 171–172
God:
  hardiness and, 99–100
  talking to, 13, 85–86, 94, 100, 121, 210–215; see also prayer
Goethe, Johann von, 180–181
golf, playing, 28–29, 51–52
grudges, holding, 72, 74
guilt, self-forgiveness and, 55–56

Hallowell, Edward, 122
Handbook to Higher Consciousness (Keyes), 122
happiness, 5, 24, 44, 102, 114
hardiness, emotional, 98–102
headaches, 84–86
hearing, sense of, 3, 232
heart, anger and, 67, 68, 71, 72, 77
help, asking for, 41
herd behavior, 182
higher value technique, 138–140
Hinduism, 13, 116–117
Hirschfeld, Al, 106
hopelessness, 206
hostility, 44, 71, 87
house cleaning, 63–64
bow technique, 11, 42

I am aware technique, 9
I choose to control myself, my negative thoughts, and my anger technique, 76–78
I choose to live each moment in an accepting, relaxed, and conscious way, 9–10
identity:
  thinking and, 119, 123–124
  see also boundaries, psychological
illness, 22
  cancer, 23, 37, 48, 71, 101–102
  chronic, 95–97, 132
  love and, 37, 48–49
  resiliency and, 100–102
I love you, 43
"I'm mildly annoyed," 80
Impartial Observer, 6–9, 205, 224
impatience, 1, 2, 14, 134
  bow technique and, 11
influence(s), 173–188
  from childhood, exercise on, 176–180
  Consistency Principle and, 185–186
  hidden rules of, 180–188
  kindness as, 187
  nature as, 173–174
  nurture as, 174–176

  Reciprocal Concession Rule and, 184–185
  Reciprocation Rule and, 182–184
  Werther Effect and, 180–182
information boundary line, 151–152
inheritance, envy and, 195
In His Image (Brand and Yancy), 210
inner-directed, 12–13, 16–26
  defined, 15
  excess of, 25–26
  factors in, 21–23
  outer-directed compared with, 19–21
  receiving by, 42
interconnectedness, 2, 4, 14
  see also oneness
interdependence, 20, 21
interrupting, 197, 198, 199
intimidation, 28, 44
introversion, 21
intuition, 3, 232
invitations, Reciprocation Rule and, 183

jealousy, 13, 14, 195–199, 222
  attention-competitive behavior and, 197–198
  defined, 195
  examples of, 195–196
  self-esteem and, 196–197
Jimmie G., 119
jobs:
  envy and, 190, 194
  loss of, 22, 89–90
  second, 175
  success at, 13
  see also work
Johnson, Catherine, 166–167
Judaism, 13
justice, right to, 55

Kettelkamp, Larry, 5
Keyes, Ken, Jr., 122
kindness, 30, 44, 88
  random acts of, 187

language learning, foreign, 8
lateness, 9, 135
leukemia, 37
license renewal, 46–47
Lincoln, Abraham, figure, 5–6
listening, 3, 114, 223
  attention-competitive people and, 198
  to God, 121
  love as, 30–32, 40, 53–54
  to music, 72, 168
lists:
  of critical comments, 136–138, 141
  to-do, 92
loneliness, pain of, 91–92
love, 12–13, 27–58
  anger and, 82
  as confronting and disciplining, 45–50
  falling back in, 92
  as forgiving, 52–57
  as giving, 36–40, 57, 58

love (*continued*)
  inner-directed people and, 19, 21
  as lifetime task, 57–58
  as listening, 30–32, 40, 53–54
  outer-directed people and, 19, 21
  as playing, 50–52, 57
  as receiving, 41–44, 57
  as remembering, 32–36, 57
  as respecting, 31, 44–45, 57
  romantic, 29–30
  self-, 14, 56–57
  self-esteem and, 197
  work and, 37, 44–46
Luzzatto, Moshe, 191

Man Who Mistook His Wife for a Hat, The
  (Sacks), 119
marriage, 26–29
  anger in, 1, 2, 7–8, 59–62, 64, 66–67, 72,
    73
  controlling behavior in, 157–158, 159
  criticism in, 125–130, 132, 135, 138
  envy and, 193–194
  forgiving in, 52–53
  giving in, 36–39, 58
  Impartial Observer and, 7–8, 9
  of inner-directed vs. outer-directed, 21
  listening in, 31, 32
  love and, 27–29, 36–39
  overgeneralizing in, 114
  psychological boundaries in, 151–152,
    156
  remembering in, 33
  Retrouvaille and, 53, 220–221
  suffering and disappointment in, 87–89, 91,
    92, 96
massage, 168
maxims, 37
media, influence of, 180–181
medication, 169, 205, 206, 208
meditation, 10–11, 79
memory:
  bad, 32, 33, 39
  loss of, 119
men:
  anger of, 72
  inner-directed, 16–22, 26
  outer-directed, 20, 22
Metta meditations, 79
Mindful Breathing, 117–118, 205
Minding the Body, Minding the Mind (Borysenko),
  203
monkey story, 24–25
mothers:
  confronting and disciplining by, 48, 49–50
  critical, 130, 131, 133, 136–138, 142
  death of, 115
  giving and, 37–40
  outer-directed, 24
  remembering, 34–36
movies, 169, 223

mumblers, 160
Murdock, Mike, 173
music, listening to, 72, 168

name-calling, 28, 59, 66
nature, 173–174
negative thinking, 2, 7–8, 103, 109–113,
  222
  anger and, 62–70, 72, 75–80
  cognitive triad and, 168
  exercise on, 110–111
  fact gathering vs., 112–113
  jumping to conclusions with, 111–113
  obsessing as, 115–118
  overgeneralizing as, 113–114
never, 114
no, saying, 17
noise, psychological boundary for, 152–154
nonverbal communication, *see* body language
nurture, 22, 174–176

obsessing, 12–13, 115–118
oneness, 2, 4, 216–223
  defined, 217
  setting the stage for, 223
  thwarting, 222
opinions of others, 20
oughts, 67, 131
outer-directed, 12–13, 16–26
  defined, 15
  excess of, 24–25
  factors in, 21–23
  giving by, 17, 42
  inner-directed compared with, 19–21
overgeneralizing, 113–114
overweight, 57, 170
  Consistency Principle and, 185

pain:
  emotional and psychic, 10, 86–95, 97–98,
    100–101, 128–130
  physical, 84–86, 88, 95–97, 100–102
  unnecessary, 114, 115
  see also suffering and disappointment
parents:
  aging, 39–40, 57
  anger of, 63–64, 67–68, 70, 72, 73
  blaming of, 179–180
  children criticized by, 126, 130, 131, 133,
    135–138, 142
  confronting and disciplining by, 47–50
  controlling behavior of, 158
  discomfort of, 193
  as influence, 174–176, 179–180
  single, 89
  suffering and disappointment of, 89, 93–95,
    97–98, 100–101
  see also fathers; mothers
past, as focus of thinking, 118–120
patience, 98
Paul, Saint, 14, 139

peace, 4, 13, 109
Peace Corps, 109
perception:
  of pictures, 5–6, 105–107
  thinking and, 105–107
personality:
  genetic factors in, 174
  nurture and, 174–176
pessimism, 174
PET (positron emission tomography), 204–205
pets, 61, 64
  depression and, 208–209
Phillips, David, 181
pictures, looking at, 5–6, 105–107
playing, love as, 50–52, 57
poems:
  gatha, 117–118
  lovingkindness, 140
politeness, 44
positive self-talk, power of, 187–188
positive thinking, 2, 63, 103, 110–111
  criticism and, 139, 140
pouting, 28, 72, 74, 81, 160–161
prayer, 88, 93–94, 116, 140, 210–215
  benefits of, 212–215
preference, craving as, 171–172
present, living in, 118, 122–123
progressive muscle relaxation, 202–203
promises:
  breaking of, 18
  keeping of, 25–26, 44
proverbs, 143
psychological boundaries, *see* boundaries, psychological
psychotherapy, 206, 208

questions:
  avoiding controlling behavior with, 159
  critical, 133
  not answering, 161
  about self-control, 164
quiet therapies, 170–171
quizzes:
  on controlling behavior, 162–163
  on psychological boundaries, 147–151

Ratey, John, 166–167
Rational Recovery, 57, 170
receiving, love as, 41–44, 57
Reciprocal Concession Rule, 184–185
Reciprocation Rule, 182–184
relaxation, progressive muscle, 202–203
Relaxation Response, The (Benson), 203
remembering, love as, 32–36, 57
resiliency, 98–102
respecting, love as, 31, 44–45, 57
responsibility:
  avoidance of, 180
  taking, 91

Retrouvaille, 53, 220–221
Reynolds, David, 37, 102, 114
Roddenberry, Gene, 186
role playing, 168
Roman Catholicism, 54
romantic love, 29–30

Sabbath, 229–230
Sacks, Oliver, 119
sadness, 13, 206
sarcasm, 28, 44, 62, 125–126
scorpion story, 173
self:
  Balanced, 23–24, 100
  of inner-directed vs. outer-directed, 20
self-control, 164–172
  cognitive-behavioral therapy and, 167–170
  preference vs. craving and, 171–172
  quiet therapies and, 170–171
self-criticism, 141–142
self-esteem, 32
  anger and, 71–72, 82
  blaming and, 180
  controlling behavior and, 161
  envy and, 190, 194
  jealousy and, 196–197
  love and, 197
selfless service, acts of, 13, 30, 95
  enlightened maturity and, 232–233
self-love, 14, 56–57
self-revelation, 26
self-talk, positive, power of, 187–188
self-therapy, 10
Seneca, 200
sense ability (awareness):
  defined, 1–3
  expansion of, 3–6
  learning use of, 6–11
  see also specific topics
Shadow Syndromes (Ratey and Johnson), 166–167
Shaw, George Bernard, vii, 216
shopping, 168
shoulds, 67, 131
shyness, 20–21
sight, sense of, 3–4, 232
situational depression, 206–207
sleep, 231–232
Smedes, Lewis, 55
smell, sense of, 3, 232
smoking, concealment of, 107
solitude, 231
Sorrows of Young Werther, The (Goethe), 180–181
Star Trek (TV show), 186
stress, reduction of, 168, 209
suffering and disappointment, 12–13, 14, 83–102
  and absence of valued person, 91–92
  chronic illness and, 95–97
  dealing with, 88–89

suffering and disappointment (*continued*)
"Drop the rock" and, 90
forgiveness and, 53–55
loss of child and, 93–95
as obsessive, 89–90
resiliency and, 98–102
taking responsibility for, 91
suicide, 180–181, 206
sulking, 74
support groups, 170, 230–231
surgery, cataract, 3–4

tai chi, 171
talk, talking, 20–21
to the dead, 95
to God, 13, 85–86, 94, 100, 121, 210–215;
see also prayer
incessant, 160, 198–199
positive self-, 187–188
refusal to, 62, 74, 81, 111, 160
see also conversation
taste, sense of, 3, 232
Tavris, Carol, 69
telephone calls, 18, 31–32, 67–68
temper tantrums, 160
Teresa, Mother, 40, 222
"thank you," saying, 33–34
therapy:
behavioral, 204–205
change and, 11–12
cognitive-behavioral, 167–170
confronting in, 49
psychotherapy, 206, 208
quiet, 170–171
reasons for, 10
therapy groups, 169–170
Thich Nhat Hanh, 50, 117
Thoreau, Henry David, 15
Thought Field Therapy, 203–204
thoughts, thinking, 103–124
behavior influenced by, 2, 104
about boundary lines, 155–156
directing of, 104–105
exercise on, 110–111
feelings created by, 2, 62–70, 104
future as focus of, 120–122
identity and, 119, 123–124
negative, *see* negative thinking
neutral, 2, 63, 68–69, 103, 109
past as focus of, 118–120
positive, *see* positive thinking
present as focus of, 118, 122–123
variety of perspectives and, 107–109
vindictive, 10–11

time:
boundary line of, 154–155
giving of, 31
for oneself, 25
to-do lists, 92
tolerance, 2
touch, sense of, 3
trust, 82, 88

ulcers, 71

vacations, 175
Velveteen Rabbit, The, 99
vengeance, 55
verbal abuse, 36, 37, 59–60, 62
vindictive thoughts, 10–11
violent behavior, 72

walking, 43, 72, 96–97, 168, 223
Mindful Breathing during, 118
weight loss, 196–197
Weight Watchers, 170
well-being, 4, 9
Werther Effect, 180–182
What About Bob? (movie), 169
why vs. *how*, 11, 42
women:
anger of, 72
inner-directed, 20, 22
outer-directed, 16–17, 20, 21, 22, 24
work:
anger at, 72–75, 77, 80–81
competition at, 191
confronting and disciplining at, 45–46
controlling behavior at, 158, 159
credit at, 192
criticism at, 126, 135, 141
giving at, 37
influences at, 181–185
jealousy at, 195, 196
negative thinking at, 111, 113–114
nurture as factor in attitude toward, 174–176
overgeneralizing about, 113–114
psychological boundaries at, 146, 152
respecting at, 44–45
suffering and disappointment at, 86, 88, 89–90, 100
see also jobs
worriers, advice for, 121–122
Worry (Hallowell), 122

Yancy, Philip, 210